The New World of
Police Accountability

By Sam Walker

Sam Walker dedicates this book to
HERMAN GOLDSTEIN who understood
these issues long before anyone else.

By Carol Archbold

I dedicate this book to Samuel Walker. Sam has drawn attention
to the topic of police accountability for more than three decades, and has
contributed some of the most influential research in this area. His work has sparked
positive change in police agencies across the country and has inspired the next
generation of policing scholars to continue developing this topic in years to come.
It is an honor to be a co-author of this book, as I know that it is a representation of
several decades of hard work and dedication by Sam. I want to thank Sam for being
a tremendous inspiration to my career, and for being a fantastic mentor and friend.

The New World of Police Accountability

Second Edition

Samuel Walker
University of Nebraska Omaha

Carol A. Archbold
North Dakota State University

Los Angeles | London | New Delhi
Singapore | Washington DC

Los Angeles | London | New Delhi
Singapore | Washington DC

FOR INFORMATION:

SAGE Publications, Inc.

2455 Teller Road

Thousand Oaks, California 91320

E-mail: order@sagepub.com

SAGE Publications Ltd.

1 Oliver's Yard

55 City Road

London EC1Y 1SP

United Kingdom

SAGE Publications India Pvt. Ltd.

B 1/I 1 Mohan Cooperative Industrial Area

Mathura Road, New Delhi 110 044

India

SAGE Publications Asia-Pacific Pte. Ltd.

3 Church Street

#10-04 Samsung Hub

Singapore 049483

Printed in the United States of America

Library of Congress Cataloging-in-Publication Data

Walker, Samuel, 1942-
The new world of police accountability / Samuel Walker, University of Nebraska, Omaha, Carol A. Archbold, North Dakota State University. — Second edition.

pages cm
Includes bibliographical references and index.

ISBN 978-1-4522-8687-7 (pbk.)
ISBN 978-1-4833-1320-7 (web pdf)

1. Police misconduct—United States. 2. Police administration—United States. I. Archbold, Carol. II. Title.

HV8141.W3458 2014
363.2'2—dc23   2013031693

This book is printed on acid-free paper.

Acquisitions Editor: Jerry Westby

Associate Editor: MaryAnn Vail

Production Editor: Libby Larson

Copy Editor: Terri Lee Paulsen

Typesetter: C&M Digitals (P) Ltd.

Proofreader: Theresa Kay

Indexer: Molly Hall

Cover Designer: Scott Van Atta

Marketing Manager: Terra Schultz

Permissions Editor: Jennifer Barron

SUSTAINABLE FORESTRY INITIATIVE
Certified Chain of Custody
Promoting Sustainable Forestry
www.sfiprogram.org
SFI-01268
SFI label applies to text stock

13 14 15 16 17 10 9 8 7 6 5 4 3 2 1

Brief Contents

Detailed Contents

Preface

This book represents the culmination of more than 25 years of intensive research and consulting on the issue of police accountability and 39 years of research and writing on policing in general. Looking back, it is astonishing how much has changed in this field just during this period. One of the most important programs described in this book—police auditors—was not even created until 1993. Early intervention systems, meanwhile, were in their infancy and had never been studied.

My own thinking about the issue of police accountability and how to achieve it has changed dramatically over this past decade and a half. One reflection of this is the change in some of the most important terminology I use. Back then, I referred to "civilian review boards"; today I refer to "citizen oversight." Only a few years ago, I undertook a study of "early warning systems" in policing. Today I refer to "early intervention systems." These changes in terminology reflect important changes in my understanding of the institutions and programs at hand. On another important issue—the one that closes this book, in fact—my thinking is profoundly mixed.

On the one hand I am optimistic about the possibilities of meaningful police reform and for achieving genuine police accountability. I think we now have a reasonably good understanding of what needs to be done, of what strategies and tools are likely to be effective. The main goal of this book is to bring these insights to a broader audience. At the same time, however, I am often pessimistic about the possibilities of lasting change. Police departments, like universities, private corporations, and all large bureaucracies, are extremely difficult to change. Although this book is cautiously optimistic, only time will tell whether that optimism is fully justified.

One thing is certain, however. This book sums up the enormous changes in the field of police accountability over the past 25 years. In light of that, it is safe to assume that the next 5 or 10 years will witness further dramatic changes. There will undoubtedly be new strategies and tools, together with new evidence on what works and what does not. The years ahead will be as exciting and challenging as were past years.

Acknowledgments

By Sam Walker

This book is dedicated to Herman Goldstein. Herman has greatly influenced my understanding of what the police do and how we might effectively control officer conduct to ensure compliance with the standards of a democratic society. Through a career that extends back almost half a century, he has shaped our thinking about the police more than any other single individual. As a member of the American Bar Foundation Survey in the mid-1950s, he helped to uncover the complexity of the police role and the pervasive exercise of discretion by police officers. He has wrestled with these issues ever since. There is a direct connection between his early work on police discretion and this book. Along the way, Herman developed the concept of problem-oriented policing, arguably the most important new idea related to how the police should address crime and disorder. I would like to thank Herman for his influence on my own career and for his immeasurable impact on the field of policing.

Many other people also contributed to the ideas expressed in this book. Merrick Bobb is simply the nation's leading expert on police accountability, and I have learned much from him. I have also learned much about policing through my many conversations with Phil Eure, head of the Washington, DC, Office of Police Complaints; Mike Gennaco, head of the Office of Independent Review for the Los Angeles Sheriff's Department; Richard Rosenthal, former head of two oversight agencies in the U.S.; Sam Pailca, former director of the Office of Professional Accountability in Seattle; Ellen Ceisler-Green, former head of the Office of Integrity and Accountability in Philadelphia; Pierce Murphy, the Boise Ombudsman; and Tristan Bonn, the former Public Safety Auditor in Omaha. Richard Jerome, formerly of the U.S. Department of Justice, has also provided useful insights into policing.

All of the people mentioned in the above paragraph have been active members of the National Association of Civilian Oversight of Law Enforcement. NACOLE has played a major role in advancing the cause of police accountability, and its annual meeting has always been for me a rich source of information into the latest developments in the field. I salute NACOLE, its leaders, and all of its members for their commitment to improving policing.

I also continue to learn much from my academic colleagues working in the field of police accountability. They include David Harris, University of Pittsburgh Law School; Lorie Fridell, University of South Florida; Roger Goldman, St. Louis University Law School, and Geoff Alpert, University of South Carolina. Charles Katz, Arizona State University, is the best student I ever had and remains a great friend and colleague.

I also want to express my admiration for Carol Archbold, North Dakota State University, a former student who is establishing an excellent record as a police scholar. It was because of her status as a scholar and her incredible work ethic that I chose her to become my co-author of this second edition.

This book is a greatly expanded version of the ideas I set forth in an article published in the *St. Louis University Law Public Law Review* (Vol. XXII, No. 1, 2003). That article, in turn, was based on the presentation I gave at a Symposium on New Approaches to Ensuring the Legitimacy of Police Conduct that the law school sponsored in April 2002. I would like to thank the law school and Professor Roger Goldman in particular for inviting me to speak at the conference and providing the opportunity to develop my ideas on this subject.

Several police departments have been particularly open and generous with their time. In particular I would like to thank officers in the Phoenix, AZ; Minneapolis, MN; and Austin, TX, police departments, as well as those in the Los Angeles Sheriff's Department who have helped me.

By Carol Archbold

I would like to thank Samuel Walker for inviting me to be his coauthor on this book. Sam's work on police accountability over the last several decades has influenced change in many police agencies across the United States. His work in this area was one of the main reasons I chose to attend the doctoral program at the University of Nebraska-Omaha. His work continues to inspire me.

I would also like to thank some of the police agencies that have allowed me to conduct research on a variety of police accountability-related topics including the use of risk management in policing, and the processing of citizen complaints filed against the police. Special thanks goes out to the staff at the Los Angeles Sheriff's Department, the Portland Police Bureau and Risk Management Division, the Charlotte Risk Management Department and Police Attorney, and the staff at the Las Vegas Metropolitan Police Department Risk Management. These agencies are some of the first to adopt risk management as part of their efforts in reducing police liability and increasing officer accountability. I would also like to thank Chief Keith Ternes of the Fargo Police Department for allowing me unlimited access to his agency's citizen complaint data. Chief Ternes is highly committed to organizational transparency and officer accountability.

Finally, I want to thank my husband, Jason Archbold and two sons, Jackson and Braeden, for being so supportive of my work. Your support and encouragement means the world to me

PART I

Introduction

ONE

Introduction to the New Police Accountability

The New Police Accountability at Work: Three Examples

Dallas Police Chief's Eight-Point Plan

In the summer of 2012 the Dallas Police Department experienced another in a series of officer-involved shootings, which represented an increase over previous years. A July 24th shooting was particularly controversial because the person shot and killed was unarmed. Two weeks later, in response to community protests, the police chief issued an Eight-Point Plan for New Policies and Strategic Directives.

The Eight-Point Plan included formalizing a relationship with the FBI for concurrent investigations of all officer-involved shootings, a more comprehensive policy for officers reporting resistance to officer incidents, revising the foot pursuit policy to reduce risks to officers and preventing escalating use of force, and most important a plan to "research Best Practices" "from around the nation."[1]

Several aspects of the Eight-Point Plan are notable. First, it represented a quick and proactive response to an immediate community controversy. Second, it went beyond the immediate issue of officer-involved shootings and addressed other issues. Third, it recognized that incidents such as a fatal shooting of an unarmed person are often the result of failures of policies, training, and supervision that need to be corrected. Fourth, it included an explicit commitment to learn from other best practices in law enforcement.

The COPS Office/Las Vegas Police Collaborative Report

In late 2012 the COPS Office of the U.S. Justice Department published a Collaborative Report on use of force by the Las Vegas Metropolitan Police Department (LVMPD). Coming in the wake of continuing controversies over officer-involved shootings, the report represented a joint effort between a new Critical Response Technical Assistance Program in the U.S. Justice Department, a private consulting firm, and the LVMPD. The 154-page report covered a wide range of policies, incident reporting procedures, and training and supervision issues related to the use of both lethal and less lethal force.[2]

The Collaborative Report recommended changes to the LVMPD's use of force policy, including adding "a mission statement that emphasizes the sanctity of human life," an emphasis on deescalating officer-citizen encounters, tighter restrictions on conducted energy devices (CEDs; known by the trademarked name "Tasers"), a broader review of shooting incidents, and improvements in the consistency, quality, and quantity of training on various issues."[3] It concluded with a detailed work plan for a continuing collaborative process through which the COPS Office would assist the LVMPD in implementing the recommendations, including a set of goals and timetables for specific tasks.

The New Orleans Consent Decree

In July 2012 the Justice Department and the New Orleans Police Department entered into a consent decree requiring sweeping accountability-related reforms in the police department. The consent decree was similar to the more than 15 such settlements negotiated by the Justice Department. The reforms included improving the department's use of force policies (including firearms, canines, CED devices, and vehicle pursuits), the development of a crisis intervention team for handling mental health cases, and new policies governing stops, searches, arrests, and custodial interrogation.[4]

The New Orleans consent decree closely resembled similar settlements between the Justice Department and local and state law enforcement agencies regarding a "pattern or practice" of violations of the constitutional rights of people. It went beyond previous settlements in two respects, however. First, it included a section devoted to gender bias, requiring new police policies related to the investigation of sexual assault cases and the handling of domestic violence incidents. Second, it included formal requirements designed to ensure greater community input into the implementation of the consent decree and into the police department once the decree was eventually lifted.

The Meaning of the Three Examples

The three examples above illustrate several themes regarding the pursuit of accountability in police departments with problems related to use of force, racial bias, community relations, and other issues.

The Dallas Eight-Point Plan represents what is arguably the ideal situation. Faced with a series of problematic incidents, the police chief responded quickly with a proactive program to address these and other issues. It was an entirely voluntary effort, initiated by the chief. Historically, on accountability issues such as shootings, allegations of excessive physical force, or racial discrimination, police departments responded with denial or half-hearted promises to investigate the issue. In the new police accountability, police departments will respond proactively, become self-monitoring, and develop into "learning organizations" where they seek to learn from problems and mistakes that occur and develop appropriate corrective responses.[5]

The Collaborative Report on the Las Vegas Metropolitan Police represents an innovative joint effort between a police department and a branch of the U.S. Justice Department, whose mission it is to assist agencies that are having problems establish appropriate accountability measures. Many police departments, some would even say most, are not in a position to undertake a thorough review of their existing policies and procedures. They are not equipped because a genuine commitment to accountability involves an organizational culture of accountability. This culture includes a willingness to ask probing, critical questions about incidents that might be embarrassing to the department and to colleagues and friends. It also includes a familiarity with various accountability procedures—an early intervention system, for example, and how it can be used to its fullest. In the transition to genuine accountability, assistance from outside experts is a valuable and possibly even necessary process. A good analogy is the annual physical exam that we regard as a sound health practice: We consult an outside expert who will identify existing or potential problems and recommend corrective action.

It should be noted that the Las Vegas collaborative effort was not entirely voluntary. A local newspaper had published a five-part series of articles on shooting incidents by LVMPD officers, the local ACLU had demanded a series of policy changes, and the Critical Response Technical Assistance Program stepped forward to offer its help. Faced with a series of local controversies over officer-involved shootings, the LVMPD responded appropriately by accepting the Justice Department's assistance.[6]

The consent decree over the New Orleans Police Department represents what should be the last resort regarding police accountability: a lawsuit by the U.S. Justice Department seeking sweeping reforms. Unfortunately, many police departments have proven to have a long history of violations of peoples' rights, of an inability to correct their own problems, and in some cases a situation of serious organizational dysfunction. While many people argue that Justice Department "pattern or practice" oversteps the bounds of federal authority, is expensive, and unnecessarily polarizes the issue of police accountability locally, advocates argue that it is a necessary remedy for deeply troubled law enforcement agencies.[7] The reports of independent court-appointed monitors in several cases found that the departments had been transformed in a positive direction. The monitor for the New Jersey State Police consent decree concluded in its final report that the agency had "become self-monitoring and self-correcting to a degree not often observed in American law enforcement."[8] The monitor for the Washington, D.C., police department reached a similarly optimistic conclusion in its final report.[9] Whether these gains will hold over the long term is an open question at this point. Sustaining reforms, in all areas of policing, is a major challenge.[10]

Even more important, at a 2012 conference on federal pattern or practice litigation sponsored by the Police Executive Research Forum, several police chiefs who had been through the consent decree experience explained how in the end it improved their departments. Charles H. Ramsey, former chief of the Washington, D.C., police department and current commissioner in Philadelphia, said that "The end result was very positive. Shootings dropped by 80 percent and have remained low. And it gave us credibility with the public." Two other officials said that because of the consent decree-mandated reforms policing improved and they were no longer paying out tens of thousands of dollars in civil suit damages as they had been beforehand.[11]

This book argues that the Dallas Eight-Point Plan represents the pursuit of police accountability at its best. If all police departments acted quickly and proactively to controversial incidents the need for litigation would be greatly reduced. The plan included many of the core ingredients of the new police accountability. The Las Vegas collaborative effort represents a promising middle ground, in which the Justice Department provides necessary expertise and technical assistance.

The Plan of This Book

This book examines the continuing developments in police accountability. The three examples discussed so far are just a few of the many new developments in the field, and the book will examine many others. As we will explain, the most important new approaches discussed in this book have certain common elements that reappear in different programs. Chapter One defines what we mean by police accountability and provides a brief introduction to the key elements of the new world of police accountability. Chapter Two provides a brief review of the most important traditional approaches to accountability, pointing out their respective strong points and weaknesses. The remaining chapters examine specific aspects of the new police accountability.

The Challenge of Police Accountability

Policing in America: Images and Reality

Police misconduct remains a serious problem in American society. Even after decades of protests, litigation, and reform, controversies continue over excessive use of force, unjustified fatal shootings, racial and ethnic bias, and other forms of mistreatment of citizens. Indelible images of police actions are seared into the American memory. Even though it is almost 25 years in the past, the March 3, 1991, beating of Rodney King by Los Angeles Police Department officers, and the trial and riots that followed, remains a well-known event in American police history.[12] Other abuses of police power, involving shootings or excessive use of physical force, regularly appear on the national news media.

Incidents of police misconduct dominate the public image of the police, and distort public perception of the current state of American policing. Ron Weitzer's study of the aftermath of the Rodney King incident documents how highly publicized incidents of misconduct adversely affect public opinion about a local police department.[13] Such unusual events, or what can be called "celebrated cases," do not fully reflect where American policing is today. They obscure important changes that occur quietly, including many important reforms. Celebrated cases are a general problem in American criminal justice. Public opinion is heavily influenced by the case of the offender recently released on bail who promptly commits a rape or armed robbery, the defendant charged with armed robbery plea bargains the case down to a misdemeanor, and similar cases.[14]

Celebrated cases of police misconduct might easily lead a reasonable person—that is, someone well informed about civic events but with no special expertise in policing—to conclude that there has been little progress in American policing since the strife-torn decade of urban riots in the 1960s.[15] That reasonable person might conclude that racial and ethnic discrimination, excessive force, and unjustified shootings are as prevalent as they were 50 years ago. He or she might then conclude that the many police reform efforts of the past half century have accomplished nothing. These efforts include the well-known Supreme Court decisions on unconstitutional police practices (e.g., *Mapp v. Ohio*, *Miranda v. Arizona*); the spread of community policing[16] and problem-oriented policing;[17] new restrictions on police use of deadly force, high speed pursuits, and other critical incidents; the growth of significant representation of African American, Hispanic, and female police officers;[18] the spread of citizen oversight of the police;[19] and dramatic improvements in police officer educational levels and training programs.[20] Did all of these reforms produce no significant or lasting improvements in American policing?

The answer is no. There been many important improvements in policing since the 1960s and they have had positive effects on day-to-day policing, as we will describe in detail in Chapter Two. In the 1960s, African Americans were barely represented on big-city police departments, police officers were given no meaningful guidance on when to use deadly force, officers routinely treated domestic violence assaults as though they were not a crime, and the concepts of community policing and problem-oriented policing were unheard of. The problem, of course, is that despite these positive developments, many problems remain. David Bayley has called the last decades of the twentieth century the most innovative period in police history.[21] The new world of police accountability represents an effort to build on past reforms and develop new strategies and programs to ensure the highest level of professionalism in American policing.

A Definition of Police Accountability

It is a basic principle of a democratic society that the police are answerable to the public.[22] That is the core meaning of police accountability. Only in totalitarian dictatorships can law enforcement agencies do whatever the supreme leader wants, with the public and individual citizens having no avenues of redress. Achieving meaningful accountability in a democracy is extremely difficult, however. Democracy is a messy process. The famous British Prime Minister Winston Churchill once said that "Democracy is the worst form of government, except for all those other forms that have been tried from time to time."[23] Achieving police accountability is an enormous challenge, in part because democracy is a challenge, but also because of the special nature of policing, which poses numerous problems.

Police accountability is a broad and multifaceted phenomenon.[24] On one level it refers to holding law enforcement *agencies* accountable for the services they deliver: crime control, order maintenance, and miscellaneous services to people and communities. The community policing movement has been a major effort to reorient what police departments do, and to develop closer relations with the communities they serve.[25] At the same time, accountability also refers to holding *individual officers* accountable for how they treat individual citizens, particularly with regard to the use of force, equal treatment of all groups, and respect for the dignity of individuals. In important respects, the agency-level and officer-level dimensions of accountability merge. Effective crime control and order maintenance depend on what individual officers do on the street. Officers who stop people because of the color of their skin rather than probable cause that they have committed a crime are not concentrating on crime. Officer misconduct, meanwhile, undermines effective police crime control. As we explain in more detail below, if people do not trust the police because of their misconduct, they will be less willing to report crimes, provide evidence of neighborhood problems, or even decline to identify offenders.

Law enforcement agencies are ultimately accountable through the political process, by which elected officials translate the will of the people into public policy. Mayors, city council members, county commissioners, governors, state legislatures, presidents, and Congress exercise control and oversight of the law enforcement agencies under their control through budgets and appointments. Mayors appoint police chiefs, governors appoint the heads of state police agencies, and the president appoints the attorney general and the director of the FBI.[26] At the same time, however, the police are also accountable to the law and should conform to established standards of lawfulness in all of their operations. The courts are the principal mechanism for holding the police accountable to the law.

One of the principal challenges of democracy is that public attitudes about the police and crime have often had a very bad impact on police practices. Public pressure to control crime has often encouraged or at least tolerated illegal searches and coercive confessions. Majority white opinion has encouraged or tolerated racial bias in policing. People do not mind the police stopping people in their neighborhood who look "different" or "dangerous," just as long as they themselves are not stopped. The worst historical example of majority rule and the misuse of police power was the era of segregation in the South, where the police and the entire criminal justice system helped to maintain a racial caste system. The courts have attempted to curb such abuses by applying constitutional standards of due process and equal protection.[27] In his classic study of policing, *Justice Without Trial*, Jerome Skolnick argued that police officers and departments are under pressure to produce results with regard to crime fighting. This pressure leads officers to cut corners or do whatever seems "necessary" to produce arrests, evidence, and convictions.[28] In a noted statement of the conflict between competing demands on the police, Herbert Packer defined it as a clash between crime control and due process perspectives on the criminal process.[29] The debate over this choice of priorities continues to rage, in public debate, in law reviews, and in the courts.

Accountability and Police Legitimacy

The most important new perspective on policing is the concept of legitimacy.[30] The concept holds that the police have legitimacy when they enjoy the understanding, trust, and support of the people they serve. Legitimacy goes far beyond the old concept of police-community relations (PCR), which focused narrowly on police relations with racial minority communities. PCR programs were never very successful in part because they were always separate from basic police operations of patrol and criminal investigation, and as a result did not address day-in, day-out police conduct on the streets. Critics labeled PCR programs an exercise in public relations, an effort to change public attitudes without changing police actions that shape those attitudes.[31]

Legitimacy takes a comprehensive view of policing, looking at individual officer conduct, police departments as organizations, and relations with the entire community. The concept of legitimacy is rooted in the academic discipline of procedural justice, which studies how people respond to the way they are treated in a particular situation and not just the outcome of that event (a traffic ticket, for example).[32] The sense of legitimacy increases the more people feel they were treated with dignity and respect, were not singled out for mistreatment, and had an opportunity to express their voice in the event.

A traffic stop illustrates how procedural justice operates. A driver is more likely to accept the legitimacy of the stop if the officer is respectful, explains the reason for the stop, and answers his or her questions. Positive feelings about the process are likely to neutralize or trump any bad feelings the person has about the outcome, a traffic ticket. If on the other hand the officer is rude, does not explain anything, and refuses to allow the driver to say anything, the driver is likely to be angry at the officer and the department. Those negative feelings will probably accentuate any negative feelings arising from a traffic ticket.

Examples from other areas of life illustrate the distinction between the process and the outcome. A student's grade on a test or paper represents the outcome. The process involves whether the teacher provided comments on what was wrong or missing, and was willing to spend some time with the student explaining a low grade. Returning something to a retail store is another good example. The outcome is whether the company accepts the return. The process is whether the clerk was friendly or rude, and accepted or questioned the customer's explanation. With respect to health care, a certain amount of public discontent is based not on the actual care provided but instead on not being able to speak to a medical professional or having to wait for a long time in the doctor's office.

Procedural justice research has found that people who trust the legal system are more likely to obey the law, cooperate with authorities, and accept the results of any proceeding (a ticket, a guilty verdict, and so on). The implications of procedural justice for policing are enormous. If people feel they are treated with respect and dignity they are more likely to regard the police as legitimate and as a consequence be more likely to trust and cooperate with police officers. For the police, that means people will be more likely to obey the law, call the police for help when they have a problem, report crimes and neighborhood problems they know about, be witnesses in criminal cases, and be more respectful and cooperative in encounters with officers on the street. Research years ago found that the most important factor in the police clearing crimes is whether there is a witness who can provide relevant information about the crime.[33] In short, legitimacy can enhance the effectiveness of the police in routine crime-fighting. The community policing movement grew out of the recognition that the police depended heavily on citizen cooperation, which has been called the "co-production" of police services, and that police departments had become insular bureaucracies that had lost touch with people in their communities.[34]

Legitimacy and the New Police Accountability

All of the policies and practices of the new world of police accountability have direct implications for police legitimacy. Police misconduct undermines respect and the belief that the police are legitimate. Simple rudeness or not answering a person's questions about a traffic stop undermines respect for the officer and ultimately the legitimacy of the police department itself. Peoples' views about the police can come from a personal experience, something they hear from someone else, or news media accounts. Every accountability-related program discussed in this book addresses police conduct that is likely to undermine public trust and the sense of legitimacy.

At a 2012 Police Executive Research Forum (PERF) conference on police use of force and de-escalation, an Arlington (Texas) police chief said that "We want this topic [legitimacy] to be on the forefront of our officers' minds. They need to ask themselves: What have I done today, in this encounter, on this traffic stop, on this call, to earn the right to police this community?" All of the policies and procedures of the new accountability discussed in this book are directed toward that end.[35] The following section examines the basic strategies and tactics of the new police accountability, each one of which has direct implications for accountability.

Strategies and Tactics of the New Police Accountability

This book focuses on the strategies and tactics of the new police accountability. As a result, it does not cover many traditional practices of professional police management that are still sound and need to be strengthened. These include the efficient organization of the department; the rational allocation of resources based on priorities and workload; rational principles of command, control, and supervision; a policy and procedure manual; preservice training of all officers; periodic personnel evaluations; investigation of alleged misconduct; and the appropriate discipline where appropriate. All of these principles were well established by the early 1960s, largely through the work of O. W. Wilson.[36] They are still sound principles—as far as they go.

And that is the problem. They do not go far enough. The crises of racial conflict, high crime rates, and loss of public confidence that began in the 1960s dramatized the inadequacy of the existing standards and practices of traditional police professionalism. The policies and practices of the new police accountability developed out of a perceived need to give closer scrutiny to routine officer-citizen contacts and to provide more meaningful controls to ensure lawful and respectful policing, and as a result to enhance police legitimacy.

New approaches to controlling police officer conduct arose in the late 1960s and early 1970s. Police departments for the first time developed meaningful controls over the use of deadly force,[37] the response to domestic violence incidents,[38] and high-speed pursuits.[39] Citizen oversight agencies spread across the country, with nearly all big cities having some form of external oversight by the 1990s.[40] Community-oriented policing (COP) and problem-oriented policing (POP) arose as new ways of thinking about the role and mission of the police, asking fundamental questions about what do the police do and how they should organize their efforts to achieve their goals.[41]

The new police accountability represents a continuation of these earlier efforts, but seeks to extend and strengthen them. The change reflects a deeper understanding of the challenge of guiding and controlling the on-the-street behavior of police officers. If we want to reduce officer use of excessive force it is not sufficient simply to have a written policy indicating what actions are approved and not approved. The new world of accountability is heavily data driven. An early intervention system relies on timely and detailed data on officer performance so that commanders can identify problematic officer actions and broader patterns of conduct that need to be addressed. (COMPSTAT and hot spots policing, which we do not cover in this book, are obviously data-driven programs.) Finally, the main argument of this book is that the various accountability measures represent a comprehensive package of policies and procedures that interact and depend on each other. An early intervention system, for example, depends on timely and accurate data on critical incidents and citizen complaints. Without them, the system cannot present a complete picture of officer performance.

Use of Force and Critical Incident Policies

The first element of the new police accountability involves written policies governing all critical incidents, not just use of force, accompanied by the requirement that police officers file official reports for each incident. A *critical incident* is defined as any police action that poses a risk to the life, liberty, or dignity of a citizen.[42] Additionally, these reports are automatically reviewed by supervisors to ensure that the officer complied with departmental policies. As we will explain in detail in Chapter Two, the movement to control critical incidents began with the use of deadly force and then slowly spread to cover other incidents such as the use of physical force, high-speed vehicle pursuits, the response to domestic violence incidents, and more. Critical incident policies are discussed in detail in Chapter Three.

This book argues that there is no fixed limit to the type and number of incidents that ideally should be covered. One of the important elements of the new police accountability is that police departments, and indeed the entire law enforcement profession, should engage in a continuous process of self-monitoring, with departments becoming "learning organizations."[43] The result of this process is that we do not know what problems will come to the attention of the public and/or police managers in the future and might lead to new understanding of what constitutes a critical incident.

One of the problems facing American policing, however, is the lack of national standards for critical incident policies. Austin (Texas) Police Chief Art Acevedo told a 2012 Police Executive Research Forum conference that "we have 18,000 police departments with 18,000 set of policies and 18,000 ways of doing business. We should come together and develop model policies. It's a matter of holding people accountable for their actions and having some consensus on model policies."[44] The lack of national standards is also true with regard to accountability. Professional associations such as PERF and the IACP (International Association of Chiefs of Police) develop model policies and sponsor discussions of accountability issues, but there is no single repository of the emerging best practices in the field. In part this is because of the fluid state of the field, with new practices continuing to develop.

Open and Accessible Citizen Complaint Procedures

An open and accessible citizen complaint process is a necessary part of a police accountability system. The citizen complaint process gives citizens a right to voice their grievances about how they were treated. Complaints against the police represent a basic First Amendment right: the right to petition government for a redress of grievances. The right to file a complaint, moreover, embodies the principle of *voice* that is central to the concept of procedural justice. People are more likely to regard an organization as legitimate if they have an opportunity to express their point of view and feel they have contributed to the ultimate outcome.[45] Finally, complaints are an important, though admittedly incomplete, indicator of police officer conduct. Even though few people who feel they have a grievance actually file complaints, and even though most complaints are not sustained, they serve a useful management purpose.

Traditionally, police departments regarded citizen complaints as virtually hostile acts, to be fended off if at all possible. The 1967 President's Crime Commission report and the 1968 Kerner Commission report both found that many departments did not have a formal complaint process and in those departments citizens were often discouraged from filing complaints, given misinformation about the process, or in some cases were threatened with arrest.[46]

In the new accountability, however, citizen complaints are regarded as an important form of *management information:* They are indicators of possible performance problems that need to be corrected. An officer who receives a higher number of complaints than peer officers, even where all of them are not sustained, may have some performance problems that need addressing. An early intervention system (see the following section) is the accountability mechanism for identifying patterns of complaints and placing those complaints in the context of an officer's overall performance so that commanders can determine what problems need to be addressed. Citizen complaints are discussed in detail in Chapter Four.

Early Intervention Systems

Early intervention systems (EISs) are widely regarded as the cornerstones of the new police accountability. An EIS involves a computerized database on officer performance for the purpose of identifying officers with performance problems that need to be corrected.[47] The database may include as many as 25 or as few as 5 performance indicators. EISs are the linchpins of an accountability system because they utilize critical incident reports on uses of force and citizen complaints, which we have already discussed. An EIS imposes new burdens on a police department. Critical incident reports need to be complete and accurate and entered into the EIS in a timely fashion. The same is true of citizen complaints. The key component of an EIS is pattern analysis. Supervisors review EIS data to look for patterns in an officer's conduct: a higher than average number of use of force incidents or citizen complaints. A pattern of incidents does not mean that the officer is guilty of an infraction or violation of department rules. It simply means that supervisors need to conduct a full review of the officer's performance to determine the underlying causes and decide whether intervention is needed.

The intervention phase of an EIS might involve merely counseling an officer about his or her performance, referral to professional counseling for substance abuse or anger management, or special training, for example, in tactics for conducting a traffic stop. Formal intervention is not recorded as a disciplinary action. EISs are designed to be *early* in terms of identifying officer performance problems and correcting them before they result in a serious use of force incident, lawsuit against the department, or other serious problem. EISs are extremely complicated and are discussed in detail in Chapter Five. Pattern analysis, a key part of an EIS, is also increasingly adopted in other accountability measures.

External and Internal Review

The fourth police accountability strategy involves both external and internal review of officer conduct. The police traditionally resisted any form of external oversight, including both citizen complaint review agencies and the Supreme Court. The new police accountability, however, recognizes the value of regular input to a police department from outside experts.

The police auditor has emerged as the most effective form of external citizen oversight. Unlike civilian complaint review boards, which review individual citizen complaints, police auditors have authority to investigate any and every issue within a law enforcement agency. Police auditors have been particularly successful in examining patterns and practices of police conduct: use of force incidents, civil suits against the department, and systemic failures to discipline officers. Police auditors are discussed in detail in Chapter Six.

The traditional dichotomy between internal and external review of the police has begun to dissolve as internal review has expanded considerably in recent years. Police internal review now goes far beyond an immediate supervisor reviewing officer critical incident reports. As we will discuss in Chapter Two, the 1972 NYPD deadly force policy initiated this development with a Firearms Discharge Review Board that examined officer firearms discharge reports. [48] Some variation of that form of review is almost standard now in large police departments. The newest form of internal review involves a procedure for examining both individual incident reports and patterns over time for the purpose of identifying issues related to policy, training, and supervision that need to be improved.

A Framework for Accountability: PTSR

As we have argued, the various elements of the new police accountability represent a package, a set of policies and programs that work together and reinforce each other. Failure to develop one of those elements weakens the other parts. Put simply, it is not sufficient to develop state-of-the-art written policies on use of force and other critical incidents if, for example, they are not reinforced by training, or if there is no early intervention system to track officer performance and identify officers with problematic performance, or if there is no meaningful discipline of officers who violate a policy. To understand the interrelatedness of the various elements of the new police accountability it is useful to think of them in terms of the acronym PTSR, which stands for *Policy, Training, Supervision,* and *Review.*

Policy

As we discussed earlier, accountability requires that departments have clear and specific policies on all critical incidents involving the life, liberty, and safety of people. Future policy development points in several directions. First, all law enforcement agencies should have state-of-the-art policies on all critical incidents. Second, the process of policy development should be recognized as an open-ended one. Not too many years ago, for example, foot pursuits were not covered by policies designed to reduce the risks to officers and citizens. Today, however, foot pursuits are recognized as potentially very dangerous, and are increasingly covered by department policies. We cannot foresee what aspects of police-citizen interaction will also be needed to be covered by policies in the future. Third, there needs to be a continuing process of refining and clarifying existing policies. The Collaborative Reform report on Las Vegas found the department's policy on deadly force to be generally sound, but it nonetheless made a series of recommendations for improvement.[49] Fourth, policies need to be made consistent throughout a department's policy manual to ensure, for example, that the less lethal force policy is not contradicted or muddied by citing it incorrectly it in another policy statement. Finally, policies need to be continually reviewed and revised (see the final section on "Review").

Training

Training, it hardly needs to be said, is a basic element of modern police administration, and it represents one of the major achievements of the police professionalization movement in the twentieth century.[50] Training, moreover, must be a continuous and comprehensive effort, including pre-service academy training, mandatory annual in-service training, roll call training, and special ad hoc training for certain officers. The importance of inservice and other forms of refresher training was highlighted by Art Acevedo, chief of the Austin (Texas) Police Department, who believes that "the vast majority of improper uses of force, especially deadly force, are a direct or indirect result of officers abandoning the tactics that we spent a lot of time and money training them on."[51]

The new police accountability has added important new dimensions to police training. One development involves having training unit officers respond to critical incidents in the field. Jerry Dyer, chief of the Fresno (California) Police Department, told a 2012 Police Executive Research Forum conference that "Our training unit responds to every officer-involved shooting. They're part of the initial walkthrough, and they're part of the review that we conduct on every officer-involved shooting. The training commander also reviews use of force reports completed by a supervisor. So they know what types of incidents are occurring out there, and they're better equipped to put together the types of training that we need."[52]

A 1980s training experiment in the Miami-Dade Police Department, called the Violence Reduction Project, provided a group of officers with a three-day training program that consisted of lectures, videotapes, and role playing on reducing conflict in encounters with citizens. Officers receiving the training were subsequently observed to use force significantly less often than a control group of officers.[53] The success of the project suggests that in the new police accountability it is possible to identify recurring police-citizen encounter problems and then design a training program that specifically addresses those problems.

A second important new dimension of training is highlighted by the 2012 Collaborative Reform Process report on the Las Vegas Metropolitan Police Department (LVMPD) (see Chapter Six).[54] The report's analysis of officer-involved shootings identified a number of officer tactical errors in both fatal and nonfatal officer-involved shootings. The most frequent errors involved radio communications (e.g., failure to provide updates on a rapidly evolving incident), defensive tactics, officer approach (e.g., failure to choose a tactic that would slow down an evolving incident), coordination among officers, and failure to use proper cover and conceal-ment tactics. All of these tactical errors and the others cited in the report are susceptible to focused training efforts. Identifying them, meanwhile, involves some of the key elements of the new police accountability, including primarily systematic data collection on critical incidents and the review and analysis of patterns of incidents. No one expects that all controversial officer-involved shooting incidents will ever be eliminated, but important parts of the new accountability, if applied to training, can certainly reduce their number.

The new accountability also imposes new training burdens on police departments, particularly with regard to data analysis. Several aspects of the new accountability rely on the systematic analysis of officer perfor-mance data: early intervention systems and trend analyses of officer-involved shootings, other uses of force, and other critical incidents. With respect to COMPSTAT (for COMPuterSTATistics), an important innova-tion for analyzing trends in crime and disorder, Michael D. White argues that existing police training programs "often fall short" in preparing offi-cers for such new demands.[55] His comments are equally relevant for the data-driven aspects of the new accountability.

Supervision

The heart of policing is the on-the-street crew of one sergeant and between eight and 10 officers (the standard generally recognized in the profession). Accountability depends heavily on how a sergeant supervises those officers. Moreover, the nature of those responsibilities has changed and expanded with new accountability mechanisms such as early intervention systems. On the street, sergeants are responsible for directly observing their officers, supporting and backing them up, monitoring their actions, and directly intervening when necessary or appropriate. When an officer violates department policy, as in using excessive force, the sergeant has a duty to report it to internal affairs for investigation. When an officer's conduct is simply less than ideal but not a violation, the sergeant may choose to advise, counsel, or mentor that officer about proper police action. Such actions represent the best kind of "early intervention" to improve officer performance.

Robin Engel's research on sergeants found several different supervisory styles used by sergeants. About a quarter of all the supervisors in the study adopted a "supportive" definition of their role, seeking to protect their officers against upper management. That approach is unacceptable in the new accountability. Similarly, about a quarter of the supervisors were defined as "traditional" in their role definition, emphasizing strict discipline of officers.[56] As we shall see later in this book, important elements of the new accountability—particularly early intervention systems—go beyond mere discipline and emphasize supervisors and the entire department's role in using problematic encounters with citizens as opportunities to counsel, coach, and train officers in how to be better officers.

The emergence of formal early intervention systems has significantly altered the role of sergeants. Sergeants are responsible for monitoring the data in the EIS to identify both individual incidents of possible misconduct and patterns of problematic performance. Without the officer in question triggering one of the thresholds in the EIS system, which would lead to a formal intervention, a sergeant can use the data to counsel the officer.[57]

Meaningful discipline of officers for violation of department policies is in many respects the crucial part of a comprehensive accountability system. Each police department has its own organizational culture (although, regrettably, we have only limited research on this subject). A key part of the culture is the "going rate," the level of discipline that is routinely meted out for certain violations of policy. The term "going rate" comes from research on sentencing in criminal courts, and refers, for example, to the normal and expected sentence for a first-offense burglary conviction where the offender has no prior felony convictions.[58] Unfortunately, we have little research on police disciplinary practices and have no good evidence on, for example, the expected punishment for a sustained rudeness complaint or a sustained excessive force complaint where there is no injury.

In departments where the going rate means that officers are rarely given meaningful discipline for misconduct, the entire accountability system begins to collapse. The formal policy on use of force, no matter how good it is by national standards, will have little meaning and impact on officers on the street if they learn by experience that no discipline will result from violating it.

Review

Review, as we have already discussed, consists of a variety of policies and practices that seek to learn from particular incidents and/or patterns of incidents. An EIS is one form of review: examining an officer's performance record to identify any pattern of problematic conduct. Another form of review that has emerged in recent years is post-incident review. It involves an *administrative* review of any critical incident and is entirely separate from the *disciplinary* review directed toward whether or not an officer violated any department policy or law. An administrative review is designed to determine whether the incident in question raises questions about the department's policies, training, or supervision that need to be revised in order to prevent serious incidents in the future. In this respect it plays a feedback role, potentially strengthening the policy, training, and supervision aspects of the PTSR framework.

Policy review, finally, involves an examination of patterns and trends in one or more areas of police activity. It might involve a review of use of force incidents, high-speed vehicle pursuits, or other incidents over the course of several years. The purpose is to identify any patterns or trends that suggest needed changes in policies, training, and supervision. At the PERF conference on Justice Department "pattern or practice" litigation, a Los Angeles police commander said that one of the "legacies" of their consent decree experience was the "audit function," in which they now do random samples of warrant applications, arrests, and other critical police actions.[59] Policy review can and should also involve learning the best practices from around the country (see the Dallas Eight-Point Plan, discussed earlier). Policy review can be conducted by an external citizen oversight agency or by the department itself. The Special Counsel to the Los Angeles Sheriff's Department has a 30-year record of policy review, with an impressive record of identifying problems related by the use of canines, civil suits against the department, use of force trends, and many other issues.[60]

Basic Themes in the New Police Accountability

Several themes emerge from the examples of the new world of police accountability that we have discussed so far. The remainder of the book will illustrate and explain them in greater detail.

A Focus on Organizational Change

One of the most important themes in the new accountability is the focus on organizations rather than individual officers. Merrick Bobb, for 20 years the Special Counsel to the Los Angeles Sheriff's Department, observed that the problem of officer-involved shootings was not a matter of a few bad officers but poor management practices.[61] Law professor Barbara Armacost agrees, arguing that police reform needs to focus on "rotten barrels" rather than rotten apples.[62] She notes the depressing cycle of scandal, reform, and subsequent scandal in Los Angeles and concludes that "reform efforts have focused too much on notorious incidents and misbehaving individuals," and not enough on police organizations that sustain a "police culture that facilitates and rewards violent conduct."[63] Changing police organizations, rather than changing single policies or prosecuting individual officers, is the focus of "pattern and practice" by the Civil Rights Division of the U.S. Department of Justice.[64]

The focus on *organizational change* is a significant departure from past reform efforts that focused too much on individual officers who may have used excessive force or made a racially biased arrest. The rotten apple theory persists and motivates many community activists because it has powerful emotional and political appeal. It personalizes misconduct by giving it a human face—the accused officer. Unfortunately, it is simplistic and ineffective. Organizational change, by contrast, involves complex administration procedures (e.g., use of force reporting requirements, early intervention systems) that lack emotional appeal, have no human face, and are often difficult for the ordinary person to immediately understand. The results, moreover, lie in the future rather than in the emotionally charged present.

Changing the organization also involves changing what is referred to as the organizational culture of a police department, or the police subculture. The police culture may be defined as the established ways of doing police work. Debra Livingston argues that the "conclusion drawn by many police scholars" is that "police reform will be most effective . . . when reform involves not simply adherence to rules in the face of punitive sanctions, but a change in the organizational values and systems to which both managers and line officers adhere."[65] It is a sad commentary on the academic field of police studies that there has been so little research on the organizational culture of policing and individual police departments.

Data Collection and Analysis

The second theme is the *central role of data collection and analysis.* Policing is an information enterprise from the bottom of the organization to the top. Patrol officers observe and collect information about their beats so that they are able to recognize events that are out of the ordinary and possibly suspicious activity. Top management today cannot effectively run a department with systematic data on officer conduct: arrests, traffic stops, uses of force, and so on. The data also needs to be detailed, including demographic data on the people who are arrested or stopped.[66]

Changing a police organization requires the systematic collection and analysis of data on officer performance. Critical incident reporting, an effective citizen complaint process, and an early intervention system are the specific tools for this purpose. The larger strategy is to develop a fact-based picture of officer activity for the purpose of identifying recurring problems that merit corrective action. To cite an important example from medicine, the collection of systematic data on deaths in hospitals produced the shocking estimate that at least 40,000 people die each year in American hospitals from preventable accidents—and some experts believe that the figure is actually much higher.[67] Chapter Seven discusses how risk management programs can prevent unnecessary deaths or other problems in medicine and policing.

Data collection is particularly relevant to the critical issues of use of force and racial profiling. The power of data to focus reform is described by Merrick Bobb, Special Counsel to the Los Angeles Sheriff's Department (LASD). He concluded his report on the troubled Century Station by observing that "this chapter began with a discussion about numbers and ended with a discussion about management. This is how it should be."[68]

In its investigation of the Seattle Police Department, the Justice Department faulted the department for not collecting demographic data on persons stopped on the street by precinct or district, which limited its ability to address allegations of racial bias. The DOJ report noted that "data collection is just one piece necessary to address policing practices."[69]

Systematic data analysis has already pervaded American policing in other areas. One of the most celebrated reforms in policing in the past decade, in fact, is COMPSTAT, a program that collects and analyzes systematic data on patterns of crime and disorder for the purpose of focusing crime reduction efforts.[70] At the same time, systematic data collection embraces the principles of problem-oriented policing (POP), the first cousin of community policing and in many respects a more specific road map for action. The action framework for POP involves the SARA model of scanning, analysis, response, and assessment.[71] Scanning, in this context, means the collection of systematic data; analysis involves the review of that data and the identification of problems that need attention; response is the action a department takes with regard to a problem; and assessment is the follow-up review on the impact of the response.[72] As we already noted with regard to training, however, the data-driven aspect of the new accountability imposes new training burdens on police departments. Few officers are proficient in systematic data analysis, and this subject has never been a part of police academy curricula. To make full use of the potential of data analysis, departments will need to revise training accordingly.[73]

Police Departments as Learning Organizations

The third theme is that police departments need to become *learning organizations.* Years ago, Bill Geller asked, "Can our police and sheriffs' departments find ways to work smarter, not just harder?" He answered his own question by arguing that police departments should "institutionalize the organizational learning process, just as our Nation's best run companies do?"[74] Working smarter involves being proactive regarding current or potential issues and developing data systems that document current operations, help to identify trends, and provide the basis for informed action.

There are many examples of police departments becoming learning organizations. At the outset of this chapter we discussed the Dallas Eight-Point Plan, where the chief planned to identify the best practices in departments around the country. The Collaboration Reform Process in Las Vegas also represented an effort to learn from both Justice Department experts and experts at the cooperating private consulting firm. Charles Ramsey, reform-minded commissioner of the Philadelphia Police Department, launched an anticorruption program saying, "a learning organization is one that has a shared vision and mission, has the means and the willingness to learn from the experiences of its members, seeks out best practices and makes changes as required."[75]

A learning organization is also a proactive one. The police have always been reactive, responding in a crisis management manner to officer-involved shootings and excessive force incidents. The sheriff in Las Vegas explains that "we don't do a good enough job of being proactive and analyzing data on situations prior to them becoming an issue."[76] Proactive response to types of incidents that have the potential to provoke community crises, utilizing data-driven analyses, is the hallmark of the new police accountability.

In the development of accountability-related policies and procedures, police departments have learned from other agencies on a number of important issues. In effect, almost all departments learned from the pioneering 1972 NYPD deadly force policy. In the 1990s, many departments developed early intervention systems by adapting some or most of the systems in the Los Angeles Sheriff's Department and the Miami-Dade Police Department. At the beginning of this chapter we described how the chief of police in Dallas, Texas, plans to examine and learn from the best practices in other departments.

There has also been an important process of cross-fertilization among different critical incident policies. The Justice Department investigation of the handling of mentally ill persons by the Portland, Oregon, police is an instructive case in point. The problems it identified involved use of force policies and the inappropriate use of conducted energy devices (CEDs) in particular. Thus, the initial issue of response to people with mental health problems directly implicates two other important issues and requires the department to develop state-of-the-art policies and practices for each one.[77]

From Punishment to Behavior Change

A relatively new theme in police accountability has been the recognition that the response to officer misconduct needs to shift from discipline to behavior change. As many observers pointed out, police departments were historically "punishment-centered," emphasizing meting out discipline for any rule violation. Mere punishment, a reprimand or suspension, for example, does not necessarily result in better conduct by the officer. A deterrent effect is assumed to occur, but there are good reasons for thinking it only creates resentment and serves to reinforce negative attitudes on the part of the officer. Darrel Stephens, the respected former police chief in Charlotte, North Carolina, and former head of PERF, points out that "alternative courses of action that would lead to behavioral change are seldom part of the sanctions imposed on officers who have had sustained misconduct charges."[78]

Early intervention systems are based on the principle of changing officer behavior by identifying problematic performance early and then intervening to provide some nondisciplinary corrective action. The Los Angeles Sheriff's Department, meanwhile, has developed an education-based discipline program designed to improve officer conduct rather than just mete out discipline.[79]

The Role of Federal Pattern or Practice Investigations

Considerable controversy surrounds federal "pattern or practice" investigations of state and local law enforcement agencies, and the consent decrees, memoranda of understanding, and investigative findings letters that have compelled departments to undertake sweeping reforms.[80] Police chiefs and local elected officials have strenuously objected that their departments have been unfairly singled out, that there are no clear standards governing which departments will be investigated, that the costs of implementing the required reforms are too costly, and that the entire process unnecessarily polarizes the community. Civil rights activists, who in many cases requested the Justice Department to act, respond that federal intervention is the only way to achieve genuine reform in police departments that have been indifferent to long-standing complaints about excessive force and discrimination.

There is no question that federal consent decrees and memoranda of understanding are expensive. The court-appointed monitor for Seattle cost nearly $1 million for its first year (2012–13). There is also no question that federal investigations generate much conflict. The mayor of Seattle fought very hard to resist a settlement with the Justice Department. The mayor of New Orleans tried in early 2013 to withdraw from a consent decree that he had previously signed. (The federal judge rejected the city's petition for withdrawal.)[81]

Law professor Rachel A. Harmon is moderately skeptical about federal intervention from a very different perspective. Given the very limited resources of the Special Litigation Section, the Justice Department would only be able to investigate a very limited number of police departments even if its current (as of 2013) resources were doubled or quadrupled.[82] Harmon argues that all federal remedies are severely limited (e.g., the exclusionary rule, prosecuting police officers for criminal offenses) and argues for exploring alternative remedies for ending civil rights abuses by local police departments.[83]

The evidence, however, indicates that federal intervention has led to significant improvements in troubled police departments. Particularly important is the testimony of police executives who have experienced consent decrees or memoranda of agreement (MOAs). Charles Ramsey, who invited the DOJ to investigate the Washington, D.C., police department, later told a PERF conference on de-escalation that "the DOJ assistance made a huge difference . . . I don't think we could have made the changes that we made without" their involvement. In the end, the department "was a far better department than it was" beforehand. A Los Angeles Police Department assistant chief told the conference that the experience "was costly but improved the department."[84] At a subsequent conference specifically on federal pattern or practice litigation, Ramsey and officials from other departments reiterated these points. Two commented that the reforms had saved them large sums of money because of reduced lawsuits and damage awards.[85]

The contributions of the federal pattern or practice effort reach beyond the results in particular cases. In the consent decrees and MOAs, the Justice Department has defined a clear set of "best practices" for all law enforcement agencies. The three key elements of these settlements include state-of-the-art use of force policies, an early intervention system, and an open and accessible citizen complaint process. (Variations on other issues exist for particular police departments.) As police experts have long noted, there are no formal national standards for police departments in the United States. (See Chapter Two for a discussion of the CALEA accreditation standards.) In an unofficial but nonetheless forceful way, the content of the consent decrees and MOAs have begun to fill that void.

An additional comment on the content of the consent decrees and MOAs is important at this point. The various provisions were not invented by Justice Department lawyers in Washington. State-of-the-art use of force policies and early intervention systems developed within the law enforcement profession over many years, and reflected the best thinking within the profession. The Justice Department simply took the best policies on a few key issues and included them in consent decrees and MOAs.

The Challenge Ahead

The new police accountability is an exciting development that holds great promise for the future. We should not, however, ignore the challenges that lie ahead. It would be easy to overestimate the significance or the long-term prospects of these promising efforts. After all, the cycle of reform and failure has been repeated many times in the history of the American police, and the challenge of sustaining reforms is enormous.[86] But there are also grounds for optimism. One of the central arguments of this book is that what is particularly new about the new police accountability is a more sophisticated understanding of the nature of the problem and a new set of tools and strategies to deal with it.

Candor requires that we emphasize the *promise* of the new accountability, as distinct from an achieved reality. By the prevailing standards of social science research there is only limited evidence that the tools and strategies described in this book in fact achieve their intended goals.

Even more disturbing, the evidence used in this book to argue for the new police accountability also includes many examples in which the new tools and strategies have not been properly implemented or have been allowed to fall into disrepair through administrative neglect. This evidence represents a substantial red flag about the prospects for meaningful and lasting reform. Will the new police accountability succeed? We cannot say at this point. It is too early in this national effort to draw any definitive conclusions about success or failure. What this book does do, however, is map the landscape: to describe the new accountability mechanisms, explain in detail how they are intended to work, and carefully weigh the available evidence on successes and failures. Some years down the road, we will be able to say whether the effort succeeded, and if the book did identify the conditions of success, and if it did not at least help to tell us where we went wrong. In the meantime, more research is needed on which accountability mechanisms work and which ones work best.

Wesley Skogan cautions us about being overly optimistic about police reform. There is a long history of reforms that have failed. In a provocative article he outlines the various reasons "Why Reform Fails."[87] They include resistance by police managers who feel threatened by change, resistance by sergeants who also feel threatened by change to their established ways of working, resistance by rank and file officers, resistance by special units, resistance by police unions, competing demands and expectations, the inability to "measure what matters," a failure of interagency cooperation (where applicable), public unresponsiveness, and leadership changes. These are formidable obstacles, and they have doomed many important reforms over the decades.[88] To the traditional list we can add the impact of the national financial crisis, which has constrained the budgets of all government agencies, and for the police has resulted in loss of police officers, delays in hiring new officers, cuts in specific programs such as training, and in general has forced police managers to focus on immediate needs rather than planning and innovation.[89]

One of the more notable examples of the failure of accountability-related reforms would be the reforms developed by New York City Police Commissioner Patrick V. Murphy in the early 1970s. In the wake of the highly publicized corruption scandal investigated by the Knapp Commission (and generally associated with the name of officer Frank Serpico), Murphy decentralized corruption control in Field Investigative Units.[90] These units were designed to be closer to streets where the problems existed than the old centralized unit, and therefore presumably more effective. Yet, as subsequent scandals and the 1994 Mollen Commission report revealed, these reforms had completely collapsed and blatant corruption flourished. Even worse, the Mollen Commission found a new and even more insidious form of corruption within the NYPD, a combination of brutality and graft.[91]

Many cynics believe that the American police are incapable of reforming themselves and that the police subculture is resistant to all efforts to achieve accountability. Regrettably, a review of police history lends an uncomfortable amount of support to this very pessimistic view. This book argues, to the contrary, that self-sustaining commitment to accountability is indeed possible and has in fact already made some important gains. A number of law enforcement agencies across the country have made a significant commitment to accountability, and in several important respects there are efforts to build upon and strengthen critical incident policies and internal review of patterns and trends in police operations that affect the lives, liberties, and safety of the American people. The remainder of this book describes the important developments in police accountability.

Notes

1   Dallas Police Department, *New Policies and Strategic Directives* (August 2012).

2   James K. Stewart et al., *Collaborative Reform Process: A Review of Officer Involved-Shootings in the Las Vegas Metropolitan Police Department*

(Washington, DC: Office of Community Oriented Policing Services, 2012). Available at http://www.cops.usdoj.gov/pdf/e10129513-Collaborative-Reform-Process_FINAL.pdf.

3 Ibid., 6–8.

4 United States v. City of New Orleans, *Consent Decree Regarding the New Orleans Police Department* (July 24, 2012). Available at http://www.justice.gov/crt/about/spl/documents/nopd_agreement_1–11–13.pdf.

5 William A. Geller, "Suppose We Were Really Serious About Police Departments Becoming 'Learning Organizations,'?" *National Institute Journal* (December 1997): 2–8.

6 The background to the report is discussed in Stewart et al., *Collaborative Reform Process,* 9–10.

7 Samuel Walker and Morgan Macdonald, "An Alternative Remedy for Police Misconduct: A Model State Pattern or Practice Statute," *George Mason Civil Rights Law Journal* 19 (Summer 2009): 479–552.

8 Public Management Resources, *Monitor's Sixteenth Report* (2007), 4. But see the reservations expressed by this author about whether the reforms endured after the consent decree was lifted. Samuel Walker, "Institutionalizing Police Accountability Reforms," *Saint Louis University Public Law Review* 32 (no. 1, 2012), 64.

9 Michael Bromwich, *Twenty-Third Quarterly Report of the Independent Monitor* (2008), 4. But see the reservations expressed above in note 8.

10 Samuel Walker, "Institutionalizing Police Accountability Reforms: The Problem of Making Police Reforms Endure," *St. Louis University Public Law Review,* 32 (no. 1, 2012): 57–92. Trent Ikerd and Samuel Walker, *Making Police Reforms Endure: The Keys for Success* (Washington, DC: Department of Justice, 2010).

11 Police Executive Research Forum, *Civil Rights Investigations of Local Police: Lessons Learned* (Washington, DC: Police Executive Research Forum, 2013), 34–5.

12 Lou Cannon, *Official Negligence: How Rodney King Changed Los Angeles and the LAPD* (New York: Times Books, 1997).

13 Ron Weitzer, "Incidents of Police Misconduct and Public Opinion," *Journal of Criminal Justice* 20 (no. 5, 2002): 397–408.

14 The celebrated case phenomenon is discussed in Samuel Walker, *Sense and Nonsense About Crime, Drugs, and Community,* 7th ed. (Belmont, CA: Cengage, 2011), 40–2.

15 A chronology of the riots is in National Advisory Commission on Civil Disorders, *Report* (New York: Bantam Books, 1968).

16 Jack Greene, "Community Policing in America: Changing the Nature, Structure, and Function of the Police," in *Criminal Justice 2000. V. 3: Policies, Processes, and Decisions of the Criminal Justice System,* ed. Julie Horney

(Washington, DC: U.S. Department of Justice, 2000), 299. www.ncjrs.org, NCJ 182410.

17 Michael S. Scott, *Problem-Oriented Policing: Reflections on the First 20 Years* (Washington, DC: Department of Justice, 2002). Available at http://www .ncjrs.org.

18 David Alan Sklansky, "Not Your Father's Police Department: Making Sense of the New Demographics of Law Enforcement," *Journal of Criminal Law and Criminology* 96 (2005): 1209.

19 Samuel Walker, *Police Accountability: The Role of Citizen Oversight* (Belmont, CA: Wadsworth, 2001).

20 David L. Carter, Allen D. Sapp, and Darrel W. Stephens, *The State of Police Education: Policy Direction for the 21st Century* (Washington, DC: Police Executive Research Forum, 1989).

21 David Bayley, *Police for the Future* (New York: Oxford University Press, 1994), 101.

22 The term *legitimacy* is increasingly used to encompass the related issues of police compliance with the law and citizen perceptions of the police. See Wesley G. Skogan and Kathleen Frydl, eds., *Fairness and Effectiveness in Policing: The Evidence* (Washington, DC: National Academy Press, 2004), chap. 8, 291–326.

23 Winston Churchill, Speech to the House of Commons, November 11, 1947.

24 The lack of research on police accountability issues is discussed in Samuel Walker, *Police Accountability: Current Issues and Research Needs*, Paper, National Institute of Justice (May 2007), available at https://www.ncjrs .gov/pdffiles1/nij/grants/218583.pdf.

25 Greene, "Community Policing in America: Changing the Nature, Structure, and Function of the Police."

26 See Sogan and Frydl, eds., *Fairness and Effectiveness in Policing*, chap. 3, 47–108.

27 This point is the basic theme of Samuel Walker, *Popular Justice: A History of American Criminal Justice*, 2nd ed. (New York: Oxford University Press, 1998).

28 The classic study is Jerome Skolnick, *Justice Without Trial: Law Enforcement in a Democratic Society*, 3rd ed. (New York: Macmillan, 1994).

29 Herbert Packer, *The Limits of the Criminal Sanction* (Stanford: Stanford University Press, 1968), chap. 8, 149–73.

30 Lorraine Mazerolle, Sarah Bennett, Matthew Manning, Patricia Ferguson, and Elise Sargeant, *Legitimacy in Policing: A Systematic Review*, Campbell Systematic Reviews 9 (no. 1, 2013). Tom R. Tyler, ed., *Legitimacy and Criminal Justice: International Perspectives* (New York: Russell Sage Press, 2007).

31 Department of Justice, *Improving Police/Community Relations* (Washington, DC: Government Printing Office, 1973). Walker, *Popular Justice*, 193–201.

32 Tom Tyler, *Why People Obey the Law* (New Haven: Yale University Press, 1990).

33 Peter W. Greenwood et al., *The Criminal Investigation Process* (Lexington: Lexington Books, 1977).

34 Wesley G. Skogan and George Antunes, "Information, Apprehension, and Deterrence: Exploring the Limits of Police Productivity," *Journal of Criminal Justice* 7 (1979): 217–41.

35 Arlington, Texas, Police Chief, quoted in Police Executive Research Forum, *An Integrated Approach to De-Escalation and Minimizing Use of Force* (Washington, DC: Police Executive Research Forum, 2012): 21.

36 O. W. Wilson and Roy C. McLaren, *Police Administration*, 4th ed. (New York: McGraw-Hill, 1977). Walker, *Popular Justice: A History of American Criminal Justice*.

37 William A. Geller and Michael S. Scott, *Deadly Force: What We Know* (Washington, DC: Police Executive Research Forum, 1992).

38 Lawrence W. Sherman, Janell D. Schmidt, and Dennis P. Rogan, *Policing Domestic Violence: Experiments and Dilemmas* (New York: The Free Press, 1992).

39 Geoffrey P. Alpert and Roger D. Dunham, *Police Pursuit Driving: Controlling Responses to Emergency Situations* (New York: Greenwood Press, 1990).

40 Walker, *Police Accountability*, chap. 1.

41 Greene, "Community Policing in America: Changing the Nature, Structure, and Function of the Police."

42 The Madison, Wisconsin, Police Department has a policy on its process for analyzing critical incidents. The definition of critical incidents is not as specific as the one offered in this book, but the Outline for Critical Incident Analysis Review is a very useful starting point. Madison Police Department, Policy 8–100, *Critical Incident Analysis*.

43 Geller, "Suppose We Were Really Serious About Police Departments Becoming 'Learning Organizations.'?"

44 Art Acevedo, quoted in Police Executive Research Forum, *An Integrated Approach to De-escalation and Minimizing Use of Force*, 11.

45 Mazerolle et al., *Legitimacy in Policing: A Systematic Review.*

46 National Advisory Commission on Civil Disorders, *Report* (New York: Bantam Books, 1968). President's Commission on Law Enforcement and Administration of Justice, *Task Force Report: The Police* (Washington, DC: Government Printing Office, 1967).

47 Samuel Walker, *Early Intervention Systems for Law Enforcement Agencies: A Planning and Management Guide* (Washington, DC: Department of Justice, 2003).

48 James J. Fyve, "Administrative Interventions on Police Shooting Discretion: An Empirical Examination," *Journal of Criminal Justice* 7 (1979): 309–24.

49 Stewart et al., *Collaborative Reform Process: A Review of Officer-Involved Shootings in the Las Vegas Metropolitan Police Department.*

50   David A. Klinger, "Police Training as an Instrument of Accountability," *Saint Louis University Public Law Review* 32 (no. 1, 2012): 111–21.

51   Acevedo, quoted in Police Executive Research Forum, *An Integrated Approach to De-Escalation and Minimizing Use of Force*, 9.

52   Chief Jerry Dyer, Fresno, California, quoted in Police Executive Research Forum, *An Integrated Approach to De-Escalation and Minimizing Use of Force*, 23.

53   David Klinger, "Can Police Training Affect the Use of Force on the Streets? The Metro-Dade Violence Reduction Field Experiment," Candace McCoy, ed., *Holding Police Accountable* (Washington, DC: Urban Institute Press, 2010): 95–107.

54   Stewart et al., *The Collaborative Reform Process,* chap. 4, 30–59.

55   Michael D. White, "Training for the Data-Driven Police Department," Candace McCoy, ed., *Holding Police Accountable*, 187–210.

56   Robin Shepard Engel, *How Police Supervisory Styles Influence Patrol Officer Behavior* (Washington, DC: Department of Justice, 2003).

57   Samuel Walker, Stacy Osnick Milligan, with Anna Berke, *Strategies for Intervening with Officers through Early Intervention Systems: A Guide for Front-Line Supervisors* (Washington, DC: Department of Justice, 2006).

58   Samuel Walker, *Sense and Nonsense About Crime, Drugs, and Community*, 7th ed. (Belmont, CA: Cengage, 2011).

59   James J. Fyfe, "Administrative Interventions on Police Shooting Discretion: An Empirical Examination."

60   The reports of the Special Counsel for the Los Angeles Sheriff's Department are available at http://www.parc.info.

61   Merrick Bobb, Special Counsel, *15th Semiannual Report* (Los Angeles: Police Executive Research Center, 2002), 16. The reports of the Special Counsel are available at http://www.parc.info. Merrick Bobb, Special Counsel, *9th Semiannual Report* (Los Angeles: Police Assessment Research Center, 1998), 8. Report available at http://www.parc.info.

62   Barbara Armacost, "Organizational Culture and Police Misconduct," *George Washington Law Review* 72 (March 2004): 457–59.

63   Ibid., 455.

64   Walker and Macdonald, "An Alternative Remedy for Police Misconduct."

65   Debra Livingston, "Police Reform and the Department of Justice: An Essay on Accountability," *Buffalo Criminal Law Review* 2 (1999): 848.

66   See, however, the provocative but skeptical discussion of the development and use of official police data in James F. Gilsinan, "The Numbers Dilemma: The Chimera of Modern Police Accountability Systems," *Saint Louis University Public Law Review* 32 (no. 1, 2012): 93–109.

67   National Institute of Medicine, *To Err Is Human* (Washington, DC: National Academy Press, 1999).

68 Merrick J. Bobb, Special Counsel, *15th Semiannual Report*, 34.

69 Department of Justice, *Investigation of the Seattle Police Department*, (2011), 30.

70 James J. Willis, Stephen D. Mastrofski, David Weisburd, and Rosann Greenspan, *Compstat and Organizational Change in the Lowell Police Department: Challenges and Opportunities* (Washington, DC: The Police Foundation, 2004).

71 Michael S. Scott, *Problem-Oriented Policing: Reflections on the First 20 Years* (Washington, DC: Department of Justice, 2002). Available at http://www .ncjrs.org.

72 Greene, "Community Policing in America: Changing the Nature, Structure, and Function of the Police," 299. See http://www.ncjrs.org, NCJ 182410. Scott, *Problem-Oriented Policing: Reflections on the First 20 Years.*

73 Michael D. White, "Training for the Data-Driven Department," McCoy, ed., *Holding Police Accountable*, 187–210.

74 Geller, "Suppose We Were Really Serious About Police Departments Becoming 'Learning Organizations'?"

75 Philadelphia Police Department, *Preventing Corruption Within Our Ranks: Creating a Values-Driven Organization* (Philadelphia: Philadelphia Police Department, 2010).

76 Police Executive Research Forum, *An Integrated Approach to De-Escalation and Minimizing Use of Force.*

77 U.S. Department of Justice, Letter to Hon. Sam Adams, *Investigation of the Portland Police Bureau* (September 12, 2012).

78 Darrel W. Stephens, *Police Discipline: A Case for Change* (Cambridge: Kennedy School of Government, 2011), 6.

79 Office of Internal Review, *Seventh Annual Report* (Los Angeles: Los Angeles Sheriff's Department, 2009), 30–4.

80 Walker and Macdonald, "An Alternative Remedy for Police Misconduct."

81 "A New Orleans–Washington Handshake Turns to Fists," *The New York Times*, February 13, 2013. The costs of consent decrees are discussed in Police Executive Research Forum, *Civil Rights Investigations of Local Police: Lessons Learned*, 34–5.

82 Rachel A. Harmon, "Limited Leverage: Federal Remedies and Policing Reform," *Saint Louis University Public Law Review* 32 (no. 1, 2012): 44.

83 Rachel A. Harmon, "The Problem of Policing," *Michigan Law Review* 110 (March 2012): 761–818.

84 Police Executive Research Forum, *An Integrated Approach to De-Escalation and Minimizing Use of Force*, 29–30.

85 Samuel Walker, Stacy Osnick Milligan, with Anna Berke, *Strategies for Intervening with Officers through Early Intervention Systems: A Guide for Front-Line Supervisors* (Washington, DC: Department of Justice, 2006).

86 Walker, "Institutionalizing Police Accountability Reforms: The Problem of Making Police Reforms Endure."

87 Wesley G. Skogan, "Why Reforms Fail," *Policing and Society* 18 (March 2008): 23–34.

88 Samuel Walker, "Institutionalizing Police Accountability Reforms: The Problem of Making Police Reforms Endure," *Saint Louis University Public Law Review* 32 (no. 1, 2012): 57–93. Trent Ikerd and Samuel Walker, *Making Police Reforms Endure: The Keys for Success* (Washington, DC: Department of Justice, 2010).

89 Police Executive Research Forum, *Is the Economic Downturn Fundamentally Changing How We Police?* (Washington, DC: PERF, 2010).

90 Knapp Commission, *Report of the Knapp Commission* (New York: Braziller, 1977). Patrick V. Murphy and Thomas Plate, *Commissioner: A View From the Top of American Law Enforcement* (New York: Simon and Schuster, 1978).

91 Commission to Investigate Allegations of Police Corruption and the Anti-Corruptions Procedures of the Police Department [Mollen Commission], *Commission Report* (New York: 1994). Available at http://www.parc.info.

TWO

The Accomplishments and Limits of Traditional Police Reforms

T he significance of the new police accountability is dramatized when we place it in the context of past police reform efforts and examine what they accomplished and where they fell short. This chapter offers a brief critical review of the principal police reform efforts of the past.

Police reform has a long history in the United States, reaching back into the middle of the nineteenth century. The early efforts achieved little in the way of lasting improvement in policing, however, and by the early twentieth century the American police were mired in corruption, brutality, and inefficiency—all the result of a pervasive system of political influence over police departments.[1] The professionalization movement arose in the 1900s and became the first police reform effort to achieve any lasting change. In the late 1950s and 1960s, civil rights and civil liberties activists turned to the courts as an instrument of police reform. These developments provoked a broader movement to reform the police through controls over deadly force, civilian review of complaints against officers, and the hiring of more African American officers. Administrative rulemaking spread in the 1970s, with new rules on deadly force, high-speed pursuits, and domestic violence. In the 1980s, community-oriented policing and problem-oriented policing rejected the operating assumptions of police professionalism, offered a new paradigm for the police role in society, and developed new police strategies designed to both bring the police into closer relations with the communities they serve and provide more effective responses to crime and disorder.[2]

While the community policing movement put much emphasis in the greater accountability of police departments to the communities they serve with regard to crime and disorder, it gave relatively little emphasis to enhancing the accountability of individual officers for their interactions with citizens. A review of the most important literature on community policing reveals little if any discussion of strategies to curb police use of deadly force, excessive physical force, or race discrimination.[3] The new police accountability movement, which was generally separate from the community policing movement, sought to fill in the missing elements.

As we explained in Chapter One, the new police accountability focuses on organizational change. Law professor Barbara Armacost argues that past police reform efforts focused too much on "notorious incidents and misbehaving individuals" and not enough on the dysfunctional aspects of police organizations that sustain serious misconduct.[4] This is not to say that past reform efforts accomplished nothing, but it does say that their achievements had important limits with respect to accountability. With that in mind, this chapter reviews the major reform movements, describing their major accomplishments and examining their limits.

Past Police Reform Strategies

The different police reform movements are each anchored in one of the three branches of government in the American system of constitutional democracy. Traditional police professionalism is anchored in the executive branch of government, with police chiefs as the principal agents of change. Suing the police over constitutional law violations or for civil damages involves private citizens and often civil rights groups utilizing the judicial branch of government. The creation of agencies to provide external citizen review of the police, as in citizen complaint review boards, is a strategy involving the legislative branch of government.

The Police Professionalization Movement

The first successful police reform effort in the United States was the police professionalization movement that emerged in the early years of the twentieth century.[5] At that time the American police were politically influenced, corrupt, and inefficient with regard to crime fighting. The core principle of police professionalism was and still remains the importance of political independence of the police, giving them the same autonomy and control over their domains that other professions enjoy.[6] To this end, generations of police managers have strenuously fought the actual or threatened intrusions into their managerial prerogatives, whether by local politicians, the U.S. Supreme Court, citizen oversight agencies, or police unions.

The reform agenda of the professionalization movement included securing expert leadership for police departments, freedom from political influence, the application of modern management principles to police organizations, and higher personnel standards for officers. The agenda of professionalization dominated police management thinking through the 1970s. The professionalization movement accomplished much in the way of improving American policing. By the 1960s, most police departments were far better managed than they had been 30 or 40 years earlier. Police departments deployed their officers on a rational basis, for example, assigning more patrol officers to high-crime areas. The advent of the telephone, the two-way radio, and the patrol car made this commitment possible as a practical matter. Personnel standards rose significantly, in terms of minimum entry requirements and formal preservice training programs. In the nineteenth century there were no standards whatsoever beyond a person's political associations. California and New York set a new standard, since adopted nationwide, in 1959 with laws requiring minimal preservice training for all sworn officers in the state.[7]

The Shortcomings of Professionalization

Despite its achievements, the professionalization movement left many problems unaddressed, the most important being the control of police officer on-the-street behavior and the growing problem of police-race relations. Two powerful external forces engulfed the police in the early 1960s and exposed the failings of the professionalism movement: a series of U.S. Supreme Court decisions regarding certain police practices and the civil rights movement. The most famous Court decisions of the 1960s—*Mapp v. Ohio* and *Miranda v. Arizona*—imposed constitutional standards on searches and police interrogations, and in the process exposed the lack of any meaningful controls over officer conduct. The civil rights movement, meanwhile, challenged use of excessive force and discriminatory practices against African Americans. The urban riots of 1964–1968 were almost always sparked by an incident involving the police. The police officer in the ghetto became the symbol of the national crisis in race relations. The principal demands of civil rights leaders became the hiring of more African American officers and the creation of civilian review boards to handle citizen complaints.[8]

One of the most devastating commentaries on police professionalization appeared in the 1968 Kerner Commission report on the 1960s riots. The report somberly observed that "many of the serious disturbances took place in cities whose police departments are among the best led, best organized, best trained and most professional in the country."[9] The comment undoubtedly referred to the Los Angeles Police Department, which had cultivated a national reputation as the most professional department in the country. Although the commission did not elaborate, its statement was clearly an indictment of the basic assumptions and accomplishments of police professionalism. In short, even the best departments had failed to serve the African American community equitably, and in particular to control the use of both deadly and physical force.

O. W. Wilson's classic textbook, *Police Administration,* generally regarded as the authoritative "bible" on the subject of police management, provides a revealing picture of the shortcomings of traditional police professionalism. It systematically ignored what we today regard as basic issues of police accountability. Even the 1977 fourth edition contains no reference to police discretion, no recognition that it is pervasive in police work, and that if left unguided it can result in serious problems. The book devotes a total of four pages (out of more than 600) to supervision through "written directives," a process that is today a basic instrument of police management.[10] Moreover, there are no specific references to such critical incidents as the use of deadly force, physical force, high-speed pursuits, or the use of race in policing. The typical police department manual was traditionally a small, vest-pocket booklet, largely devoted to petty administrative rules about such things as grooming.

Wilson focused on the purely formal aspects of police management, such as the proper organizational structure, the chain of command, and the rational allocation of patrol officers. Missing from this approach to police management was any explicit attention to what police officers actually *do* on the street.[11] By the 1970s the emerging research on the police revealed that officers routinely encounter a wide range of complex and ambiguous situations, exercise broad discretion in handling them, and, in the absence of meaningful guidance, can engage in questionable actions.[12]

This point is commonplace today, but it was a startling revelation when it first began to appear in the late 1950s and 1960s. Kenneth C. Davis's 1975 book, *Police Discretion,* was the first serious discussion of this all-important topic.[13] Wilson's formalistic approach simply assumed that the proper organizational arrangements would necessarily result in the correct officer behavior. As we now know, and as this book argues in detail, the control of police officer behavior requires a complex array of detailed rules and procedures.

Evidence of the Shortcomings of Traditional Professionalism

Even in the 1980s and 1990s, it was easy to find evidence of how many police departments had failed to comply with even their own standards of traditional police professionalism. The follow list illustrates the point.

- A 1987 investigation found that the Philadelphia Police Department had not redrawn its patrol district boundaries in 16 years. Officers in the 35th district handled an average of 494 calls for service, whereas officers in the 5th district averaged 225.[14]
- Investigations of the Los Angeles Sheriff's Department and the Riverside, California, police department in the late 1990s found that the ratio of sergeants to officers under their command exceeded their own recommended standard of 1:8.[15]
- In the wake of the 1999 Rampart scandal, the Los Angeles Police Department's own internal Board of Inquiry Report concluded that the department's own personnel evaluation system was worthless. The report bluntly declared that "our personnel evaluations have little or no credibility at any level in the organization."[16]
- The 1994 Mollen Commission report on corruption in the New York City Police Department found that officer Michael Dowd's performance evaluation described him as having "excellent street knowledge" and said he could "easily become a role model for others to emulate." The report, however, also cited him as possibly the most corrupt and brutal police officer in the entire NYPD.[17]
- A 1997 report by the Police Executive Research Forum (PERF) concluded that "most performance evaluations currently used by police do not reflect the work officers do." A 1976 report had reached a similar conclusion, suggesting that virtually no progress had been made in the intervening two decades.[18]
- In 2011 the Justice Department found that the Seattle Police Department's policies on the classification of and findings regarding citizen complaints were "so complex that they damage [the department's] credibility and undermine public confidence."[19]

The list of shortcomings of traditional professionalism (see Figure 2.1) reveals two separate problems. In some instances, previous generations of police chiefs did not do certain things because no one had thought of them yet (for example, early intervention systems). More telling, however, are the instances where they failed to fully implement their own standards, as in maintaining a proper span of control regarding the number of officers supervised by each sergeant. How was this allowed to occur? One explanation is the nature of complex bureaucracies. Failure to ensure full compliance with all written policies and procedures is probably endemic in private corporations, hospitals, universities, and so on. A 2000 report by the Institute of Medicine found that an estimated 40,000 die accidentally in hospitals every year (and that was a low, conservative estimate).[20] In short, the medical profession had left a very serious problem unacknowledged and uncorrected.

Figure 2.1   Missing From Traditional Police Professionalism

** Mandatory incident reports of use of deadly force, vehicle pursuits

** Citizen complaint procedures

** Systematic data collection on officer performance

** Systematic review of officer performance indicators

** Pattern analyses of incidents

Another explanation is the crisis management tradition in American policing. Police leaders are regularly buffeted by emergencies that require their attention: a particularly vicious crime, public demands for more police protection, a shooting incident, an allegation of excessive force, a rumor about some other embarrassing officer misconduct, a budget crisis, and so on. In this atmosphere it is easy not to think proactively and fail to anticipate future problems and take the necessary preventive steps. Additionally, in the political environment of American policing, moreover, where departments face embarrassing news media exposés and accusations of brutality by civil rights activists, police chiefs typically fall into a defensive mode, denying or diminishing the seriousness of the allegations. It is not a habit that encourages reflection, examination of existing procedures, and corrective action.

Public demands to "do something" about crime pressures police chiefs to put more officers on the street rather than to invest in the training and research and planning that are likely to pay off in the future.

A Comment on Accreditation of Law Enforcement Agencies

Accreditation is a process of professional self-regulation that exists in most professions and has been adopted by law enforcement. It is important to examine its achievements and shortcomings. In policing, the process is administered by the Commission on Accreditation for Law Enforcement Agencies (CALEA), created in 1979.[21] To date, however, only about 600 of the nearly 18,000 law enforcement agencies in the United States are accredited.

Several factors explain this low number. Accreditation is voluntary and there is no penalty for not being accredited. In social work, by comparison, a degree from an accredited social work school is required for many jobs. Law enforcement agencies do not face loss of federal funds for not being accredited.

The standards for accreditation are also cause for concern. With only a few exceptions, the standards are procedural rather than substantive. Typically, they require that an agency "have a written policy on" a particular subject, or that a particular staff member be responsible for that issue. They do not specify what that policy should be. Standard 41.2.2 on vehicle pursuits, for example, requires that the department have a written directive on the subject and that it cover "evaluating the circumstances" of a potential pursuit.[22] But it provides no substantive guidance on what circumstances to consider (e.g., road conditions) or how to weigh conditions if faced with a pursuit decision (e.g., balancing bad roads against the dangerousness of the fleeing suspect). The standard on inservice training (Standard 35.1.1) requires that all sworn officers receive inservice training annually. It does not, however, specify how many hours of training they should receive or on what subjects. A department, for example, could conceivably maintain a police academy with no coverage of human relations, communication skills, traffic stops, or the use of informants, and still be accredited.

With respect to the investigation of alleged officer misconduct—a key element of accountability—the CALEA Standards do not specify any details about a department's Internal Affairs or Professional Standards unit. The CALEA Standards require only that a department have such a unit but do not specify how many investigators it should have relative to the size of the department or how they should be selected and trained.[23]

Only a few CALEA Standards prescribe a substantive standard of care, and only one of those is very specific. The Standard on use of deadly force (Standard 1.3.2) embodies the prevailing defense of life standard.[24] With regard to the recruitment of racial and ethnic minority and female officers, the CALEA Standards (Standard 31.2) state that the composition of an agency should reflect the composition of the community served.[25] This is consistent with the standard recommended by other experts and is roughly comparable to the standard used by the courts in affirmative action cases. The existing American Correctional Association (ACA) Standards, by contrast, are very specific on these and other issues, providing a definite standard of care that must be met.[26]

The Judicial Strategy: The Courts as an Instrument of Police Reform

The failure of police professionalization to address critical issues of police searches and seizures, interrogations, and other uses of police power led civil liberties and civil rights activists to turn to the courts as instruments of police reform.[27] The resulting judicial strategy of reform consisted of three different avenues for pursuing higher standards of police accountability: constitutional law, tort litigation, and criminal prosecution.

The Supreme Court and the Police

The U.S. Supreme Court emerged as a potent force for police reform during the 1960s, and its impact continues today, even though the Court has turned in a conservative direction. A series of well-known decisions are among the most controversial in the history of the Warren Court (1953–1969), which issued many controversial decisions. The Court intervened in previously hidden matters of routine police work, especially in-custody interrogations, and imposed constitutional standards that limited police officer conduct. The Court's decisions relating to the police were only one part of a larger due process revolution affecting the entire criminal justice system. Prisoners' rights litigation, for example, ended many traditional prison practices and established a broad array of rights for prisoners based the First, Fourth, and Eighth Amendments to the Constitution.[28] The criminal justice decisions of the Supreme Court were only one part of its rights-oriented activism that also had a profound impact on race relations, freedom of speech, privacy, and other areas of American life.[29]

The impact of the major Supreme Court decisions on the police was profound and multifaceted. At the basic level, the Court created a set of rules for the police that included meaningful penalties. And because it was the Supreme Court, the rules were national standards. This was particularly significant given the highly decentralized structure of American policing, with nearly 18,000 independent state and local agencies and no process for establishing national standards such as exists in other countries with national police forces.[30] In a similar fashion, the federal courts fashioned national standards for correctional institutions between the late 1960s and the mid-1980s.[31] The Court's decisions also increased public awareness of important aspects of policing, throwing a spotlight on previously hidden areas of police work such as in-custody interrogations. Ordinary people came to understand that they had a right to remain silent if arrested. The Court stimulated significant improvements in police personnel standards and police training, as departments found they had to train their officers to comply with Court decisions.[32] Finally, as mentioned earlier, the police accreditation movement was a direct outgrowth of the new standards imposed by the Supreme Court.

All of the positive developments have continued to the present day, long after the Supreme Court began to withdraw from an activist role as watchdog of the police in the 1970s. By establishing constitutional principles as a minimum standard for police work, the Court reshaped the debate over police reform and stimulated lasting reform efforts.[33]

Scholars have examined the impact of Supreme Court decisions on police operations. With regard to *Mapp* and *Miranda*, for example, they have sought to measure the number of criminal cases "lost" as a result of constitutional law violations related to unconstitutional searches or interrogations.[34] As law professor Rachel Harmon argues, however, the debate over the impact of Supreme Court decisions, and the decisions themselves, have distorted discussions of police problems and police reform efforts, leading to a concentration on only those areas addressed by the courts and only those issues that can be addressed through constitutional law. The new police accountability involves developing policies and practices that are sound and reasonable, that are likely to reduce officer use of force, that enhance community relations and protect officer safety, but cannot necessarily be addressed as matters of constitutional law.[35] We now turn our attention to the limits of the courts as a means of police accountability.

The Limits of the Supreme Court as a Mechanism for Police Accountability

During the heyday of the Warren Court, civil rights and civil liberties advocates saw the Supreme Court as perhaps the best possible instrument of police reform. Law professor Rachel Harmon argues that for many people this belief has become "the conventional paradigm" about the role of law and police reform.[36] The famous Court decisions of the Warren Court era—*Mapp, Miranda*, and others—had an enormous impact on the police. For the first time there was a clear mandate that basic police operations had to conform to constitutional standards. The impact of the major decisions went far beyond actual on-the-street police conduct. Police departments significantly raised recruitment and training standards to ensure that officers would be able to comply with court rulings. The publicity surrounding *Miranda* in particular brought long-hidden police procedures to public attention and in the process taught millions of Americans (often imperfectly) that they had rights vis-à-vis a police officer. The long-term result was a significant rise in public expectations about the quality of policing.

In the 1970s, the Supreme Court turned in a conservative direction and withdrew from the role of active oversight of the police, for example, scaling back the application of *Mapp* and *Miranda*. Inevitably, those activists who had invested their hopes for police reform in the Supreme Court were dismayed. Even at the height of the Court's activism, however, a number of perceptive experts recognized the limits of the Court as an instrument of police reform. This included observers who fully supported the intent and the result of the Court's activist role.[37]

The principal limit on the Court is that it lacks the institutional capacity to ensure compliance with its own decisions on a day-to-day basis.[38] While it is true that both *Mapp* and *Miranda* include penalties—the exclusion of evidence or confessions—the impact is limited. First, criminal law enforcement represents only a small percentage of police work, and few cases ever go to trial where the exclusion of evidence or confessions would be a factor. Additionally, there are abundant opportunities for evading the rules laid down by both *Mapp* and *Miranda*. Following *Mapp*, for example, experts identified the "dropsy" phenomenon where officers claimed that they did not conduct a search because the suspect "dropped" the drugs or other contraband.[39] Studies of *Miranda* found that a high percentage of suspects voluntarily confess and that in many cases the interrogating officers lie to suspects (e.g., claiming that their partner had already confessed) or manipulate them in other ways.[40]

Rachel Harmon has introduced a more serious argument, that the focus on the Supreme Court and constitutional law has seriously distorted police reform efforts by directing attention away from other strategies for ending police misconduct and improving the quality of policing. A number of factors inherent in the Supreme Court as an institution of government severely limit its capacity to effectively promote police reform.[41] As some other police scholars had previously argued, many critical aspects of routine policing fall outside the scope of constitutional law. For example, although police experts recognize that a proper ratio of sergeants to patrol officers is a key element of good supervision, it is doubtful whether failure to meet that standard rises to the level of a constitutional law issue. Similarly, few of the details of an effective citizen complaint review process rise to the level of constitutional law (for example, whether review by internal affairs or by a citizen review agency). It is difficult to imagine, for example, the Supreme Court holding that an early intervention system is required by the Constitution. Yet, in the new police accountability an EIS is a central element. The challenge facing the new accountability is to achieve such important reforms as an EIS or trend analyses of force data by means other than depending on the Supreme Court.[42]

Suing the Cops: Reform Through Civil Litigation

Civil rights and civil liberties activists also adopted the strategy of suing the police as a way to increase police accountability. The assumption has always been that by raising the dollar cost of police misconduct local elected officials will respond by instituting reforms that will curb misconduct and the resulting costs.[43]

There is at best mixed evidence that civil litigation has been successful as a strategy for reforming the police. Academic studies evaluating the impact of strategy have generally found little direct impact on police reform.[44] In 2009–2011 Chicago paid out more than $45 million in damage awards because of police abuse. Detroit paid out an average of over $10 million a year for 10 years, but no meaningful effort to improve the police resulted. Detroit, in fact, was eventually sued by the federal government

over its abuses. (Risk management as a strategy to reform police departments and end costly abuses is discussed in Chapter Seven.) There are
some instances where lawsuits forced local police departments to adopt a
new or revised policy on a particular aspect of police operations, but these
cases are the exceptions and not the rule. The most positive example was
when the Los Angeles County Board of Supervisors created a police auditor for the Sheriff's Department. The mandate of the Special Counsel
included tracking litigation against the department and the resulting payouts as a way of reducing those costs.[45] (The Special Counsel is discussed
later in Chapter Six.)

Candace McCoy argues that federal Section 1983 litigation (violation
of civil rights while acting under color of law) has in fact been a positive
force for police reform between 1978 and 2005.[46] She cites the number of
police-related cases in federal court jurisdictions, changing insurance
industry practices that demanded improved policies and training, and
the emergence of model policies that departments could adopt. Along
with political scientist Charles Epp, she argues that the insurance industry played a particularly important role in goading police departments
to reform.[47] McCoy concedes, however, that 1983 litigation has been successful primarily with regard to police use of force cases, particularly
deadly force. The reason is simple: that's where plaintiffs and their
attorneys can recover significant monetary damages. McCoy acknowl-
edges that 1983 litigation has not had a significant impact with respect
to violations of the Fourth Amendment by the police. The reason?
There's no money in it.

The flaw in the civil litigation strategy is the assumption that public
officials will necessarily act in a rational and coordinated manner in
response to a problem. Instead, the response to lawsuits against the police
has been indifference and disconnection. Human Rights Watch, for example, quoted one police internal affairs officer as saying "civil cases are not
our problem."[48] Barbara Armacost argues that "many police departments
apparently consider the money they pay out in damages and settlements
as simply a "cost of doing business," quoting former LAPD Police Chief
Daryl Gates to that effect.[49] Generally, one agency of government (the
police) perpetrates the harm, another agency defends it in court (the law
department), and a third agency writes the check (the treasurer). The
missing element has been a coordinated risk management strategy that
seeks to identify the sources of litigation costs and then correct the underlying problems. Why several generations of mayors have failed in this

regard is both an intriguing question and a sad commentary on municipal government in America. A survey of police risk management programs, moreover, found that even those programs that claim to have reduced litigation costs do not collect and publish data that would verify these claims.[50] Risk management is discussed in detail in Chapter Seven.

Law professor Joanna Schwartz examined the impact of lawsuits against the police from the perspective of deterrence. The litigation strategy assumes that successful suits will deter police misconduct. Specific deterrence theory holds that lawsuits will deter individual officers from misconduct. General deterrence theory holds that successful suits will affect the behavior of other officers not directly involved in any suit. In theory, the general deterrent effect will operate because cities and police departments will take steps to control misconduct. She noted that assumptions about deterrence are "deeply ingrained" in American criminal justice, yet there is little if any empirical evidence to support the theory.[51]

Schwartz studied 26 departments to determine whether police departments made specific attempts to heighten the deterrent effect through the use of information about lawsuits. She found that police officials "rarely have information about suits brought against their departments and officers."[52] The problems included a lack of computerized data on lawsuits, and the failure of departments to investigate claims made in suits, and that departments that do have such data fail to make use of it.[53] Six of the 26 departments did not gather any information about suits, and she cited the New York Police Department as a "prime example" of this failure. The specific failures included the fact that an officer who was named in a lawsuit was not recorded in the officer's file; the allegations made in a suit were not investigated by the department (e.g., that an officer used excessive force); the city law department did not inform Internal Affairs when a suit is filed; no details about the suit and its allegations were available in over 90 percent of all cases, and were collected in only 1 percent or 2 percent of the cases expected to result in a settlement for the plaintiffs of $250,000 or more; and the resolution of suits (dismissed; victory for the department; settlement or trial victory for the plaintiff) was not recorded or analyzed. Finally, there was no examination of cases for its "personnel and policy implications," which might include identifying an officer with a very problematic performance history or a shortcoming in a department policy (e.g., regarding homeless people).[54]

Schwartz identified five different policies that potentially could use lawsuit information to heighten accountability. They include some of the most important new accountability measures. The first is an early intervention system that includes lawsuit data as a performance indicator. Some current EISs do in fact incorporate such data. A second policy is to undertake a trend analysis to determine patterns that indicate a need for departmental intervention. A third approach is for departments to investigate the specific claims (not just use of force, but accompanying verbal abuse or ethnic slurs charges) made in lawsuits for possible action by the department independent of the suit. Schwartz notes that many departments were already conducting such investigations at the time of her study. A fourth approach involves departments reviewing closed lawsuit case files for information about an officer's conduct that might warrant further investigation by the department. Finally, in cases where a suit resulted in a finding of liability on the part of the officer, the department could determine if such a finding could be the basis for discipline of the officer after the trial.[55]

In essence, Schwartz outlines some of the review procedures that are discussed in Chapter Six. Some, such as EIS, are already being done. Others, such as revisiting closed cases for relevant information about officers' conduct, are not known to be currently done but are a creative suggestion for the future.

Federal Pattern or Practice Litigation

A new form of civil litigation against the police emerged in 1994 with Section 14141 of the 1994 Violent Crime Control Act. The law authorizes the U.S. Department of Justice to bring civil suits against law enforcement agencies where there is a "pattern or practice" of abuse of citizens' rights. The purpose of such suits is to bring about organizational change. To date, the Justice Department has reached settlements with about 20 enforcement agencies, either through consent decrees, memoranda of understanding, or settlement letters.[56]

The Justice Department settlements are all very similar and, with only slight variation, require the core elements of the new police accountability: improved policies on officer use of force (including procedures for reporting and investigating of force incidents), improved citizen complaint procedures, and an early intervention system. It is worth noting that litigation under Section 14141 represents an approach to systemic organizational reform for law enforcement agencies that the federal courts began with respect to prisons in the late 1960s. The prisoners' rights movement effected sweeping changes in prison practices, eliminating many unjust practices, revolutionizing the authority structure within prisons, and setting in motion an accreditation process that far exceeds law enforcement accreditation in its scope.[57]

One might ask, why did the federal courts ignore police organizations while ordering sweeping reforms in prisons despite the fact that they were ordering prison reforms through prisoners' rights litigation?[58] Herman Goldstein argues that the critical turning point was the Court's 1976 decision in *Rizzo v. Goode*, in which it declined to order administrative reforms in the Philadelphia Police Department.[59] The District Court had heard what the Supreme Court termed a "staggering amount of evidence," including 250 witnesses over a 21-day period. Yet the Court held that none of the plaintiffs could show that they had been harmed by the police practices cited and, further, that none of the city officials named as defendants were alleged to have "acted affirmatively" in depriving the plaintiffs of constitutional rights. The Court declined to accept the role of "fashioning of prophylactic procedures" designed to minimize employee misconduct. Why the Court declined to address deficiencies in police policy and practices while at the same time choosing to address similar kinds of failures in prisons is a question that is beyond the scope of this book but one that legal historians can address. One possible explanation is the deeply ingrained deference to the police. After all, the federal courts were then in the business of ordering all manner of administrative reforms in prisons designed to minimize misconduct, and to appoint special masters to oversee their orders.[60] One can only speculate about how the history of American policing might have been different had the Supreme Court decided *Rizzo* differently in 1976 and as a consequence the federal courts had ordered numerous police reforms over the course of the following decades, as they did with prison conditions.

In the end, federal pattern or practice litigation has had an impact on American policing far beyond the small number of police departments directly affected. Perhaps most important, it has defined a short list of basic accountability procedures: state-of-the-art use of force policies, an open and accessible citizen complaint procedure, and an early intervention system. There is no other official or even semi-official document or statement that defines an equivalent set of minimum standards. In effect, all law enforcement agencies are on notice regarding the standards for constitutional policing.

Criminal Prosecution of Police Officers

Another strategy for curbing police misconduct is through criminal prosecution of officers guilty of criminal acts related to excessive physical force or unjustified shootings. The underlying assumption of this strategy is that a successful conviction of officers will both remove bad officers from a police department and deter future misconduct by other officers. Criminal prosecution has a deep emotional appeal among people who have been the victims of police misconduct, and want *that* officer punished for what he or she did.

Criminal prosecution, however, has been an extremely weak instrument of reform. One report noted "the sheer difficulty of obtaining a conviction is another hurdle that leads civil rights prosecutors to wonder if criminal prosecution is ultimately their best option." [61] Convictions of police officers are extremely difficult to obtain. Local prosecutors, by the very nature of their role, have close working relationships with local police departments and are reluctant to file criminal charges against them, except in the most extreme cases. The resources of the Criminal Section of the Civil Rights Division of the U.S. Department of Justice, meanwhile, are extremely limited, given the more than 18,000 local law enforcement agencies in the United States. In 2011, for example, the Criminal Division prosecuted a grand total of 45 law enforcement officers (including correctional officers).[62] Additionally, prosecutors must prove beyond a reasonable doubt that an officer had criminal intent, and this is an extremely high bar. In excessive force or deadly force cases, officers can always claim that they faced a threat to their own lives and were therefore justified in using force. Judges and juries are extremely deferential to these claims and to the police in general. Corruption cases are easier to win than excessive force cases because it is easier to prove first that money changed hands, and second that there could have been no other intent other than corruption. Even though there have been successful prosecutions of officers, they do not appear to have any deterrent effect. In both New York City and Philadelphia, for example, many officers have been convicted over the past three decades, yet both departments have been beset by repeated scandals involving both corruption and brutality.[63]

Summary

The judicial strategy for reforming the police has had a very mixed record of success. Earlier Supreme Court rulings on police conduct had a major impact that continues today. But only a limited range of police activities are likely to be dealt with by this strategy. Civil suits against police departments to raise the cost of misconduct and force departments to change has proven to have a very limited impact. Criminal prosecution of officers has proven completely inadequate. More recent Justice Department pattern or practice suits under Section 14141 appear to have the greatest success in making significant reforms in the police departments the Civil Rights Division of the Justice Department investigated and sued. The very limited resources of the Division mean that it can affect only a very small number of police departments at best, but as we argued earlier the federal litigation, by defining a set of accountability standards, has had a very broad impact.[64]

The Legislative Strategy: External Oversight of the Police

Community activists have also turned to the legislative arena in response to police misconduct, demanding external oversight of the police. In a familiar process known as "scandal and reform,"[65] the exposure of police abuse (corruption, excessive force, etc.) mobilizes public opinion and forces elected officials to take some kind of action. External oversight has taken two different forms: one-time, blue-ribbon commissions and permanent external oversight agencies that either handle citizen complaints against police officers or serve as permanent auditors of a police department.

Blue-Ribbon Commissions

Blue-ribbon commissions are a familiar feature of the American political landscape. Although they have rarely been acts of legislative bodies, it is useful to consider them here because as a form of external oversight of the police they resemble the legislative measures we do consider. In response to a perceived social problem, presidents, governors, or mayors appoint a panel of experts to investigate the problem and recommend solutions to the problem. There is a long history in American policing of commissions appointed in response to racial problems,[66] exposés of police corruption, or serious incidents of excessive force. The Christopher Commission (1991), appointed in the wake of the Rodney King beating in Los Angeles, is the best-known recent example.[67] National-level blue-ribbon commissions have made important contributions to American policing. The Wickersham Commission (1931) exposed the "third degree," the practice of forcing suspects to confess;[68] the 1968 Kerner Commission report on race relations;[69] the President's Crime Commission (1967), which recommended a broad range of criminal justice reforms including for policing;[70] and the American Bar Association *Standards Relating to the Urban Police Function* (1974),[71] which recommended a set of standards for police operations.

On the positive side, blue-ribbon commissions have the capacity to study a problem in depth, particularly when they have been given sufficient staff and resources, to retain the best experts in the field, and to make recommendations for change that elected officials are often reluctant to make. Many blue-ribbon commission reports are valuable resources, even years after they have been published. The Kerner Commission report documented the state of police-community relations in the mid-1960s with regard to race relations.[72] The Christopher Commission provided valuable insights into the operations of the Los Angeles Police Department, many of which are relevant today for other departments. By documenting the "problem officer" phenomenon, the report gave a strong boost to the development of early intervention systems. The report also found that evidence of officer misconduct is rarely used in regular performance evaluations and promotions.

Blue-ribbon commissions suffer from certain inherent and serious weakness, however. By their very nature they lack any capacity to implement their own recommendations and ensure that reform occurs.[73] Commissions are temporary bodies that disband once their final report is released. (The reports do become useful sources of information for academic studies of the police, however.) Implementation depends on a voluntary effort by a police department itself. In some instances, the original scandal results in the appointment of a new police chief who makes a sincere effort to implement the recommended reforms. The typical result is that the political momentum for reform wanes as the original crisis fades into memory and public attention (particularly the attention of the news media) moves on to new crises.

Events in Los Angeles in the decade of the 1990s offer one notable example of the consequences of the inability of blue-ribbon commissions to compel adoption of their recommendations. The 1991 beating of Rodney King led to the Christopher Commission, which thoroughly documented the problems in the LAPD and offered a strong set of recommendations. Two separate follow-up reports found that while some changes had been made in the LAPD there was a general failure of the LAPD to implement most of the Christopher Commission recommendations. A few years later the Rampart scandal erupted, prompting three additional investigations. Finally, in 2001 the Justice Department intervened and secured a consent decree mandating a series of accountability-related reforms. Even then, the LAPD did not fully complete the implementation process within the required five years, and the consent decree was extended.[74]

A notable exception to the failure of blue-ribbon commissions to achieve implementation of their reforms is Los Angeles County. Also in response to the Rodney King beating and subsequent riot, the County Board of Supervisors established the Kolts Commission to study the Los Angeles Sheriff's Department, and its 1992 report led to the creation of the office of the Special Counsel as a permanent external oversight agency for the Sheriff's Department. The Special Counsel became arguably the most effective such agency in the country (see Chapter Six).[75]

Chapter Six of this book argues that police auditors, a form of external citizen oversight, overcome the inherent limitations of blue-ribbon commissions by virtue of being permanent government agencies. They have the capacity to revisit issues and monitor implementation of their recommendations and also to investigate new issues that arise.

Citizen Oversight of the Police

The most important legislative strategy for curbing police misconduct involves creating a permanent external oversight agency to handle citizen complaints and/or to audit or monitor a law enforcement agency. In the police-community relations crisis of the 1960s, the creation of "civilian review boards" was one of the principal demands of civil rights groups.[76] (This book uses the term *citizen oversight* because it is more representative of the variety of external agencies and procedures that have developed in recent years, including both citizen complaint review boards and police auditors.)[77] The civilian review board movement suffered seemingly fatal blows in the late 1960s when both the New York City and Philadelphia review boards were abolished. The movement quietly revived in the early 1970s, however, and by the mid-1980s, citizen oversight was an established part of American policing. By 2000, virtually all big-city police departments in the United States were subject to some form of citizen oversight.[78] By 1991 citizen oversight had grown sufficiently that a professional association, the National Association for Citizen Oversight of Law Enforcement (NACOLE), was established.[79]

Citizen review of complaints against police officers is based on the assumption that police departments are inherently unable to police themselves, as a result of both bureaucratic self-interest and the power of the police subculture. Critics have long charged that complaint investigations by internal affairs units or professional standards units do not investigate complaints thoroughly, are biased in favor of the officer, often fail to sustain complaints when there is sufficient evidence, and do not impose appropriate discipline in cases where a complaint is sustained. Advocates of external citizen review of complaints argue that it will be more independent, objective, and thorough because it is staffed by people who are not sworn officers. As a result, they will sustain more complaints, which will result in more discipline of officers, that this will deter future misconduct more effectively than internal complaint procedures, and that all of these factors will lead to higher levels of citizen satisfaction.

In practice, civilian complaint review agencies vary considerably in terms of their authority and resources. The New York City Civilian Complaint Review Board (CCRB) and the San Francisco Office of Citizen Complaints (OCC) are among the few that have original jurisdiction to investigate complaints. Most review boards, however, review only the investigative file compiled by the police department's internal affairs unit. They can disagree with the police report, and some can request additional investigation, but they do not have the authority to conduct their own investigations. All review boards, including those with original jurisdiction, have the power only to make a recommendation about the disposition of the complaint. The final authority remains with the chief of police. Many review boards, moreover, have lacked the necessary staff and budgetary resources to function effectively, while some agencies suffered from poor management. Others have failed because of a lack of political support, disinterest by police management, or staunch opposition from the local police union.[80]

The performance of citizen review boards has left some of their advocates with a bitter taste, however. The New York Civil Liberties Union, for decades the leading advocate of citizen oversight in New York City, has been very critical of the CCRB, which it was instrumental in creating.[81] A 1998 NYCLU report found the CCRB "understaffed and underfunded," to an extent that "virtually ensured that it would not provide oversight" as originally intended. Only 1.5 percent of all complaints that were finally disposed of resulted in the discipline of an officer. The Police Commissioner had rejected CCRB findings in 66 percent of all cases. The

San Francisco Office of Citizen Complaints, which also has original jurisdiction to investigate complaints, sustained only 7 percent of the 848 complaints it disposed of in 2011.[82]

There have been no comparative evaluations of citizen review agencies
that meet the minimal standards of research. One problem is that agencies
vary in the mandate, staffing, and activities to the extent that comparisons
are inherently difficult.[83] Citizen complaint data are so complex and vari-
able that they are not useful measures of the quality of investigations. Many
factors explain why there is a high rate of citizen complaints against one
department, for example. It could be that the department has a very open
and accessible complaint process that encourages citizens to file complaints. But it could also be that there is a very high level of police misconduct. The data themselves cannot tell us which reason it is. Also, as already
noted, citizen oversight agencies have multiple goals and any comprehensive attempt to measure effectiveness would have to take into account all of
them. Most discussions of citizen review effectiveness have focused exclusively on the sustain rate, the percentage of all complaints sustained in
favor of the complainant. Yet, as we have already noted, official complaint
data is extremely problematic and it represents only one of the many goals.
Finally, sustain rates for citizen review agencies are very low, and there is no
consistent evidence that they are higher than internal affairs units.[84]

In a broader sense, focusing exclusively on citizen complaints makes
rank-and-file officers the scapegoats for police misconduct. The new
police accountability, as we explained in Chapter One, emphasizes management failures and seeks to remedy the problem of misconduct through
organizational change. It does relatively little good to sustain a complaint
and discipline an officer when the causes of misconduct are organizational failures related to policies, training, and supervision (the PTSR
framework), as discussed in Chapter One.

The Auditor Model of Citizen Oversight

An alternative form of external citizen oversight appeared in 1993 in
the form of the police auditor, with the creation of the Special Counsel to
the Los Angeles Sheriff's Department, the San Jose Independent Police
Auditor, and the Seattle Police Auditor. The auditor model of oversight
recognizes the inherent limits of focusing on individual citizen complaints and argues that it is more productive to review policies and procedures for the purpose of changing the police organization and preventing
future misconduct.[85] As we argued in Chapter One, that conclusion is one

of the core elements of the new world of police accountability, and for that reason it is discussed in detail in Chapter Six.

Conclusion: The Lessons of the Past

The new police accountability builds on the lessons of these past reform efforts. The following section attempts to identify the most important of those lessons.

First, many past reforms failed to change officer behavior in day-to-day police work on the street. One popular reform illustrates the point. For the past 100 years, reformers have urged higher educational requirements for police officers. This book argues, however, is that in a poorly managed department, with no meaningful standards of accountability, even the better educated officers will sink to a low standard of performance.

Second and closely related to the first point, many reforms designed to achieve greater accountability failed to reach deep into the police organization and affect police officer behavior on the street. The most notable example would be Supreme Court decisions on such issues as searches and seizures or interrogations. As many critics have pointed out, the Court has no mechanism for enforcing its decisions (apart from ruling in a subsequent appeal in a new case). Ultimately, it falls to police departments to develop the internal procedures for ensuring officer compliance with Supreme Court decisions and other legal mandates.

Third, past reform efforts largely neglected the role of supervisors in controlling the critical actions by officers on the street. In all of the literature on policing there is an alarming shortage of research about street-level sergeants.[86] This is particularly surprising because all police commanders and most outside experts agree that the sergeant is the key to day-to-day policing. Yet we have precious little information about what sergeants do, how they think about their role, their activities that are most effective in improving the performance of officers under their command, the nature and quality of their training, variations in sergeants' activities across departments, and so on. Fourth, piecemeal reform, with no overarching strategy for organizational reform, failed to appreciate the interconnectedness of various aspects of police work. It does little good to improve police training, for example, if officers know that the department tolerates use of excessive force on a routine basis.

Reversing the order changes the role of training dramatically. If a department makes a strong effort to control the use of force, and officers see this happening, training over the use of force becomes very meaningful. Along the same lines, a department can adopt a state-of-the-art policy on use of force, but if sergeants do not effectively supervise and review force reports as intended, the written policies become empty bureaucratic gestures.

Finally, past reform efforts never developed institutionalized procedures for sustaining reform over time.[87] There were no procedures for monitoring reforms that were instituted and for ensuring that they are implemented and that the reform process continues over time. One of the most notable examples of this failure is the fate of the corruption control measures instituted by Commissioner Pat Murphy in the New York City Police Department in the early 1970s. Widely hailed at the time, they had completely vanished by the early 1990s according to the Mollen Commission, appointed in the wake of another corruption scandal.[88]

The new police accountability addresses the historic shortcomings in police reform. New approaches to critical incident reporting (Chapter Three) reach deeper into police organizations in an effort to control officer behavior. Early intervention systems (Chapter Five) are designed to track officer performance over time and to identify any potentially problematic patterns or trends. External review of police departments, along with some new internal self-monitoring procedures, are also designed to identify problems that are the result of earlier reforms being allowed to deteriorate. And in a more general sense, as was argued in Chapter One, the new police accountability involves an awareness of the need to change organizations and not simply make one or more incremental changes. Also, the new accountability is data driven and in that respect provides chiefs and mid-managers with a kind of evidence about police practices that previous generations did not enjoy.

Notes

1 Samuel Walker, *A Critical History of Police Reform* (Lexington, MA: Lexington Books, 1977).

2 David Bayley, *Police for the Future* (New York: Oxford University Press, 1994).

3 Jack Greene, "Community Policing in America: Changing the Nature, Structure, and Function of the Police," in *Criminal Justice 2000. V. 3: Policies, Processes, and Decisions of the Criminal Justice System,* ed. Julie

Horney (Washington, DC: U.S. Department of Justice, 2000), 299. http://www.ncjrs.org, NCJ 182410.

4 Barbara Armacost, "Organizational Culture and Police Misconduct," *George Washington Law Review* 72 (March 2004): 455.

5 Walker, *A Critical History of Police Reform.*

6 See the provocative discussion of the development of a police monopoly over their professional mandate in Peter K. Manning, *Police Work* (Cambridge: MIT Press, 1977). A critique of this insular professional monopoly over the delivery of public services is one of the core principles of the community policing movement. George L. Kelling and Mark H. Moore, *The Evolving Strategy of Policing,* Perspectives on Policing, no. 4 (Washington, DC: U.S. Justice Department, 1988).

7 It is possible to benchmark improvements in policing by comparing the data on police in The Cleveland Foundation, *Cleveland Survey of Criminal Justice* (Cleveland: Cleveland Foundation, 1922) (the first of the modern crime commissions), National Commission on Law Observance and Enforcement, *The Police* (Washington, DC: Government Printing Office, 1931) (the first national crime commission), and the President's Commission on Law Enforcement, *Task Force Report: The Police* (Washington, DC: Government Printing Office, 1967).

8 National Advisory Commission on Civil Disorders, *Report* (New York: Bantam Books, 1968). Samuel Walker, *Popular Justice: A History of American Criminal Justice,* 2nd ed. (New York: Oxford University Press, 1998), 193–201.

9 National Advisory Commission on Civil Disorders, *Report,* 301.

10 O. W. Wilson and Roy C. McLaren, *Police Administration,* 4th ed. (New York: McGraw-Hill, 1977), 136–41.

11 Samuel Walker, "The Creation of the Contemporary Criminal Justice Paradigm: The American Bar Foundation Survey of Criminal Justice, 1956–1969," *Justice Quarterly,* 9 (1992): 201.

12 Wesley G. Skogan and Kathlee Frydl, eds., *Fairness and Effectiveness in Policing: The Evidence* (Washington, DC: National Academy Press, 2004), 34.

13 Kenneth Culp Davis, *Police Discretion* (St. Paul: West, 1975). Samuel Walker, "The Creation of the Contemporary Criminal Justice Paradigm: The American Bar Foundation Survey of Criminal Justice, 1956–1969."

14 Philadelphia Police Study Task Force, *Philadelphia and Its Police* (Philadelphia, 1987), 48–9.

15 Merrick Bobb, *9th Semiannual Report* (Los Angeles: Police Executive Research Forum, 1998). Available at http://www.parc.info. *People of California v. City of Riverside, Stipulated Judgment* (March 2001), Para 58. Available at http://www.ci.riverside.ca.us/rpd.

16 Los Angeles Police Department, *Board of Inquiry Report on the Rampart Incident* (Los Angeles: Los Angeles Police Department, 2000), 335.

17 Commission to Investigate Allegations of Police Corruption and the Anti-Corruption Procedures of the Department [Mollen Commission], *Commission Report* (New York, City of New York, 1994), p. 81. Available at http://www.parc.info.

18 Timothy Oettmeier and Mary Ann Wycoff, *Personnel Performance Evaluations in the Community Policing Context* (Washington, DC: Police Executive Research Forum, 1997), 5. Frank Landy, *Performance Appraisal in Police Departments* (Washington, DC: The Police Foundation, 1977).

19 U.S. Department of Justice, Investigation of the Seattle Police Department (December 16, 2011).

20 See, for example, the shocking report by the National Academy of Sciences on accidental deaths in American hospitals: Institute of Medicine, *To Err Is Human: Building a Safer Health System* (Washington, DC: National Academy Press, 2000).

21 Commission on Accreditation for Law Enforcement Agencies (CALEA), *Standards for Law Enforcement Agencies*, 4th ed. (Fairfax, VA: CALEA, 1998). http://www.calea.org.

22 Commission on Accreditation for Law Enforcement Agencies, *Standards for Law Enforcement Agencies*, Standard 41.2.2.

23 Ibid.

24 Ibid.

25 Ibid.

26 American Correctional Association, *Performance-Based Standards for Adult Community Residential Services*, 4th ed. (Lanham, MD: American Correctional Association, 2000).

27 See the commentary on the failure of the law enforcement profession and state governments in this regard in American Bar Association, *Standards Relating to the Urban Police Function*, 2nd ed. (Boston: Little, Brown, 1980), Standard 1-5.3.

28 Malcolm M. Feeley and Edward L. Rubin, *Judicial Policy Making and the Modern State* (New York: Cambridge University Press, 1998).

29 On the development of a pervasive "rights culture" in America, see Samuel Walker, *The Rights Revolution* (New York: Oxford University Press, 1994).

30 On the structure of American policing and its impact, see Skogan and Frydl, eds., *Fairness and Effectiveness in Policing: The Evidence*, chap. 3.

31 Feeley and Rubin, *Judicial Policy Making and the Modern State.*

32 Myron Orfield, "The Exclusionary Rule and Deterrence: An Empirical Study of Chicago Narcotics Officers," *University of Chicago Law Review* 54

(Summer 1983): 1016–55. This study has one of the most detailed and illuminating accounts of the changes in training and relationships between
the police and local prosecutors as a result of the *Mapp* decision.

33   Samuel Walker, "Historical Roots of the Legal Control of Police Behavior,"
in *Police Innovation and the Control of the Police,* ed. David Weisburd and
Craig Uchida (New York: Springer-Verlag, 1993), 32–55. *Walker, Popular
Justice,* 181–93.

34   Dallin H. Oaks, "Studying the Exclusionary Rule in Search and Seizure,"
University of Chicago Law Review 37 (Summer 1970): 665–757. Richard Leo
and George C. Thomas, III, eds., *The Miranda Debate: Law, Justice, and
Policing* (Boston: Northeastern University Press, 1998).

35   Rachel A. Harmon, "The Problem of Policing," *Michigan Law Review,* 110
(March 2012): 761–818.

36   Ibid, 765.

37   Anthony M. Amsterdam, "Perspectives on the Fourth Amendment,"
Minnesota Law Review 58 (1973–74): 349–577. American Bar Association,
Standards Relating to the Urban Police Function, Standard 1-5.3, "Sanctions,"
and accompanying commentary.

38   Harmon, "The Problem of Policing."

39   Oaks, "Studying the Exclusionary Rule in Search and Seizure."

40   Leo and Thomas, eds., *The Miranda Debate.*

41   Harmon, "The Problem of Policing," 772–81.

42   Rachel A. Harmon, "Promoting Civil Rights Through Proactive Policing
Reform," *Stanford Law Review,* 62 (no. 1, 2009): 1–70.

43   Mary M. Cheh, "Are Law Suits an Answer to Police Brutality?" in *And
Justice for All: Understanding and Controlling Police Abuse of Force,* ed.
William A. Geller and Hans Toch, 256–8 (Washington, DC: Police
Executive Research Forum, 1995).

44   "Project: Suing the Police in Federal Court," *Yale Law Journal* 88 (1979):
781. Candace McCoy, "Lawsuits Against Police: What Impact Do They
Really Have," *Criminal Law Bulletin* 20 (1984): 53. Human Rights Watch
concluded that civil litigation "must always be available, but cannot be a
substitute for police departmental mechanisms of accountability or prose-
cutorial action." Human Rights Watch, *Shielded from Justice* (Washington,
DC: Human Rights Watch, 1998), 85.

45   James G. Kolts, *The Los Angeles Sheriff's Department* (Los Angeles: County
of Los Angeles, 1992). Available at http://www.parc.info. See the Special
Counsel's website at http://www.parc.info and look for its annual
reports under "Publications."

46   Candace McCoy, "How Civil Rights Lawsuits Improve American
Policing," in McCoy, ed., *Holding Police Accountable* (Washington, DC:
Urban Institute Press, 2010), 111–60.

47 Charles Epp, *Making Rights Real: Activists, Bureaucrats, and the Creation of the Legalistic State* (Chicago: University of Chicago Press, 2010).

48 Human Rights Watch, *Shielded from Justice*, 81.

49 Armacost, "Organizational Culture and Police Misconduct," 474–5.

50 Carol Archbold, *Police Accountability, Risk Management, and Legal Advising* (New York: LFB Scholarly Publishing, 2004).

51 Joanna C. Schwartz, "Myths and Mechanics of Deterrence: The Role of Lawsuits in Law Enforcement Decisionmaking," *UCLA Law Review* 57 (April 2010): 1031.

52 Ibid., 1028.

53 Ibid.

54 Ibid., 1045–8.

55 Ibid., 1052–6.

56 Samuel Walker and Morgan Macdonald, "An Alternative Remedy for Police Misconduct: A Model State 'Pattern or Practice' Statute," *George Mason University Civil Rights Law Journal* 19 (no. 3, 2008–2009): 479–552. See the U.S. Department of Justice Special Litigation Section website: http://www.justice.gov/crt/about/spl/.

57 Feeley and Rubin, *Judicial Policy Making and the Modern State.*

58 Ibid.

59 *Rizzo v. Goode,* 423 U.S. 362 (1976).

60 Feeley and Rubin, *Judicial Policy Making and the Modern State,* especially the reference to *Rizzo v. Goode* on pages 250–1.

61 Vera Institute of Justice, *Prosecuting Police Misconduct* (New York: Vera Institute of Justice, 1998). Available at http://www.vera.org. "Securing Police Compliance With Constitutional Limitations: The Exclusionary Rule and Other Devices," in National Advisory Commission on the Causes and Prevention of Violence, *Report* (New York: Bantam Books, 1970), 405–7. Human Rights Watch, *Shielded from Justice,* 85–103. "Criminal prosecutions and Other kinds of law suits have not played a major role in addressing the problem of excessive force by the police . . ." Cheh, "Are Law Suits an Answer to Police Brutality?," 234.

62 Cited in Rachel A. Harmon, "Limited Leverage" *Saint Louis Public Law Review* 32 (no. 1, 2012): 48, esp. note 59.

63 New York City, Commission to Investigate Allegations of Police Corruption and the Anti-Corruption Procedures of the Police Department [Mollen Commission], *Report* (New York: City of New York, 1994).

64 Walker and Macdonald, "An Alternative Remedy for Police Misconduct."

65 The phrase is from Lawrence W. Sherman's study of police corruption. Lawrence W. Sherman, *Scandal and Reform: Controlling Police Corruption* (Berkeley: University of California Press, 1978).

66 A useful collection and analysis is Anthony M. Platt, ed., *The Politics of Riot Commissions, 1917–1970* (New York: Collier Books, 1971).

67 Christopher Commission, *Report of the Independent Commission on the Los Angeles Police Department* (Los Angeles, 1991). Available at http://www .parc.info. Human Rights Watch, *Shielded from Justice*, 44–6.

68 National Commission on Law Observance and Enforcement, *Lawlessness in Law Enforcement* (Washington, DC: Government Printing Office, 1931).

69 National Advisory Commission on Civil Disorders, *Report* (New York: Bantam Books, 1968).

70 President's Commission on Law Enforcement and Administration of Justice, *The Challenge of Crime in a Free Society* (Washington, DC: Government Printing Office, 1967). See also the accompanying *Task Force Report: The Police* (Washington, DC: Government Printing Office, 1967).

71 American Bar Association, *Standards Relating to the Urban Police Function*, 2nd ed.

72 National Advisory Commission on Civil Disorders, *Report*.

73 Samuel Walker, "Setting the Standards: The Efforts and Impact of Blue-Ribbon Commissions on the Police," in *Police Leadership in America: Crisis and Opportunity*, ed. William A. Geller (New York: Praeger, 1985), 354–70.

74 *United States v. Los Angeles* Consent Decree (2001). Christopher Stone et al., *Policing Los Angeles Under a Consent Decree: The Dynamics of Change at the LAPD* (Cambridge: Harvard University Press, 2009).

75 Kolts, *The Los Angeles Sheriff's Department*.

76 Walker, *Popular Justice*, pp. 193–9.

77 Samuel Walker, *Police Accountability: The Role of Citizen Oversight* (Belmont: Thomson, 2001), chap. 1.

78 The history of citizen oversight is in Walker, *Police Accountability*, chap 1.

79 The NACOLE website is http://www.nacole.org.

80 Walker, *Police Accountability*. A visit to the New Orleans Office of Municipal Investigations (since abolished) in 1995 by a Human Rights Watch investigator found that "the office was absolutely silent, no phones were ringing, and some staffers were playing computer video games." *Human Rights Watch, Shielded from Justice*, 259.

81 New York Civil Liberties Union, *Five Years of Civilian Review: A Mandate Unfulfilled* (New York: New York Civil Liberties Union, 1998).

82 San Francisco, Office of Citizen Complaints, *2011 Annual Report* (2012). http://www.sfgov3.org/modules/showdocument.aspx?documentid=1938.

83 Walker, *Police Accountability*.

84 The problems with complaint data and with evaluating citizen oversight agencies are discussed in Walker, *Police Accountability*, 120–42.

85 Walker, *Police Accountability*.

86   The exception to this rule is the work of Robin Engel, *How Police Supervisory Styles Influence Patrol Officer Behavior* (Washington, DC: Department of Justice, 2003). Available at http://www.ncjrs.org, NCJ 194078. The scant body of literature she is able to cite is eloquent testimony to the neglect of this critical subject.

87   Samuel Walker, "Institutionalizing Police Accountability Reforms: The Problem of Making Police Reforms Endure," *Saint Louis University Public Law Review* 32 (no. 1, 2012): 57–92.

88   Lawrence W. Sherman, *Scandal and Reform: Controlling Police Corruption* (Berkeley: University of California Press, 1978). Patrick V. Murphy and Thomas Plate, Commissioner: *A View from the Top of American Law Enforcement* (New York: Simon and Schuster, 1978). New York City, Commission to Investigate Allegations of Police Corruption and the Anti-Corruption Procedures of the Police Department [Mollen Commission], *Commission Report* (1994).

PART II

The Elements of the New Police Accountability

THREE

Critical
Incident Policies

Holding Officers Accountable:
Controlling Critical Incidents

Police officers hold awesome powers—powers that are not granted to any other public or private officials. They have the power to deprive people of their liberty through arrest, to intrude into their privacy through a stop and frisk, to physically harm them through the use of force, to engage in racial or ethnic discrimination through the discretionary use of these powers, and they have the ultimate power to take human life through the use of deadly force. It is essential in a free society that these powers are used only when absolutely necessary and legally justified.[1]

Looking back over police history, it is astonishing how comparatively recently police departments have developed formal policies to control officers' use of their powers. As late as the early 1970s, departments sent their officers out onto the streets with hours of training about how to fire their weapons but no meaningful guidelines on when to shoot. In 1965, for example, the American Bar Foundation praised the Milwaukee Police Department's policy that permitted shooting in cases of "any felony" for the simple reason that it was a *written* policy.[2] Departments typically kept no records on officers' use of force and made no effort to learn about which officers used force more than others.[3] The Supreme Court did not address the use of deadly force until the 1985 case of *Tennessee v. Garner,* where Memphis officers had shot and killed an unarmed 14-year-old named Edward Garner who was fleeing a building. The Court declared unconstitutional the existing "fleeing felon" rule on the use of deadly force, and departments rapidly replaced it with the "defense of life" standard.[4]

The law and police policy and practice have changed dramatically since the early 1970s. It is now well established that police departments must take the necessary steps to ensure that officers are held accountable for their actions. In practice, this means that police departments have a *written policy* clearly specifying, for example, what amount of force is permissible in particular situations, or when officers may engage in a high-speed vehicle chase. Officers must then complete a *written report* after each critical incident, describing what they did and the justification for it. Finally, all incident reports are *reviewed* by supervisors to determine that the officer or officers complied with the law and department policy. The report and review process is now a recognized best practice in policing and is at the heart of the PTSR accountability framework described in Chapter One.

The Department of Justice 2001 report *Principles for Promoting Police Integrity* recommends that "Agencies should develop use of force policies that address use of firearms and other weapons and particular use of force issues such as: firing at moving vehicles, verbal warnings, positional asphyxia, bar arm restraints, and the use of chemical agents."[5] Even by 2001 most departments had gone far beyond the DOJ recommendation and adopted policies covering a wider range of police critical incidents. As we discussed in Chapter One, this book defines a critical incident as *any police action that poses a risk to the life, liberty, or dignity of a person.* The list of critical incidents covered by the PTSR framework should continue to grow as new issues surrounding the use of police powers arise. This chapter examines some of the more important critical incidents to illustrate how police departments have addressed (or not addressed) them through formal policies.

Administrative Rulemaking: The Basic Accountability Process

The policy, report, and review process for critical incidents in policing is a part of a general legal process known as administrative rulemaking. It is standard practice in large organizations in both the public and private sectors. The following section examines the history of rulemaking in policing and how it has been applied to policing.

Turning Point: The New Deadly Force Policy in New York City, 1972

The historic turning point in police accountability occurred in 1972 when New York City Police Commissioner Patrick V. Murphy adopted a new use of deadly force policy. A few departments had already begun to develop more restrictive policies in the 1960s, and at least six national-level blue-ribbon commissions recommended change in the 1960s and early 1970s as a result of the riots of the 1960s.[6] The NYPD policy had the most impact on local police departments, however, mainly because of its status as the largest department in the country. Additionally, the policy was evaluated by Professor James Fyfe (himself a former NYPD officer and future deputy commissioner), and his finding that the policy reduced firearms discharges gave important support to the idea that formal policies can have a positive impact on officer discretion.[7]

The NYPD's policy did not emerge out of thin air. In response to the riots of the 1960s, there was growing awareness among police experts of the need to control shootings and other police actions through detailed rules. Lorie Fridell identified four factors contributing to the movement for new deadly force policies: the broader movement to control police discretion, demands for racial justice arising from the disproportionate number of African Americans shot and killed, court rulings that expanded municipal liability for unjustified police shootings, and the growing social science research on officer-involved shootings that documented the racial disparities in shootings.[8] The President's Crime Commission in 1967 recommended "The Development of Guidelines for Police Action," and the following year the Kerner Commission cited "The Need for Policy Guidelines" that would cover a short but important list of police actions.[9]

NYPD policy TOP 237 had the basic elements that have shaped use of force policies over the past 40 years and the entire police accountability movement. Substantively, the policy limited discretion by clearly specifying when force can be used and when it is not appropriate, replacing the very permissive *fleeing felon rule* with the restrictive *defense of life* rule. Officers were permitted to use deadly force only in the defense of life, either their own lives or the life of another person. In addition, the policy prohibited firing a weapon for a number of specific purposes, including warning shots, shots intended to wound a suspect, and shots at or from moving vehicles. Procedurally, the policy required officers to complete a written report for each firearms discharge and mandated an automatic review of each report by supervisors.[10]

The NYPD policy quickly won favor within the law enforcement profession and spread to other departments. A 1977 report on police use of deadly force by the Police Foundation endorsed the mandatory reporting and review requirements.[11] The U.S. Civil Rights Commission's influential 1981 report, *Who Is Guarding the Guardians?*, recommended that "Unnecessary police use of excessive or deadly force could be curtailed by . . . strict procedures for reporting firearms discharges."[12] By the time of the Supreme Court's 1985 decision in *Tennessee v. Garner*, most big-city police departments had already adopted deadly force policies that were more detailed and restrictive than the *Garner* decision. This development reflected a new national consensus on the basic elements of the original 1972 NYPD policy.

Fyfe's evaluation of the 1972 NYPD policy found that it reduced firearms discharges by 30 percent over the next three years. Additionally, there was an increase in the number of "accidental" shootings but they were still only 9 percent of all discharges, which suggested that officers were not systematically trying to evade the new restrictions falsely reporting unauthorized discharges as accidents. Fyfe's findings, in short, suggested a high rate of officer compliance with a restrictive policy that significantly intruded on their traditional discretion.[13]

It is important to note in this regard that the NYPD policy required officers to report *all firearms discharges*, and not just shootings where someone was injured or killed. This approach recognizes that all discharges are potentially dangerous—to the officer and others—and that the control of firearms requires a complete picture of firearms usage.

By the 1980s, national data on persons shot and killed suggested that as more police departments adopted the defense of life policy significant reductions in police shootings had occurred. Additionally, the racial disparity in persons shot and killed has narrowed from a ratio of 6 or 8 African Americans for every white person shot in the mid-1970s to a ratio of 3 to 1 by the late 1990s. In Memphis, where the old fleeing felon rule had resulted in 13 African Americans and only 1 white person shot and killed in the "unarmed and non-assaultive" category, the new restrictive policy resulted in no fatal shootings of any people, white or African American, in this category by the late 1980s. In short, the defense of life rule not only achieved its intended goal of eliminating fleeing felon shootings but had the collateral positive effect of reducing racial disparities in persons shot and killed.[14]

The positive impact of the initial restrictive deadly force policies is easy to understand. As we pointed out, police departments traditionally sent their police officers out onto crime-ridden streets trained in *how* to fire those weapons but with absolutely no guidance on *when* to fire those weapons. A 1961 survey found that about half of departments surveyed relied on an "oral policy."[15] The 1963 edition of O. W. Wilson's influential textbook *Police Administration* said nothing about the use of deadly force.[16] A 1999 report by the Philadelphia Police Department's Integrity and Accountability Office quoted officers who recalled the 1970s as the "wild west," where it was "open season" and a "free for all." Warning shots and shots at fleeing suspects (two actions now prohibited by all departments) "occurred with alarming frequency."[17] In short, given the near total lack of controls over shootings, one could reasonably expect that even minimal controls would have a significant impact. In addition to the lack of written policies, prior to the 1970s most police officers did not have to complete detailed reports about use of force incidents. A 1968 book on Los Angeles pointed out that for years the LAPD conducted an automatic investigation if an officer damaged a patrol car, but not until March 1965 did it require a board on inquiry investigation if an officer shot and wounded a person.[18] Even in those departments in which some kind of formal reports was required, supervisors generally did not conduct rigorous reviews of those reports with an eye toward disciplining officers who violated policy. The lack of a formal policy and review process presumed that officers would use good judgment and should not be second-guessed in dangerous encounters. In effect, they were literally unaccountable for their behavior.[19]

The Administrative Rulemaking Framework

Confine, Structure, and Check Discretion

The framework for administrative rulemaking in policing was developed by law professor Kenneth Culp Davis in his short 1975 book, *Police Discretion*. His framework consists of three elements: confining, structuring, and checking discretion.[20]

Confining Discretion

Confining discretion involves having a written policy that clearly defines what an officer can and cannot do in a particular situation. This approach does not attempt to abolish discretion but only to limit its use to a narrow range of situations where judgment is still called for. In the entire criminal justice system, the idea of attempting to abolish discretion, in plea bargaining and sentencing, for example, has been rejected as futile and unwise. Confining discretion through clear and reasonable rules preserves a necessary amount of discretion to accommodate particular circumstances while enhancing consistency and equity in decision making.[21] Davis puts it bluntly: discretion "cannot be eliminated. Any attempt to eliminate it would be ridiculous."[22]

The principle of confining police discretion is illustrated by the following examples.

** Use of deadly force policies prohibits firing warning shots.
**Police policies that mandate an arrest in a domestic violence incident where there is evidence of a felonious assault.[23]

Structuring Discretion

Discretion is structured in the Davis model by allowing a certain amount of discretion while specifying the factors that an officer should consider in making a decision. The admonition to "use good judgment" is too vague and does not give officers meaningful guidance on when they can and cannot shoot. As Davis explains, policy should advise officers to "let your discretion be guided by these goals, policies, and principles."[24] For example:

** Vehicle pursuit policies that instruct officers to consider road conditions and the potential risk to pedestrians or other vehicles before initiating a pursuit.[25]
** A use of force continuum that instructs officers to use a certain level of force in response to a specific form of resistance.

In all of these examples, officers retain considerable discretion in choosing a response, but their response is guided by considerations that enhance compliance with the law and department policy.

Checking Discretion

Discretion is checked in the Davis model by having incident reports reviewed by supervisors and other higher command officers. In the original 1972 NYPD, deadly force policy, reports were reviewed both by an officer's immediate supervisor and by a departmental Use of Force Review Board. Since that time, the review/checking process has expanded in important ways.

> ** Some police departments conduct two parallel investigations of shooting incidents, with one directed toward whether the officer violated law or department policy and the other directed toward identifying any possible deficiencies in department policy, training, or supervision.[26]
> ** An early intervention system (see Chapter Five) that tracks officer-involved shootings can identify officers who have an unusually high rate of such incidents, even where no citizen has been shot and killed.[27]

The checking procedures described above all involve a commander or committee of supervisors of higher authority than an officer's immediate supervisor. This approach recognizes the fact that in policing, sergeants develop close relations with the officers under their command, and as a result might not be completely objective when evaluating whether an officer violated the law or department policy. Robin Engel's research on supervisors, for example, found that almost a quarter (23 percent) played a "supportive" role, seeking to protect officers under their command from "unfair" discipline, and acting as a "buffer" between them and upper management.[28] Sergeants' knowledge that the review of their incident reports by higher ranking officers is likely to enhance their objectivity in reviewing incident reports.

Collateral Aspects of Rulemaking

The administrative rulemaking process has several collateral effects in addition to guiding police officer behavior and controlling discretion.

Rules as Statements of Values

Rules governing police actions in critical incidents are statements of values. Use of force policies typically begin with the statement about the importance of protecting human life. The Use of Force Policy of the Metropolitan Police Department of Washington, D.C., for example, states that

> The policy of the Metropolitan Police Department is to value and preserve human life when using lawful authority to use force. Therefore, officers of the Metropolitan Police Department shall use the minimum amount of force that the objectively reasonable officer would use in light

of the circumstances to effectively bring an incident or person under control, while protecting the lives of the member or others.[29]

The 2012 Las Vegas Collaborative Reform Process report found that the Las Vegas Metropolitan Police Department's policy on deadly force, while good in many respects, lacked a statement on respect for the sanctity of human life, and recommended that one be added.[30]

The typical defense of life policy affirmation of the value of life stands in sharp contrast to the implicit values of the old fleeing felon rule. The latter prioritized arrest, communicating the message that arrest of a fleeing suspect was highest priority and that if the wrong person was sometimes shot and killed, that was just one of the mistakes we have to live with. The defense of life standard reverses the order of priority, indicating that the possible escape of a genuine felon is the mistake we are willing to pay in order to ensure the protection of life. Similarly, restrictive vehicle pursuit policies communicate the message that the safety of bystanders and other drivers is a higher value in certain circumstances than the arrest of a fleeing suspect.[31] The San Jose (California) Police Department vehicle pursuit policy states that:

> The primary purpose of this policy is to protect the public by assisting Department members in making reasonable pursuit related decisions that emphasize the importance of protecting the public. This requires balancing the known or reasonably suspected offenses and the apparent need for immediate capture against the risks to peace officers, innocent motorists, and others.[32]

Rules as the Basis for Training

It goes without saying that policies on critical incidents serve as the basis for officer training. Preservice academy training, however, is only one part of a comprehensive training program that should include regular inservice training. Academy training is easily forgotten once an officer hits the streets. In fact, policing has been notorious for having veteran officers tell the new recruit, "forget all that academy crap, this is how we really do it." The California P.O.S.T. program recognizes the special legal and social significance of certain policies and has a required inservice component labeled "Perishable Skills." Every two years, officers are required to complete 12 hours of training, with 4 hours each over arrest and control, driver training/awareness, and tactical firearms or force options.[33] This requirement recognizes that under the pressure of routine police work policies can easily erode and that it is necessary to provide regular refresher training.

Rules and Contributions to Openness and Transparency

Departments can enhance openness and transparency and build public trust and legitimacy by making their rules public. In the crisis atmosphere of the 1960s, one of the common criticisms of the police was that they were closed, secretive bureaucracies. Today, openness and transparency are recognized as important values, and an increasing number of departments place their policy manuals on their websites. Making public a department's policies on use of force or domestic violence, for example, allows people to understand why officers acted as they did in a controversial incident, or to see how a particular officer violated department policy. With policies public, moreover, it is then possible for community activists, civic leaders, and elected officials to engage in an informed debate over whether a revised policy is needed. In Los Angeles Sheriff's Department, the Office of Independent Review (OIR) recommended placing the Manual of Policies and Procedures on the department website and the sheriff quickly agreed. The OIR explained that "the public has an interest in being able to know the internal rules that govern the actions of the Sheriff's Department."[34]

Critical Incidents

As we have already mentioned, the control of police officer conduct in critical incidents through written policies has expanded considerably since the early 1970s. They now cover a wide range of incidents. This book argues that there is no known limit to how many incidents should be covered. Many police actions that were barely even thought of as raising potential legal and practical problems a few years ago (foot pursuits are a good example) are now regarded as matters of great concern and are covered by written policies. The following section discusses police policies in a selected group of critical incidents. It is not meant to be an exhaustive list.

Use of Deadly Force

The first and most important development of administrative rulemaking in policing applied to the use of deadly force. We have already discussed the influence of the 1972 New York City policy on the entire administrative rulemaking process. The 1985 Supreme Court decision in *Tennessee v. Garner* illustrates one of the great virtues of department rulemaking: its flexibility and capacity for specificity. By the time of *Garner*, the defense of life rule had already been widely adopted by police departments and went further in terms of the range of issues covered—the prohibition on warning shots and shooting at moving vehicles, for example. Supreme Court decisions are necessarily limited by the terms of constitutional law (and how a minimum of five Justices interpret the Constitution).[35] A police department, however, can develop administrative rules that cover issues that are simply good policy but do not necessarily raise issues of constitutional law. Moreover, a police department can act quickly on a particular issue that comes up without waiting for a court ruling.

Deadly force policies typically allow some limited exceptions to the strict defense of life rule, authorizing the use of deadly force where the officer believes a suspect has committed a felony involving the use of deadly force and is likely to commit another violent crime. The third paragraph of the Minneapolis Police Department policy is typical in this regard in allowing deadly force:

> To effect the arrest or capture, or prevent the escape, of a person who the officer knows or has reasonable grounds to believe has committed or attempted to commit a felony if the officer reasonably believes that the person will cause death or great bodily harm if the person's apprehension is delayed.[36]

It is important to note that while the policy creates an exception, it structures discretion by specifying that there must be reasonable grounds to believe there is a serious potential threat to someone's life ("will cause. . . if . . ."). It does not represent a return to the old fleeing felon rule.

One collateral issue regarding police use of firearms involves the display of a firearm in encounters with citizens. Some departments now explicitly prohibit the display of an officer's handgun. The Washington, D.C., police department use for force policy, for example, directs that no officer "shall draw and point a firearm at or in the direction of a person" unless a substantial risk of harm exists. Additionally, officers are required to complete a use of force report for "drawing and pointing their weapon at another person."[37] Two considerations underlie this policy. First, there is the risk of an accidental discharge that could result in the unintended injury or death of a citizen or another police officer. Second, an officer displaying a handgun in a contact with a citizen is an intimidating expression of police power. This practice strained police-community relations in some cities, notably Cincinnati in the events leading up to the riot in 2001 and the resulting federal consent decree in 2002.[38]

Less-Lethal Force

In an effort to reduce the use of deadly force, police departments adopted various forms of less-lethal force. These include chemical sprays, conducted energy devices (CEDs, popularly known by their trademarked name Tasers),[39] and others devices. Providing alternatives to the use of deadly force had the laudable goal of reducing officer-involved shootings and saving lives. The Department of Justice in 2003 faulted the Detroit police for having only "a limited array of [nonlethal] force options available," providing only firearms and chemical spray.[40] The new devices, however, introduced new issues regarding their use that needed to be addressed. As a result, they too are now covered by written policies governing their proper use.

When first introduced into policing, CEDs were greeted with both enormous popularity and controversy. Aggressively promoted by their manufacturers, they were quickly adopted by police departments.[41] The two most popular CED models were introduced in 1999 and 2003, and by 2007 an estimated 8,000 law enforcement agencies had adopted them, covering the majority of the people in the United States. Very quickly, however, there were a number of deaths of people against whom police CEDs had been used, and civil rights groups protested their use.[42] The protests led to the first research on the potential lethality of CEDs. In most of the initial publicized cases it was not clear that the victim's death was directly caused by the CED or was the result of other medical factors. Recognition of the potential lethality had one important effect on generally used terminology. Initially, CEDS and other weapons had been referred to as "less-than-lethal" weapons, suggesting that they were not potentially lethal. The commonly used terminology today is "less lethal" weapons, in recognition that they can result in death in certain circumstances.

Some police departments adopted CEDS without detailed policies governing their use. In response to the public controversy, formal policies are now standard and a national consensus over the content of those policies has emerged. The model policy developed by the Police Executive Research

Forum (PERF) and the COPS office appears in Figure 3.1. The policy *confines* CED use by limiting use to incidents involving active resistance, active aggression, and also by limiting it to one officer per incident and prohibiting use against pregnant women, the elderly, children, and frail persons.[43] CED deployment is *checked* by requiring an officer report on every

Figure 3.1 Model CED Policy (Excerpts)

1. CEDs should only be used against persons who are actively resisting or exhibiting active aggression, or to prevent individuals from harming themselves or others. CEDs should not be used against a passive suspect.

2. No more than one officer at a time should activate a CED against a person.

3. When activating a CED, law enforcement officers should use it for one standard cycle and stop to evaluate the situation (a standard cycle is five seconds). . . .

7. CEDs should not generally be used against pregnant women, elderly persons, young children, and visibly frail persons unless exigent circumstances exist.

8. CEDs should not be used on handcuffed persons unless they are actively resisting or exhibiting active aggression, and/or to prevent individuals from harming themselves or others. . . .

12. Officers should avoid firing darts at a subject's head, neck, and genitalia.

13. All persons who have been exposed to a CED activation should receive a medical evaluation. Agencies shall consult with local medical personnel to develop appropriate police-medical protocols. . . .

16. Following a CED activation, officers should use a restraint technique that does not impair respiration.

18. Agencies should create stand-alone policies and training curriculum for CEDs and all less-lethal weapons, and ensure that they are integrated with the department's overall use-of-force policy. . . .

32. Every instance of CED use, including an accidental discharge, should be accounted for in a use-of-force report.

Source: James M. Cronin and Joshua A. Ederheimer, *Conducted Energy Devices: Development of Standards for Consistency and Guidance* (Washington, DC: Department of Justice and the Police Executive Research Forum, 2006).

usage and also by creating a special out-of-chain-of-command review for any deployment that results in death.[44]

One of the main concerns regarding CED deployment is that instead of being an alternative to use of a firearm they become a substitute for less serious uses of force, with the result that more serious force is used than would be the case if CEDs were not available. One example would be using a CED against a suspect who becomes passively resistant by going into a fetal position. The model policy addresses that concern by limiting CED use to incidents of aggressive resistance. Nonetheless, the national survey of CED use found that almost half of all agencies permitted the use of CEDs against persons who only passively resisted an officer's commands.[45] Concerns about inappropriate use of CEDs were confirmed by a 2011 Justice Department investigation of the Portland, Oregon, police department that found a pattern of inappropriate CED use against mentally disturbed people. "These practices," the report concluded, "engender fear and distrust in the Portland community," which adversely affects the department's "ability to police effectively."[46]

On the positive side, the national survey of CED use found that CED deployment incidents involved far fewer injuries to both citizens and officers than did officer use of physical force. Citizens were injured in 25.1 percent of CED incidents, compared with 48.9 percent of officer use of physical force incidents. Officers, meanwhile, experienced injury in 7.6 percent of CED incidents, compared with 21.2 percent of physical force incidents.[47]

Use of Physical Force

Allegations of "police brutality"—meaning the use of excessive physical force—have been as much a volatile civil rights issue as deadly force. Police use of force is a relatively rare event. Research has consistently found that officers use force in only between 1 and 2 percent of all citizen encounters. Nonetheless, force has a significance far exceeding its numbers. It represents a visible exercise of coercive police power and is one of the flash points of police tensions with communities of color, along with arrests and officer-involved shootings. Not only are citizens often injured but police officers are most likely to be injured in incidents where they use force.[48]

In several important respects, physical force is more difficult to control than deadly force. It includes a wide range of actions, ranging from verbal commands through "soft empty hand" control to the use of a baton. There is no consensus over whether routine handcuffing is a form of force that officers should be required to report. Additionally, the number of nonlethal force incidents in any given year far exceeds the number of shooting incidents, which greatly complicates the task of reporting, reviewing, and controlling such incidents.[49] Finally, and perhaps most important, "excessive" force is typically a matter of perception. What the officer regards as necessary to overcome a suspect's resistance, the person involved often regards as excessive. In one revealing study of comparative perspectives on incidents that involved force, 33.4 percent of officers reported either active aggression or a deadly threat by the citizen, while no citizen reported such behavior. And no officers, meanwhile, reported that they faced no resistance or passive resistance, while 76.7 percent of the citizens reported that they did not resist.[50] Other studies reviewed by Alpert and Dunham, however, found higher levels of agreement between officer and citizen accounts of incidents.[51] The prevailing standard is that an officer may use the *minimum amount of force necessary for achieving a lawful purpose.* The Washington, D.C., police department limits lawful purposes as *"(a) To protect life or property, (b) To make a lawful arrest, (c) To prevent the escape of a person in custody, [and] (d) To control a situation and/or subdue and restrain a resisting individual."*[52]

The Supreme Court standard in *Graham v. Connor*[53] provides some guidance regarding the use of force but does not completely resolve all the issues. In brief, the Court held that the use of force is objectively reasonable depending on the severity of the crime in the precipitating incident, whether the suspect poses an immediate threat to the officer, and whether he or she is actively resisting arrest. A Supreme Court decision, however, is based on constitutional law. As discussed earlier with regard to *Tennessee v. Garner,* however, police departments can go further than a Supreme Court decision (without, of course, countermanding any part of the decision) with more detailed and more restrictive policies, providing additional guidance for officers.

One recurring problem is that police departments fail to clearly define uses of force. In 2002, for example, the Justice Department found that the Detroit Police Department policy "does not define 'use of force' nor adequately address when and in what manner the use of less-than-lethal force is permitted."[54] Similarly, the DOJ found that the Schenectady, New York, use of force policy "contains vague language and undefined terms," it "fails to identify specific uses of physical force that may be prohibited or restricted to limited circumstances," and it does not specify whether officers may use carotid holds or hog-tying—two types of force that have caused serious injury and death.[55] As recently as 2012, the Spokane (Washington) Police Department's policy required officers to complete a report only when physical force resulted in injury, or the person complained of an injury, or was rendered unconscious or experienced some other adverse consequence. A city commission recommended expanding the list of reportable force incidents to include "head strikes, knee strikes, elbow strikes, open and closed hand strikes; baton/flashlight strikes; all applications of less lethal devices (OC spray, foam or wood rounds, beanbag rounds, etc.); carotid neck restraint (Level I) ...; [and] all takedowns and prone handcuffing incidents that result in any head or facial injury."[56]

The Use of Force Continuum

In terms of administrative rulemaking, the *use of force continuum* emerged as a strategy for structuring officers' discretion in the use of force. Continua vary from department to department but all are designed to correlate the level of force used by an officer to the conduct of the citizen.[57] A model continuum developed by the U.S. Department of Justice begins with Officer Presence, noting that "The mere presence of a law enforcement officer works to deter crime or diffuse a situation." It then proceeds upwards to verbal questions or commands, to "empty hand control," such as grabbing or holding a person, and on to less-lethal devices and finally the use of deadly force.[58]

An officer does not have to begin at the bottom of the use of force continuum (officer presence) and work his or her way up to higher levels of force. If the person is immediately aggressively resistant, the officer can and should begin at that point on the continuum. Some departments use a "plus one" rule, which means that the officer can use one level of force higher than that prescribed by the continuum for a given level of resistance. (The "plus one" rule, however, does not apply to the use of deadly force. An officer may not use deadly force where there is no threat to life, as described in the earlier section of this chapter.)

De-escalation, Disengagement

The idea of de-escalating encounters with people that have the potential for conflict has emerged as a best practice in policing. A long-standing problem in American policing has been the tendency of officers to escalate an encounter in response to their perception of disrespect or lack of cooperation on the part of a citizen. Critics have labeled the practice "contempt of cop," meaning that in response to disrespect or noncooperation an officer is more likely to reply with verbal abuse, use of force, and/or an arrest.[59] Research on police-citizen interactions has consistently found that citizen disrespect increases the probability of an officer using force and/or making an arrest.[60] The Justice Department found that Seattle police officers used excessive force against citizens who "talk back" to officers and express their discontent with the situation. The DOJ labeled this practice an unconstitutional and unreasonable attack on freedom of speech.[61] In some cases the officer files resisting arrest charges (often referred to as "cover" charges since they are designed to cover an arrest that lacks justification). The practice is considered sufficiently common that many early intervention systems include resisting arrest charges as a performance indicator (see Chapter Five). Philadelphia Police Commissioner Charles Ramsey argues that "a large number of 'contempt of cop' arrests is a hint that officers may not be going in the right direction," and recommends close scrutiny of data on such arrests.[62]

De-escalation is a tactic designed to reduce conflict and reduce police officer use of force in situations where it was not really necessary. The Kansas City (Missouri) Police Department policy explains that in many situations "mere police presence often avoids the need for any force."[63] Philadelphia Police Commissioner Charles Ramsey told a PERF meeting that "one of the things that I have discovered during my time as a police officer is that it's easy for us to go up the use-of-force continuum, but the hard part is bringing it back down, and de-escalating situations effectively."[64] In the most detailed analysis of the sequence of events in police use of force incidents, Alpert and Dunham agree. "Once a cycle of force is initiated," they argue, "there appears to be only limited opportunity to deescalate the level of force."[65]

A Justice Department investigation of the Portland, Oregon, police department found that the lack of policy and training on de-escalation was partly responsible for a pattern of excessive force against mentally ill persons. (See the discussion below, pp. 89–91). The report concluded that "strategic disengagement—a practice of withdrawing from a situation to avoid use of force when a subject does not appear in imminent danger to harm to self or others"—is a valuable tactic. Also important, "properly applied, de-escalation begins long before the officer is faced with the choice of using force and will often make that decision unnecessary."[66]

The idea of de-escalation illustrates the crucial point that police-citizen encounters are fluid events that can go in different directions and that officers have some capacity to shape the outcome. Peter Scharf and Arnold Binder identified four stages of police-citizen encounters: *Anticipation, Entry and Initial Contact, Dialogue and Information Exchange,* and *Final Decision.* Each stage includes actions by the citizen, the perception of those actions by the officer, the officer's response, and the person's response to the officer's initial action.[67] Although the scenario originated in a study of deadly force, it is relevant to all police-citizen encounters. Alpert and Dunham developed the most sophisticated analysis of the sequence of events in police-citizen encounters involving force, identifying 10 different steps in the entire sequence.[68] As we have already noted, the Justice Department 2012 report on a pattern of excessive and unnecessary use of force against mentally ill persons in Portland emphasized that "properly applied, de-escalation begins long before the officer is faced with the choice of using force and will often make that decision unnecessary."[69]

Mike Gennaco, head of the Office of Independent Review in the Los Angeles Sheriff's Department, explains how de-escalation increases officer control of situations. Many officers, he points out, argue that the resistant person controls the encounter. Gennaco explains that

> A progressive policing model [of officer use of force] equips officers with strategies that do not allow subjects to dictate the response. It is the peace officer that must effectuate an effective plan of detention that avoids the use of deadly force if at all possible and still safely takes a dangerous individual into custody. The police should dictate the situation; not the subject, and should approach any tactical situation with that mindset.[70]

The fluidity of police-citizen encounters, meanwhile, highlights the importance of communication between an officer and a citizen. Officers can de-escalate an encounter in several ways. One is by giving the citizen clear and firm direction as to what to do. Another is by not using language likely to insult or anger a citizen and cause him or her to exert a higher level of resistance. The Las Vegas Collaborative Reform Process report found that verbal commands to citizens were "insufficient" in about 15 percent of officer-involved shootings [OIS]. It concluded that explicit, clear, and direct commands produce higher levels of citizen compliance in all types of encounters, both violent and nonviolent. Additionally, in 21 percent of the OIS incidents, a flawed approach by the officer "failed to slow the momentum of the incident," and allowed it to escalate to the point where deadly force was used.[71] The report recommended that one quarter of training on defensive tactics should be devoted to de-escalation.[72]

De-escalation can also contribute to a reduction in injuries to both citizens and police officers. A national survey of CED use found that citizens experienced injury in 48.9 percent of the incidents where an officer used hands-on physical force, and officers experienced injury in 21.2 percent of the incidents. Most of the injuries were minor, but they were injuries nonetheless. Injuries were also lower when officers used OC chemical spray. It follows that de-escalation techniques that can avoid any officer use of force can significantly reduce injuries to all parties.[73]

Vehicle Pursuits

High-speed vehicle pursuits are extremely dangerous events. The first study to gain national attention, by the Physicians for Automotive Safety, reported the alarming estimate that 20 percent of all pursuits ended in someone being killed, 50 percent ended in at least one serious injury, and 70 percent ended in an accident. Subsequent studies produced much lower estimates but nonetheless confirmed that pursuits are highly dangerous. Alpert and Dunham's study of 952 pursuits in Dade County, Florida, in the mid-1980s found that 33 percent of all pursuits ended in an accident, and 17 percent ended with someone being injured (11 percent ended with an injury to the driver or passenger in the fleeing vehicle, and 2 percent ended with an injury to the police officer); seven of the 952 ended in a fatality.[74] It should be noted, moreover, that Alpert and Dunham conducted their study *after* the Miami-Dade Police Department had instituted a restrictive pursuit policy.

As with deadly force, vehicle pursuits were essentially uncontrolled until the 1970s. Officers were free to pursue a fleeing vehicle regardless of the circumstances if they simply chose to do so. High-speed pursuits became a part of the culture of policing, with flight defined as a direct challenge to an officer's authority (another version of "contempt of cop").[75] With the development of media technology (helicopters, more mobile cameras) high-speed pursuits became a part of the public image of policing, featured on the news ironically just as police departments have begun to limit them.

The new controls over high-speed pursuits follow the basic administrative rulemaking model. Written policies *confine* officer discretion by forbidding pursuits in certain situations (e.g., for suspected minor offenses) and *structure* it by directing officers to consider dangerous road conditions, school zones, or other risk factors before initiating a pursuit.[76]

Discretion is *checked* by giving supervisors and/or dispatchers authority to terminate a pursuit and requiring officers to complete pursuit reports.

Research on vehicle pursuit policies indicates that restrictive policies effectively reduce the number of pursuits, accidents, injuries, and deaths. Alpert found that a new restrictive policy in the Miami-Dade Police Department in 1992 reduced pursuits by 82 percent. Training also had a dramatic effect on officer attitudes. Prior to training, in St. Petersburg, Florida, 58 percent of officers would pursue in the case of a "low risk" traffic violation; following training, only 24 percent would pursue in such cases.[77]

Foot Pursuits

Until a few years ago, foot pursuits by officers were rarely discussed in terms of either officer safety, effectiveness, or legal liability. Today, they are recognized as highly dangerous events that need to be governed by detailed policies providing guidance for officers and encouraging restraint. Foot pursuits typically occur when a police officer stops a motor vehicle and the driver flees on foot. Because they do not involve the use of a vehicle, they are not covered by a department's vehicle pursuit policy. Nor did departments require reports on such events. The Special Counsel to the Los Angeles Sheriff's Department in 2003, for example, found that "in contrast to vehicle pursuits, which are reliably tracked, the LASD does not keep tabs on foot pursuits and currently cannot state how many foot pursuits occur each year, or result in a use of force, or lead to an injury to a deputy."[78] Pursuing the person on foot is motivated by both an officer's understandable desire to apprehend a fleeing suspect and also to assert the officer's authority over what is regarded as "contempt of cop."

A 2003 study by the LASD Special Counsel brought the issue of foot pursuits to public attention, finding them to be extremely dangerous. About 22 percent of all LASD officer-involved shooting cases between 1997 and 2002 (52 of 239 incidents) involved "shots fired by deputies during or at the conclusion of a foot pursuit."[79] One case study illustrated the problems and dangers with foot pursuits:

> 1. The deputy was all alone; 2. It was dark; 3. The stop was made in a high crime area; 4. Until the suspect ran, he had engaged in no illegal activity more serious than driving without a license and running a stop sign; 5. No one from the deputy's station knew his whereabouts or that he was chasing a suspect on foot; 6. The suspect was taller and heavier than the deputy and

was on parole; 7. The deputy lost sight of the suspect in the darkness before starting to run after him; 8. The deputy evidently had no clear plan of action other than to chase the suspect; 9. The deputy apparently failed to follow his training, in which case he would have established contact with his station, resisted the impulse to run after the suspect, and would have coordinated a containment to isolate the suspect and prevent his escape. He should have summoned other deputies to the scene and established a plan to search for and capture the suspect that posed the minimum possible risk to the suspect's or the deputies' lives.[80]

Compounding the problem, the LASD had been extremely "reluctant" to discipline officers for "tactically reckless foot pursuit that puts the deputy himself in real danger." One lieutenant explained that it was punishment enough for a deputy to later realize that "his ass could have been dead out there," and therefore he would "not act like an idiot again."[81]

In response to growing awareness of the dangers of foot pursuits, the IACP (International Association of Chiefs of Police) issued a model policy. (See Figure 3.2, which follows the administrative rulemaking model of confining and structuring officers' discretion.)

Gender Bias Issues: Domestic Violence and Sexual Assaults

While use of force issues often involve questions of racial or ethnic bias, gender bias is also a matter of concern in terms of equity in policing. The most serious involve the failure of police officers to respond appropriately to incidents of domestic violence and sexual assault allegations.

Research established that the traditional (that is, pre-1970s) police response to domestic violence incidents involved a practice of not making arrests, even where there was evidence of a felonious assault of a woman. The no-arrest practice reflected the prevailing social attitude that domestic violence against a woman was a private matter and not a crime.[82] In the 1970s, the women's movement identified domestic violence as a serious problem and began challenging traditional police no-arrest practices. Several early lawsuits alleging denial of equal protection of the law to domestic violence victims resulted in court decisions requiring police department policies that mandated arrests where there was evidence of a felonious assault. The Oakland, California, police department was required in 1979 to adopt a policy directing that "arrest shall be presumed to be the most appropriate response in domestic violence cases which involve an alleged felony."[83] The Oakland suit and other cases, along with

Figure 3.2   IACP Model Policy on Foot Pursuits (*with emphases added*)

2. Unless there are exigent circumstances such as an immediate threat to the safety of other officers or civilians, officers shall not engage in or continue a foot pursuit under the following conditions:

   a. If the officer believes the *danger to pursuing officers or the public* outweighs the necessity for immediate apprehension.
   b. If the officer becomes aware of any unanticipated circumstances that substantially increases the *risk to public safety* inherent in the pursuit.
   c. While acting alone. If exigent circumstances warrant, *the lone officer shall keep the suspect in sight from a safe distance* and coordinating containment.
   d. *Into buildings, structures, confined spaces, or into wooded or otherwise isolated areas without sufficient backup and containment of the area.* The primary officer shall stand by, radio his or her location, and await the arrival of officers to establish a containment perimeter. At this point, incident shall be considered a barricaded or otherwise noncompliant suspect, and officers shall consider using specialized units such as SWAT, crisis response team, aerial support, or police canines.
   e. If the officer loses possession of his firearm.
   f. If *the suspect's identity is established* or other information exists that allows for the suspect's probable apprehension at a later time and there is no immediate threat to the public or police officers.
   g. If the suspect's location is no longer known.

Source: International Association of Chiefs of Police, Model Policy, *Foot Pursuits* (2003).

political activity by the new women's movement, provoked a national debate over the best approach to handling domestic violence incidents. While some activists wanted *mandatory arrest* in all cases of alleged domestic violence, a consensus developed in favor of an *arrest preferred* policy that allowed the officer some discretion where there was no clear evidence of a felonious assault.[84]

Although most departments today have a domestic violence policy, some still lag behind in terms of policy and actual practice. A 2011 Justice Department investigation of the New Orleans Police Department found serious deficiencies in the department's handling of domestic violence incidents. Both the department's main policy and a separate Domestic Violence Unit's manual were vague and inadequate with regard to how

911 operators should take calls, procedures for preliminary investigations of crime scenes, the identification and documentation of victim injuries, and procedures for follow-up investigations. The Domestic Violence Unit, moreover, lacked sufficient staff, with only three detectives attempting to handle the 6,200 domestic violence calls received in the first half of 2010. Incident reports, moreover, did not indicate follow-up interviews of witnesses. Most of the follow-up work was done by the prosecution unit in the District Attorney's office. The DOJ report concluded that the department's "involvement in investigating a case appears to end at the point of arrest."[85]

A subsequent DOJ consent decree for the New Orleans Police Department mandated a series of reforms, including "clear and detailed guidelines" for each stage in the handling of domestic violence incidents, prioritizing victim safety, discouraging dual arrest of both alleged victim and offender, requiring custodial arrest for violating an outstanding protection order, developing a working relationship with the New Orleans Family Justice Center, assigning "sufficient staff" to the Domestic Violence Unit, and additional training for all officers related to their specific duties.[86]

The Justice Department investigation of the New Orleans Police Department's handling of sexual assault cases closely paralleled its findings related to domestic violence. The department misclassified many rape and attempted rape cases, with the result that they were not investigated; among those cases that were investigated there were patterns of inadequate documentation in reports, including failure to locate and interview witnesses, and there was heavy influence of "stereotypical assumptions and judgments about sex crimes and victims of sex crimes." The department's policies on sexual assaults were "outdated and in need of revision," and supervision was inadequate. The resulting consent decree mandated a set of reforms designed to overcome these deficiencies.[87]

The mandated reforms in the consent decree dramatize a number of issues related to a comprehensive accountability process. It demonstrates that simply having a written policy and even a special unit for a particular issue is not sufficient. Departments need to commit sufficient resources to be able to carry out its mission. Finally, for many issues a department's effectiveness is greatly enhanced by developing partnerships with social service agencies. These issues include police responses to mentally disturbed persons (see below) and homeless people.

Deployment of Canines

Police use of canines has a long history of controversy with the African American community. Police dogs evoke memories of the 1960s civil rights movement, particularly the famous newsreel footage of dogs attacking civil rights demonstrators in Birmingham, Alabama, in 1963. The more recent problem has been police departments maintaining canine units with either inadequate policies or no formal policies at all governing their deployment.

The Department of Justice 2001 report *Principles for Promoting Police Integrity* unequivocally states that "the use of a canine to attempt to apprehend or seize a civilian is a use of force," and should be incorporated into a department's general use of force policy.[88] In Philadelphia in the 1970s, "several hundred police canines were trained to bite first and bark second."[89] The Department of Justice found that the Miami Police Department did not "specify whether it uses a 'find and bite' policy (which allows dogs to bite upon locating a subject) or a 'find and bark' policy (requiring a dog to bark, rather than bite)." Interviews with canine unit officers indicated that in practice the department used a "find and bite" policy. Dogs were trained to bite subjects "regardless of whether the subject is actively resisting or attempting to flee."[90]

The case of canines in the Los Angeles Sheriff's Department illustrates both the impact of a new restrictive policy and the difficulties in maintaining the positive effects that were initially achieved. The Special Counsel to the LASD examined the use of canines in 11 different reports over 11 years. These reports provide an illuminating picture of how a policy does not remain fixed, but changes in response to developing circumstances, some of which include lobbying by department stakeholders.

The issue of canine policy in the LASD arose with the 1992 Kolts Report, which found many lawsuits arising from canine-involved incidents. The Special Counsel, created as a result of the Kolts Report, immediately took up the issue and in 1993 recommended changes in the department's canine policy. Perhaps the most important change involved substituting "find and bark" for the existing "find and bite" policy. As a result of this and other changes, the number of canine deployments dropped by almost half from 1991 to 2001, and the average number of bites over three-year periods dropped by two-thirds (from about 50 to about 20 per year). One change was an end to deployment of canines regarding auto theft suspects. The department's data indicated that many of these cases involved teenage joy rides, where there was no serious danger requiring a canine. The ban eliminated about 25 percent of all canine deployments.[91]

After the initial successes in reducing canine deployments and bites, however, canine unit handlers and canine trainers lobbied successfully for loosening some of the new restrictions. The Special Counsel reported that the department's "guard and bark" policy had become indistinguishable from "find and bite." By 2004 the number of deployments and bites was rising, although the Special Counsel was unable to identify any specific cause. It continued the dialogue with the LASD over canine deployments, recommending consideration of alternative technologies such as clear-out gas to remove people from buildings or hiding places, pole cameras to permit viewing around corners, and night-vision technologies.[92]

The story of the continuing struggle over of the LASD canine policy has a number of important lessons that are relevant to other critical incidents. First, the initial successes indicate that a properly designed restrictive policy can successfully reduce potentially harmful police activities. Second, even good policies can and do change over time. In this instance, the unit officers affected by new restrictions fought back and successfully won revisions loosening some of the new restrictions. With various interests and perspectives at stake, we should never assume that any policy remains the same. Third, the Special Counsel played a particularly important role in continuously monitoring the changes in both policy and practice over time. It helped to bring about the initial policy changes, analyzed department data on deployments and bites, monitored subsequent changes in policy and their impact, and was an active player in the ongoing debate over policy. The role of external review is discussed in greater detail in Chapter Six.

As a final note, the story of LASD canine policy illustrates the importance of systematic data in the new police accountability. The incident reports, which provided data on deployments, bites, bite ratios, and the racial and ethnic background of people bitten, tracked the department's performance over time and allowed for informed discussions over policy and policy changes.

Responding to People With Mental Disorders

Responding to people with mental health issues is a routine part of policing. Such incidents sometimes require the use of force. Persons with mental health problems may pose a threat to themselves or other persons, including police officers. In some cases the person has a weapon or object that could cause harm. The problem of police encounters with mentally ill persons has been accentuated in recent years because of cuts in social services for the mentally ill, leaving people without proper treatment. The Justice Department investigation of the Portland, Oregon, police department found "serious deficiencies in the mental health system," which resulted in increased burdens on law enforcement agencies. One veteran Portland police officer commented that over the course of his career the number of encounters with mentally ill people had gone from "a couple of times a month to a couple of times a day."[93]

When police officers do use force in mental illness encounters, department force incident investigations often focus narrowly on the final moments of the encounter. At this point, the mentally ill person with a weapon probably poses a threat to the officer's safety and the officer's force was justified. This is true of many use of force incidents not involving mentally ill people. The best practice regarding encounters with mentally ill persons emphasizes examining the full scenario of the encounter to determine whether the officer could have taken some action at an earlier stage that would have de-escalated the encounter and avoided any serious use of force by the officer.

The Justice Department investigation of the Portland, Oregon, police department found a number of serious "deficiencies in policy, training, and supervision" with regard to the handling of mentally ill persons. It concluded that officers "often do not adequately consider a person's mental state before using force and that there is instead a pattern of responding inappropriately to persons in mental health crisis, resulting in a practice of excessive use of force, including deadly force, against them." It particularly noted the inappropriate use of CEDs in response to mentally ill persons. The report noted both "the absence of officers specially trained in and proficient at responding to mental health crisis," and "the lack of strategic disengagement protocols involving mental health providers." De-escalation and disengagement, which we discussed earlier in this chapter, are particularly relevant with regard to police-citizen encounters involving mental health issues.[94]

The most widely used program for improving police response to people with mental disorders is the Crisis Intervention Team (CIT) program developed by the Memphis (Tennessee) Police Department. It involves a collaborative arrangement with mental health professionals and special training for officers in dealing with mentally disturbed persons. CIT has gained national recognition and has been copied by a number of other police departments.[95] The Justice Department report on Portland found that while the department trained all officers in crisis intervention, it did not have a specialized CIT of officers "who have expressed a desire to specialize in crisis intervention and have demonstrated a proficiency at responding to individuals in mental health crisis." The Justice Department argued that mere academy training was inadequate and that "expertise requires vast field experience" acquired over time in real-life situations. And paralleling the recommendation in the report on gender issues in the New Orleans Police Department (see above, pp. 86–87), it noted a lack of engagement with mental health services providers.[96]

The case of police handling of mentally ill people in Portland illustrates an important point about critical incident policies. In practice, policies are not isolated issues, but in most cases implicate other policies. Police handling of mentally ill people involved the department's policies on use of force and CEDs in particular, and raised broader policy questions related to the creation and use of a special unit and relations with community social service providers.

Ensuring Bias-Free Policing

Allegations of discrimination based on race and ethnicity are recurring police controversies in every type of police-citizen encounter. Indeed, race and ethnicity are a central issue in the entire criminal justice system.[97] The problem of eliminating discrimination in policing is complicated, however, by the complex nature of police-citizen encounters, in which many factors are often at work simultaneously that make it difficult to conclude that race was the sole or even the primary factor in, for example, a pedestrian stop or a traffic stop. Police officers can easily claim that a car was weaving or that a pedestrian made a furtive movement to justify a stop. In such circumstances, it is difficult if not impossible to say for certain that race or ethnicity was the sole reason for the stop.

The debate over the legitimate use of race or ethnicity in policing has resulted in a consensus of opinion that is well stated in a model policy by the Police Executive Research Forum (Figure 3.3).[98] Officers may not use race or ethnicity as the *sole* factor in any enforcement decision, but they may use it as one of several factors related to an individual suspect. Following the administrative rulemaking approach, the policy *confines*

Figure 3.3   Model Policy on the Use of Race or Ethnicity in Police Work

Except as provided below, officers shall not consider race/ethnicity in establishing either reasonable suspicion or probable cause. Similarly, except as provided below, officers shall not consider race/ethnicity in deciding to initiate even those nonconsensual encounters that do not amount to legal detentions or to request consent to search.

Officers may take into account the reported race or ethnicity of a specific suspect or suspects based on trustworthy, locally relevant information that links a person or persons of a specific race/ethnicity to a particular unlawful incident(s).

Race/ethnicity can never be used as the sole basis for probable cause or reasonable suspicion.

Source: Lorie A. Fridell et al., *Racially Biased Policing: A Principled Response* (Washington, DC: Police Executive Research Forum, 2001).

discretion by forbidding the use of race or ethnicity as the exclusive factor, and then *structures* discretion by describing the circumstances under which race and ethnicity may be used. Thus, police officers may not stop all young African American men in a neighborhood but may stop a young African American man who, as described by witnesses, is tall, thin, and bald. The use of race is appropriate here because it is linked to other characteristics. Similarly, police officers may not stop all young white men in a neighborhood, but may stop a middle-aged white man who was short and overweight, as described by witnesses.

The Washington, D.C., police department adopted a policy on Unbiased Policing based on the PERF model, which includes a broad list of categories that officers may not use as the sole criterion for arrest *(race, color, ethnicity, national origin, religion, age, gender, gender identity, sexual orientation, family responsibilities, disability, educational level, political affiliation, source of income, and place of residence or business of an individual),* and states that an officer may use any one of them only "in combination with other identifying factors when the law enforcement member is seeking to apprehend a specific suspect."[99]

Complicating the issue of race and ethnicity in policing is the fact that bias can be unconscious as well as conscious. That is, a person may act in a racially biased way without being aware of the influence of race or ethnicity when it is buried in deeply held assumptions and stereotypes. Social science research has explored the phenomenon of unconscious racism, and there is now an area of social psychology known as the "science of bias." The Fair and Impartial Policing (FAIP) project explains that "even well-intentioned humans (and thus, officers) manifest biases that can impact on their perceptions and behavior." These biases, moreover, can express themselves below the level of consciousness. "Implicit" or "unconscious" bias affects what people think and do even among "people who consciously hold non-prejudiced attitudes." An officer, for example, might perceive a potential crime when he or she "observes two young Hispanic males driving in an all-Caucasian neighborhood or lead an officer to be 'under-vigilant' with a female subject because he associates crime and violence with males."[100]

Many people have trouble accepting the idea of unconscious or implicit bias. The science of bias research, however, offers persuasive research evidence that it exists and affects perceptions and decisions. One study first collected self-reported beliefs and attitudes about African American suspects compared to white suspects among a group of police officers and then, using a computer simulation, examined their decisions to shoot or not shoot criminal suspects. Officers with negative attitudes toward African American suspects and negative beliefs about the alleged criminality of African Americans were more likely to shoot unarmed African American suspects than officers with more positive attitudes.[101] Another study used simulations to compare police officers to community members with regard to their decisions to shoot or not shoot in simulations involving African American and white armed and unarmed targets. Both the police and community members exhibited racial bias with respect to how quickly they made a decision to shoot. Police officers were better able to distinguish between armed and unarmed persons, and community members were more likely to shoot African Americans than whites. The study's authors linked the more positive officer results to high-quality police use-of-force training, which the community member suspects in the study had not had.[102]

More police departments are incorporating the issue of unconscious bias into their training, in some cases contracting with FAIP. The Las Vegas Collaborative Reform report, after finding a pattern of potential racial bias in officer-involved shootings, recommended fair and impartial policing training for the department.[103] The FAIP program offers a six-hour training program for recruit and patrol officers that is designed to (a) "Understand that even well-intentioned people have biases";

(b) "Understand how implicit biases impact on what we *perceive/see* and can (unless prevented) impact on what we *do*"; (c) "Understand that fair and impartial policing leads to *effective policing*"; and (d) help officers "(1) recognize his/her conscious and implicit biases, and (2) implement 'controlled' (unbiased) behavioral responses."[104]

The principal significance of training on unconscious bias for the issues in this book is that formal policies on use of force, foot pursuit, and the handling of mentally ill persons, to name only three, may properly address the objective conditions of a police-citizen encounter but not take into account how unconscious bias may at times be the determining factor in an officer's action. That is, they may be more likely to perceive a threat from the African American person compared with the white person, and as a result be more likely to use deadly force, a less lethal weapon, or physical force.

Additional Critical Incident Issues

Failure to Report Incidents and Incomplete Reports

Critical incidents are a crucial element of police accountability tools, but if officers fail to complete required reports or do not provide complete and accurate data the entire accountability system begins to collapse. An early intervention system (Chapter Five), for example, is useless without timely and accurate incident reports. There is evidence that officers do not always file required reports. The Justice Department's 2011 investigation of the Seattle Police Department found "multiple cases" where officers failed to report force incidents. There were also incidents where a second officer used force but was not named in the primary officer's report. A related problem is the use of what the DOJ called "patterned and non-descriptive language" in force reports. Officers, for example, reported that people "struggled," without specifying the exact nature and seriousness of their resistance.[105] In New York City, more than half of stop and frisk reports said that the stop was prompted by "furtive movements," without describing the exact movements and why they justified a stop and frisk. In short, a reporting requirement is an important advance in police accountability but it is not always sufficient in and of itself.[106]

Ensuring full compliance with critical incident reporting requirements is a major challenge for which there is no easy solution. Much depends on the culture of a police department. Ideally, officers would feel a professional commitment to file required reports; in a less than ideal organization, they would file reports out of fear of being reported by other officers. Close supervision and enforcement of department rules is also likely to ensure compliance.

Officers in Critical Incidents

A long-neglected issue in policing involves how departments respond to officers involved in shootings and other critical incidents. Typically, officers remained on the job in their regular assignment. This approach reflected two aspects of traditional police culture. The first is that officer-involved shootings were simply not considered that important. The second is that in the traditional macho culture of policing, no one wanted to acknowledge the emotional impact of a shooting on an officer who did the shooting and take steps to reduce an officer's stress level.

Police practices have changed dramatically on this subject. Officers involved in officer-involved shooting incidents and other critical incidents where discipline may result are typically placed on administrative assignment pending the outcome of the investigation of the incident. It recognizes that sending an officer back onto the streets is unfair to the officer and creates potential risks to the public should the incident affect his or her conduct in subsequent contacts with the public. Additionally, an officer is under investigation for an action that might result in departmental or even possible criminal charges and should not be on duty until the investigation of the incident is concluded.

The Phoenix Police Department's Serious Incident Policy represents an emerging best practice in this area. A supervisor "will accompany the involved employee away from the scene to a quiet place . . . as soon as possible." When more than one officer is involved in an incident, they are to be separated "to avoid common discussion." Also, "When practical, every effort will be made to provide one-on-one support" to the involved officers. Finally, access to the officers is restricted to a designated supervisor, other department officials involved in investigating the incident, family members, and a designated officer union official. Officers are not to discuss the incident with other officers involved in it.[107] The Phoenix policy simply respects the humanity of officers involved in critical incidents.

A related issued involves the integrity of incident investigations, especially officer-involved shootings. The practice of officers talking among each other immediately after an incident in order to create an agreed-upon version of the incident and to cover for violations of law or policy has been an unfortunate tradition in American policing. The Los Angeles Police Department was required by the 2001 consent decree to develop a post-incident "no huddling" policy for this reason.[108]

Ensuring Consistency Among Policies

Critical incident policies, along with all other department policies, are collected in the policy and procedure manual (which is known by various names). The manual itself raises a number of important issues requiring close administrative attention.

The first issue is that to be useful, a policy and procedure manual needs to be organized on a rational basis so that officers and others can quickly find a policy they need to consult. This simple proposition is not as easy to achieve as one might think. In the Kansas City (Missouri) Police Department, policies are spread among 12 different categories: Procedural Instructions, Administrative Bureau Memorandums, Board Resolutions, Chief's Memorandums, Department Memorandums, Executive Services Bureau Memorandums, Investigative Bureau Memorandums, Legal Bulletins, Patrol Bureau Memorandums, Professional Development and Research Memorandums, Special Orders, and finally a Personnel and Policy Benefit Manual.[109] An alphabetical index helps one find a particular policy, but overall the body of policies and procedures is disorganized and incoherent.

A second issue is that many policies implicate several other policies. A policy on arrest procedures, for example, may include a section on the use of force when making an arrest. It is a best practice for policy manuals to cross-reference all the relevant policies. Departments typically revise a policy in a crisis atmosphere without also updating the other related policies. The resulting lack of consistency between policies creates confusion for officers. The Justice Department, for example, found in 2003 that while one policy on use of force in the Miami Police Department embodied a state-of-the-art definition of when force could be used, the policy on arrests contained a vague and far more permissive definition. The DOJ concluded that "The MPD . . . fails to provide officers with clear guidance on what constitutes a reasonable use of force."[110]

Conclusion

The American police have made enormous progress in developing meaningful controls over officer conduct in critical incidents where the lives, liberty, and safety of citizens are potentially at risk. That progress is comparatively recent, however. There are many people today who were adults and even police officers at a time when police departments provided no guidance on when their officers could use deadly force. There has been considerable progress in recent years over emerging issues such as foot pursuits and the value of de-escalation as a tactic for minimizing use of force. The administrative rulemaking process of confining, structuring, and checking officer discretion, as described in this chapter, is firmly established in American policing and provides a framework for responding to future issues as they may arise.

It is worth noting that the experience with critical incident policies over the last 40 years offers an optimistic view of the capacity to change and improve policing. It is an old cliché that the American police are resistant to change, and this view is firmly held by some critics of the police. The evidence does not support this interpretation. Change has been positive in two respects. First, departments have adopted a wide range of policies covering critical incidents. To be sure, they typically had to be dragged kicking and screaming into the future through community protests, media exposes, and litigation. But change they did. Second, there is good evidence that officers generally, although certainly not always, conform to new restrictive policies, albeit often reluctantly and not completely, as each week's media headlines remind us. Nonetheless, the evidence clearly indicates that American policing is extremely fluid and constantly changing. This conclusion should encourage efforts to make still more changes in the near future.

Despite this progress, however, a number of significant challenges remain. The first challenge is to continue the expansion of the list of critical incidents that need to be covered by a detailed policy and articulated with existing policies. As we argued at the beginning of this chapter, no one knows what tomorrow's list of critical incidents might look like. Recent experience teaches us that events continue to cause us to look anew at familiar events and assess them from a different perspective. Just as a few years ago not many people thought foot pursuits were dangerous events that needed to be governed by strict policies, so additional issues will arise in the near future.

Second, we have learned that even with respect to one issue, reassessment and revision is a continuous process. Policies on use of force and the handling of people with mental health issues have changed over time. Consequently, it is safe to assume that these and other policies will also change, in response to new perspectives and new evidence on the implementation of existing policies.

Third, the search for new and better policies requires a police department commitment to becoming a "learning organization," as described in Chapter One. Individual departments and the law enforcement profession as a whole need to develop institutionalized procedures for developing and disseminating best practices.

Notes

1   The classic discussion, which is still relevant today, is Egon Bittner, "The Capacity to Use Force as the Core of the Police Role," in *Aspects of Police Work* (Boston: Northeastern University Press, 1990), 120–32.

2   William A. Geller and Michael S. Scott, *Deadly Force: What We* (Washington, DC: Police Executive Research Forum, 1992), 251.

3   Geller and Scott, *Deadly Force: What We Know* (pp. 248–57), discusses the history of the "long march" toward the current defense of life rule.

4   *Tennessee v. Garner,* 471 U. S. 1 (1985).

5   Department of Justice, *Principles for Promoting Police Integrity* (Washington, DC: Department of Justice, 2001).

6   Geller and Scott, *Deadly Force: What We Know,* 253–54.

7   James J. Fyfe, "Administrative Interventions on Police Shooting Discretion: An Empirical Examination," *Journal of Criminal Justice* 7 (Winter 1979): 309–23. Curiously, Murphy did not mention this historic achievement in his memoirs: Patrick V. Murphy and Thomas Plate, *Commissioner: A View from the Top of American Law Enforcement* (New York: Simon and Schuster, 1978).

8   Lorie A. Fridell, "Deadly Force Policy and Practice: The Forces for Change," in Candace McCoy, ed., *Holding Police Accountable* (Washington, DC: Urban Institute Press, 2010): 29–51.

9   President's Commission on Law Enforcement and Administration of Justice, *The Challenge of Crime in a Free Society* (Washington, DC: Government Printing Office, 1967), 103–6. National Advisory Commission on Civil Disorders, *Report* (Washington, DC: Bantam Books, 1968), 312–15.

10 Fyfe, "Administrative Interventions on Police Shooting Discretion."

11 Catherine H. Milton et al., *Police Use of Deadly Force* (Washington, DC: The Police Foundation, 1977), 138.

12 U.S. Commission on Civil Rights, *Who Is Guarding the Guardians? A Report on Police Practices* (Washington, DC: Government Printing Office, 1981), Finding 3.1,136.

13 Fyfe, "Administrative Interventions on Police Shooting Discretions." The most comprehensive review of the deadly force policy is Geller and Scott, *Deadly Force: What We Know.*

14 Geller and Scott, *Deadly Force, What We Know.* Bureau of Justice Statistics, *Policing and Homicide, 1976–98: Justifiable Homicide by Police, Police Officers Murdered by Felons* (Washington, DC: Department of Justice, 2001). http://www.ncjrs.org, NCJ 180987. Jerry R. Sparger and David J. Giacopassi, "Memphis Revisited: A Reexamination of Police Shootings After the Garner Decision," *Justice Quart*erly 9 (June 1992): 211–25.

15 James J. Fyfe, "Police Use of Deadly Force: Research and Reform," *Justice Quarterly* 5 (June 1988): 168–9.

16 O. W. Wilson, *Police Administration,* 2nd ed. (New York: McGraw-Hill, 1963).

17 Philadelphia Police Department, Integrity and Accountability Office, *Use of Force* (Philadelphia: Philadelphia Police Department, July 1999), 10. The Office has since been abolished.

18 Paul Jacobs, *Prelude to Riot: A View of Urban America from the Bottom* (New York: Vintage Books, 1968), 38.

19 James J. Fyfe, "Police Use of Deadly Force: Research and Reform," 168–9.

20 Kenneth Culp Davis, *Police Discretion* (St. Paul: West, 1975).

21 Samuel Walker, *Taming the System: The Control of Discretion in Criminal Justice, 1950–1990* (New York: Oxford University Press, 1993).

22 Davis, *Police Discretion,* 140.

23 Lawrence W. Sherman, Janell D. Schmidt, and Dennis P. Rogan, *Policing Domestic Violence: Experiments and Dilemmas* (New York: The Free Press, 1992).

24 Davis, *Police Discretion,* 145.

25 Geoffrey P. Alpert and Roger G. Dunham, *Police Pursuit Driving: Controlling Responses to Emergency Situations* (New York: Greenwood Press, 1990).

26 Police Assessment Resource Center, *The Portland Police Bureau: Officer-Involved Shootings and In-Custody Deaths* (Los Angeles: Police Assessment Resource Center, 2003).

27 Samuel Walker, *Early Intervention Systems for Law Enforcement Agencies: A Planning and Management Guide* (Washington, DC: Department of Justice, 2003).

28 Robin Shepard Engel, *How Police Supervisory Styles Influence Patrol Officer Behavior* (Washington, DC: Department of Justice, 2003).

29   Metropolitan Police Department of Washington, DC, GO-RAR-901.07, Use of Force, October 7, 2002.

30   James K. Stewart et al., *Collaborative Reform Process: A Review of Officer-Involved Shootings in the Las Vegas Metropolitan Police Department* (Washington, DC: Department of Justice, 2012), 22–5.

31   Ibid.

32   San Jose Police Department, *Duty Manual*, Policy L 2100.

33   California POST, Perishable Skills Program at http://www.post.ca.gov/perishable-skills-program.aspx.

34   Los Angeles Sheriff's Department, Office of Independent Review, *Tenth Annual Report* (Los Angeles: Sheriff's Department, 2012), 107.

35   The point is argued in Rachel A. Harmon, "The Problem of Policing," *Michigan Law Review* 110 (March 2012): 761–818, and discussed in Chapter 2 of this book.

36   Minneapolis Police Department, *Policy and Procedure Manual*, Policy 5-305, August 17, 2007.

37   Washington, DC, Metropolitan Police Department, General Order RAR – 901.07, October 7, 2002.

38   United States v. City of Cincinnati, *Memorandum of Agreement* (April 12, 2002).

39   Taser, Inc. http://www.taser.com/.

40   *United States v. City of Detroit, Consent Judgment* (June 12, 2003). Available at http://www.usdoj.gov/crt/split.

41   By one estimate, Taser, Inc. controls over 90 percent of the American CED law enforcement market.

42   Amnesty International, *"Less Than Lethal"? The Use of Stun Weapons in US Law Enforcement* (New York: Amnesty International, 2008).

43   James M. Cronin and Joshua A. Ederheimer, *Conducted Energy Devices: Development of Standards for Consistency and Guidance* (Washington, DC: Department of Justice and the Police Executive Research Forum, 2006).

44   See, for example, Phoenix Police Department, Operations Order 1.5, *Use of Force*, 25–9.

45   Geoffrey P. Alpert and Roger G. Dunham, "Policy and Training Recommendations Related to Police Use of CEDs: Overview of Findings from a Comprehensive National Study," *Police Quarterly* 13 (no. 3, 2010), 243.

46   U.S. Department of Justice, Letter to Hon. Sam Adams, Mayor, City of Portland, Oregon, *Investigation of the Portland Police Bureau*, September 12, 2012.

47   Alpert and Dunham, "Policy and Training Recommendations Related to Police Use of CEDs."

48   Geoffrey P. Alpert and Roger G. Dunham, *Understanding Police Use of Force: Officers, Suspects, and Reciprocity* (New York: Cambridge University Press, 2004).

49   Department of Justice, *Principles for Promoting Police Integrity*, 5–6.

50   Jeff Rojek, Geoffrey P. Alpert, and Hayden P. Smith, "Examining Officer and Citizen Accounts of Police Use-of Force-Incidents," *Crime and Delinquency* 58 (no. 2, 2012): 301–27.

51   Alpert and Dunham, *Understanding Police Use of Force*, 124–34.

52   Metropolitan Police Department of the District of Columbia, General Order RAR 901.07, "Use of Force."

53   *Graham v. Connor*, 490 U.S. 386 (1989).

54   *United States v. City of Detroit, Consent Judgment* (June 12, 2003). Available at http://www.usdoj.gov/crt/split.

55   U.S. Department of Justice, *Investigation of the Schenectady Police Department*, Letter to Michael T. Brockbanck, Schenectady Corporation Counsel, March 19, 2003.

56   City of Spokane, *Draft Report of the City of Spokane Use of Force Commission* (Spokane: December 20, 2012), 20.

57   Joel H. Garner and Christopher D. Maxwell, "Measuring the Amount of Force Used by and Against the Police in Six Jurisdictions," Bureau of Justice Statistics, *Use of Force by Police: Overview of National and Local Data*, 37–39, http://www.ncjrs.org, NCJ 176330. The use of force continuum is recommended by the Department of Justice, *Principles for Promoting Police Integrity*, 4.

58   National Institute of Justice, *The Use-of-Force Continuum* (Washington, DC: Department of Justice, 2009).

59   Christy E. Lopez, *Disorderly (mis)Conduct: The Problem with Contempt of Cop Arrests* (Washington, DC: American Constitution Society, June 2010).

60   Alpert and Dunham, *Understanding Police Use of Force*.

61   Department of Justice, *Investigation of the Seattle Police Department*, 14.

62   Charles Ramsey, Comments, Police Executive Research Forum, *An Integrated Approach to De-Escalation and Minimizing Use of Force* (Washington, DC: PERF, 2012), 31.

63   Kansas City Police Department, Procedural Instruction C 01-3, "Use of Force." Available at http://www.kcpd.org.

64   Ramsey, Police Executive Research Forum, *An Integrated Approach to De-Escalation and Minimizing Use of Force*, 1.

65   Alpert and Dunham, *Understanding Police Use of Force*, 122.

66   U.S. Department of Justice, Letter to Hon. Sam Adams, Mayor, City of Portland, Oregon, September 12, 2012, pp. 11, 22.

67   Peter Scharf and Arnold Binder, *The Badge and the Bullet: Police Use of Deadly Force* (New York: Praeger, 1983), chap. 5, but especially p. 117.

68   Alpert and Dunham, *Understanding Police Use of Force*, 87–123.

69   Department of Justice, *Investigation of the Portland Police Bureau*, 22.

70   Gennaco quoted in City of Spokane, *Draft Report of the City of Spokane Use of Force Commission* (Spokane: City of Spokane, 2012), 19.

71   Stewart et al., *Collaborative Reform Process*, 44–51.

72   Stewart et al., *Collaborative Reform Process*, 79.

73   Alpert and Dunham, "Policy and Training Recommendations Related to Police Use of CEDs."

74   Geoffrey P. Alpert and Roger Dunham, *Police Pursuit Driving: Controlling Responses to Emergency Situations.*

75   Lopez, "Disorderly (mis)Conduct."

76   Alpert and Dunham, *Police Pursuit Driving: Controlling Responses to Emergency Situations.*

77   Geoffrey P. Alpert, *Police Pursuit: Policies and Training* (Washington, DC: U.S. Department of Justice, 1997).

78   Merrick Bobb, *16th Semiannual Report* (Los Angeles: Police Assessment Resource Center, 2003), 11. Available at http://www.parc.info.

79   Ibid., 5.

80   Ibid., 10.

81   Ibid., 7.

82   Donald J. Black, *The Manners and Customs of the Police* (New York: Academic Press, 1980), 109–92.

83   Nancy Loving, *Responding to Spouse Abuse and Wife Beating: A Guide for Police* (Washington, DC: Police Executive Research Forum, 1980), Appendix D, p. 163.

84   Sherman et al., *Policing Domestic Violence: Experiments and Dilemmas.*

85   Department of Justice, *Investigation of the New Orleans Police Department* (Washington, DC; Department of Justice, March 16, 2011), pp. 43–51.

86   United States v. City of New Orleans, *Consent Decree* (July 24, 2012), 58–9. After the Consent Decree was signed, the Mayor of New Orleans changed his mind and asked to withdraw from the Decree but the motion was denied.

87   Department of Justice, *Investigation of the New Orleans Police Department*, 43–51. United States v. City of New Orleans, *Consent Decree*, 54–7.

88   Department of Justice, *Principles for Promoting Police Integrity*, 4.

89   Philadelphia, Integrity and Accountability Office, *Use of Force* (Philadelphia: Integrity and Accountability Office, July 1999), 10.

90   Department of Justice, Letter to Alejandro Vilarello, City Attorney, City of Miami, March 13, 2003. Available at http://www.usdoj.gov/crt/split.

91   Merrick Bobb, *1st Semiannual Report* (Los Angeles: Police Assessment Resource Center, 1993), 69–75. Merrick Bobb, *15th Semiannual Report* (Los Angeles: Police Assessment Resource Center, 2002), 99.

92   Merrick Bobb, *18th Semiannual Report* (Los Angeles: Police Assessment Resource Center, 2004), 9.

93   Department of Justice, *Investigation of the Portland Police Bureau*, 6–7.

94   Department of Justice, *Investigation of the Portland Police Bureau*, 10, 12.

95 Bureau of Justice Assistance, Practitioners Perspectives, *The Memphis, Tennessee, Police Department's Crisis Intervention Team* (Washington, DC: Department of Justice, 2000). Available at http://www.ncjrs.org, NCJ 182501.

96 Department of Justice, *Investigation of the Portland Police Bureau*, 19–22.

97 Samuel Walker, Cassia Spohn, and Miriam A. DeLone, *The Color of Justice*, 5th ed. (Belmont, CA: Cengage, 2012).

98 Fridell et al., *Racially Biased Policing*.

99 Metropolitan Police Department of Washington, DC, GS-OPS-304.15, Unbiased Policing (March 19, 2007).

100 http://fairandimpartialpolicing.com/

101 B. M. Peruche and E. A. Plant, "The Correlates of Law Enforcement Officers' Automatic and Controlled Race-based Responses to Criminal Suspects," *Basic and Applied Social Psychology* 28 (2, 2006), 193–9.

102 J. Correll, B. Park, C. M. Judd, B. Wittenbrink, and M. S. Sadler, "Across the Thin Blue Line: Police Officers and Racial Bias in the Decision to Shoot," *Journal of Personality and Social Psychology* 92(6, 2007), 1006–23.

103 Stewart et al., *Collaborative Reform Process. United States v. City of Cincinnati*, Collaborative Agreement, p. 54.

104 http://fairandimpartialpolicing.com/

105 Department of Justice, *Investigation of the Seattle Police Department*, 15.

106 New York Civil Liberties Union, *Stop and Frisk Fact Sheet* (New York: New York Civil Liberties Union, 2012).

107 Phoenix Police Department, Operations Order 3.1, *Serious Incident Policy* (08/01).

108 *United States v. Los Angeles*, Consent Decree, Para. 61.

109 Kansas City Police, Missouri Department, *Policies and Procedures*. http://kcmo.org/police.

110 U.S. Department of Justice, *Investigation of the Miami Police Department*, Letter to Alejandro Vilarello, City Attorney, March 13, 2003. Available at http://www.usdoj.gov/crt/split.

FOUR

Citizen Complaints and Complaint Investigation Procedures

The New Paradigm of Citizen Complaints

A dramatic change has occurred in the status of citizen complaints in policing since the turbulent 1960s. At that time, many police departments did not have a formal process for handling citizen complaints. Even in police departments where formal procedures did exist, they often discouraged citizens from filing complaints, in some cases even threatening people who attempted to file them. Civil rights groups, moreover, argued that internal affairs units did not investigate citizen complaints thoroughly and generally found in favor of the officer.[1]

The new paradigm for citizen complaints regards citizen complaints as important *management information*, data that are an important part of accountability. Even complaints that are not sustained in favor of the citizen represent information about officer performance that supervisors need to know about. The San Jose, California, Independent Police Auditor argues that each complaint "matters" (Figure 4.1).

Figure 4.1 San Jose Independent Police Auditor

WHY EACH COMPLAINT MATTERS

The complaint process is an important tool because it strives to hold SJPD officers accountable to the communities that they serve. While a small minority of officers receive formal discipline as a result of complaints, complainants can influence SJPD policy and practice when they make their concerns known. Here are some of the reasons why complaints matter, regardless of their outcomes:

- Officers receive Intervention Counseling when their work prompts multiple complaints—even when the complaints are not sustained.
- Some complaints are selected for mediation, an invaluable opportunity for both complainants and the officers to gain deeper understandings of their experiences.
- The IPA tracks trends in complaints that often shape our policy recommendations to SJPD.

Source: San Jose Independent Police Auditor, *2011 Year End Report* (2012), p. 29.

Many people are surprised at the idea that unsustained complaints have value. What can unsustained complaints tell us that is useful? The answer is that a pattern of unsustained complaints may be an indicator of an officer's performance problems. Sustaining a complaint is difficult, particularly since many complaints are "swearing contests," with no witnesses or forensic evidence. A pattern of complaints, particularly in combination with other performance indicators, may suggest the need to examine an officer's performance. Early intervention systems (see Chapter Five) operate on this principle.

Police departments have a duty to investigate complaints against their officers in a thorough, fair, and unbiased manner, and to impose appropriate discipline when allegations are sustained. Investigating complaints is an extremely complex process, and achieving a high level of professionalism requires a set of appropriate policies and procedures. Despite much progress since the turbulent 1960s, many police departments lag behind in developing professional citizen complaint procedures. In 1992, for example, the Kolts report on the Los Angeles Sheriff's Department found that problems with complaint procedures still existed in that department. It found "explicit and implicit biases against civilian complainants at every level of the complaint process." The problems included investigations being conducted by the supervisor of the officer in question, with resulting evidence of bias, investigations being "closed before completion—at times under highly suspicious circumstances," and a failure to sustain complaints that are "corroborated by physical evidence and independent witnesses."[2] More recently, a Justice Department investigation of the Seattle Police Department found that complaints brought to precinct stations did not reach police headquarters and were not entered into the citizen complaint database.[3]

Preliminary Considerations

It is important at the outset to clarify three important issues. The first is that complaints against officers come from two different sources. Citizen complaints are those initiated by citizens. Internal complaints are those filed by supervisors or other officers. Many of the issues regarding the complaint process discussed in this chapter apply with equal force to both types of complaints.

Second, a single *complaint* may include several *allegations.* A complaint, for example, may allege that the officer used excessive force and also used a racial slur. Additionally, a single complaint may involve allegations against two or more officers. It might, for example, allege that two officers used excessive force, or that one used force and the other used a racial slur. In 2011, for example, the New York City Civilian Complaint Review Board (CCRB) received 5,966 complaints that included 17,867 separate allegations.[4]

Third, responsibility for investigating complaints varies from department to department. All police departments maintain an internal affairs unit, although they may be called by some other name, such as a professional standards unit. They are responsible for all internally generated complaints, and in most departments they also handle citizen complaints. In a few jurisdictions, San Francisco and New York City, for example, original jurisdiction for investigating complaints lies with an external citizen oversight agency. Most external citizen oversight agencies (generally referred to as citizen review boards), however, only review the complaint investigations conducted by the police department's internal affairs unit.[5]

In an important policy statement on police discipline, Darrel Stephens, the respected former police chief in Charlotte, North Carolina, sums up the new standard for police citizen complaint procedures:[6]

The department must have effective complaint reception protocols and investigative procedures. It should not be overly difficult for a citizen to lodge a complaint against a police employee. Like employees, citizens should be informed of the steps that will be taken to follow up on the complaint and should also be informed of the outcome. The investigative process should also have defined time frames for completion, with complainants notified of any delays.

Consistent with the principles articulated by Stephens, a number of departments now publicly state that they welcome citizen complaints. The Washington, D.C., police department in 2013 stated on its website that "if you believe you have been subjected to, or witnessed, police misconduct of any type, the MPD encourages you to report the incident," to either the department's internal affairs unit or the Office of Police Complaints, the city's external citizen complaint review agency.[7] The Department of Justice report, *Principles for Promoting Police Integrity*, recommends that police departments "provide a readily accessible process in which community and agency members can have confidence that complaints against agency actions and procedures will be given prompt and fair attention."[8]

Citizen Complaints as a First Amendment Right

Citizen complaints against police officers are also protected by the First Amendment to the Constitution. They are an expression of the right to "petition government for a redress of grievances." Any attempt to restrict or even deny that right would be a violation of that right.

Constitutional protection for citizen complaints is important because police officers and police unions at times accuse complainants of making "false" statements about an officer or the incident. Many citizen complaints involve allegations of "excessive force." What level of force is "excessive" is typically a matter of perception: The complainant believes the force was excessive, and the officer argues that it was necessary and reasonable given the circumstances.[9] The complainant has a First Amendment right to make the allegation if he or she feels the level of force was excessive. It is the function of the complaint investigation process to determine the truth of the matter and make a determination. A citizen cannot be denied the right to make an assertion he or she believes to be true.

Basic Principles for Citizen Complaint Procedures

The operating principles of an effective citizen complaint procedure are openness, integrity, and accountability. *Openness* means that the process makes an effort to inform citizens about the complaint process and to receive all citizen complaints, no matter how frivolous some might seem. *Integrity* means that the complaint investigations are conducted in a manner that is thorough and unbiased. *Accountability* means that the complaint process itself is subject to review to ensure that it operates properly and effectively. The remainder of this chapter discusses in detail the various factors that serve to promote these principles.

The Lack of National Standards

Despite the importance of complaint investigation procedures, both internal and external, there are no generally accepted standards for complaint procedures. This is only one part of the lack of formal national standards in policing with respect to police management issues and accountability procedures in particular, as we have already mentioned in Chapters One and Three.

Some authoritative statements about citizen complaint procedures exist, but they lack specificity. The Commission on Accreditation for Law Enforcement Agencies (CALEA) Standards Chapter 52, for example, holds that departments should have a formal complaint process, but it provides no details on such critical questions as minimum staffing levels; the selection, training, and supervision of complaint investigators; or protocols for complaint investigations.[10] The International Association of Chiefs of Police (IACP) policy paper, *The Investigation of Misconduct*, meanwhile, addresses a number of *legal* issues surrounding complaint investigations but ignores most of the *administrative* issues referred to above regarding the complaint process.[11]

The void left by the absence of a set of professional standards has been partially filled in two ways. First, a number of citizen oversight agencies have developed detailed policies and procedures of their own. Second, the consent decrees negotiated by the Justice Department settling pattern or practice suits mandate a number of specific policies and procedures for handling citizen complaints. In this regard, law professor Debra Livingston points out that one of the positive benefits of federal pattern or practice litigation may be to stimulate "the articulations and dissemination of national standards governing core police managerial responsibilities."[12]

The Citizen Complaint Process

Handling allegations about officer misconduct, whether they arise from a citizen complaint or an internal action, is a very complex process that involves many important policy issues. The following section of this chapter examines the most important of these issues.

Public Information About the Complaint Process

The starting point for an open and accessible complaint procedure involves a sincere effort to publicize the process and inform citizens about how to file a complaint. A complaint procedure is an important part of the organizational "face" that a department presents to the public. The information should include (1) a description of the formal complaint process, (2) how and where to file a complaint, (3) the complaint forms themselves, and (4) what a complainant can expect in the way of possible outcome, including the timetable for a final disposition. In the digital age, a police department's website, or a citizen review agency website, has become the principal means of providing public information.

While many police departments have proactively made information about the complaint process widely available, many others have lagged behind. The U.S. Justice Department consent decree covering the New Jersey State Police required the department to "develop a program of community outreach to inform the public about State Police functions and procedures, including motor vehicle stops, searches and seizures, and the methods for reporting civilian complaints or compliments regarding officers." Complaint forms and informational materials were required to be available "at State Police headquarters, all State Police stations, and such other locations around New Jersey as it may determine from time to time," and that information be provided on the Internet, and at state-operated rest stops located on limited-access highways.[13] In addition, the State Police was required to place posters around the state indicating the availability of the toll-free "hotline" for filing complaints. The Denver Office of the Independent Monitor lists 32 locations where complaint and officer commendation forms are available.[14]

Information in All Relevant Languages

Immigration is changing the face of the United States, and except for many small towns and rural areas virtually all communities contain recent immigrants who either have very limited command of the English language or do not speak English at all. Many people do not understand the nature of the citizen complaint process and think it is similar to the criminal process that requires an attorney. Some recent immigrants are extremely fearful of police retaliation because of experiences in their home countries. To serve these communities, citizen complaint procedures need to provide informational material in all the languages spoken in the local community. The Web page of the Washington, D.C., Office of Police Complaints, for example, has a prominently displayed announcement "Forms in Multiple Languages." Clicking on it leads to information in 14 different languages, including Spanish, Chinese, Russian, and others.[15]

Officer Responsibility to Provide Information About the Complaint Process

Rank-and-file police officers have an important role with regard to informing citizens about the complaint process. Traditionally, officers on the street responded in an unprofessional and hostile manner when citizens expressed dissatisfaction with their experience and indicated a desire to file a complaint. Officers often provided no information about the complaint process, told them it would do no good to file a complaint, or possibly even threatened the citizen with some kind of retaliation. In the 1960s, the refusal of officers to even provide their name and badge number to citizens was a major source of police–community relations tensions.[16]

The new police accountability requires officers to respond in a polite, professional, and informative manner to all citizens, regardless of the circumstances of the encounter, and to respond professionally when citizens say they want to file a complaint. The Cincinnati Memorandum of Agreement with the Justice Department, for example, required "all officers to carry informational brochures and complaint forms in their vehicles at all times while on duty. If a citizen objects to an officer's conduct, that officer will inform the citizen of his or her right to make a complaint. Officers will not discourage any person from making a complaint."[17] Along the same lines, New Jersey state troopers were required "to carry fact sheets and complaint forms in their vehicles at all times while on duty," and shall "inform civilians who object to a trooper's conduct that civilians have a right to make a complaint."[18]

Multiple and Convenient Methods of Filing Complaints

An open and accessible complaint process is one that provides multiple and convenient ways of filing a complaint. Traditionally, complaints could only be filed at police headquarters. Because many people regard police headquarters as a hostile and threatening environment, however, many complainants are discouraged from filing complaints.

In recent years, police departments have expanded the options for filing complaints. Some departments have moved their internal affairs unit to a separate location. Others have made it possible to file complaints at the mayor's office or other official government facility. Some accept complaints by mail and/or phone, and an increasing number now accept electronically filed complaints. The Los Angeles Police Department and the New Jersey State Police maintain toll-free telephone numbers to receive complaints. The LAPD consent decree required that complaints could be filed in person, by mail, telephone, fax, or electronic mail.[19] In-person complaints can be filed at LAPD headquarters, any department station or substation, or the offices of the Police Commission or the Inspector General. In New York City, 82 percent of the complaints filed with the CCRB were filed by telephone, 12.7 percent electronically, 3.6 percent in person, and 1.8 percent were submitted by mail or fax.[20]

The Issue of Anonymous Complaints

Anonymous citizen complaints raise some difficult issues. Traditionally, the police did not accept anonymous complaints. Many police departments and some citizen oversight agencies, in fact, require the complainant to sign the complaint form before they will investigate it. This practice has begun to change. Some police departments and oversight agencies have begun accepting anonymous complaints, whereas others are compelled to do so by consent decrees (e.g., the New Jersey State Police, Los Angeles).[21]

Whether or not to accept anonymous complaints depends on how one views the complaint process. If it is narrowly defined as analogous to the criminal process, with the goal of adjudicating guilt or innocence, then one could argue that complaints should be signed. But if complaints are viewed as management information that helps a department search for potential performance problems, then it makes sense to accept anonymous complaints. A number of anonymous complaints about police officers harassing homeless people or young African American men in certain locations, for example, would be sufficient for the department to initiate an undercover investigation to confirm or refute the allegations.

Citizen Inquiries, Questions, and Complaints

People contact police departments and citizen review agencies with questions and complaints about many different things, some of which do not involve a complaint about an officer's conduct. Some do not even involve the police department. Many people do not understand the law or police policy. Some people, for example, seeking to complain about an arrest or citation do not understand that they violated the law. Additionally, protesting an arrest is not a function of citizen complaint procedures. Others complain about being handcuffed, not understanding that it is department policy to handcuff all persons arrested for a felony. Some people are distraught and simply want to vent their anger or frustration at some public official. In 2011–2012, for example, the Washington, D.C., Office of Police Complaints was contacted by 1,241 people, only 574 of whom filed a formal citizen complaint against an officer.[22]

Handling all citizen inquiries, no matter how irrelevant or ludicrous they may be, is an important public service. Each inquiry represents an unhappy citizen who deserves an explanation or just a chance to express his or her frustration. The Boise Ombudsman recognizes the importance of such inquiries, and its official procedures state that it "will make every attempt to answer or resolve Citizen Inquiries."[23]

Investigating Complaints

Investigating citizen complaints involves a number of different stages, each one of which involves complex issues. The discussion of the different stages that follows is relevant to both internal and external citizen complaint procedures.

Accepting and Classifying Complaints

The first stage in the complaint investigation process is for the agency to accept and properly classify each complaint. Historically, police departments were guilty of often not accepting complaints from people who appeared at police headquarters or a precinct station seeking to file a complaint. In some cases the response was crude, and people were rebuffed, told they had come to the wrong place, or threatened and ordered out of the building. Not accepting complaints is a device for keeping the official number of complaints low. At the same time, it is a power play in which the police refuse to acknowledge the legitimacy of any criticism. In the highly publicized 1991 beating of Rodney King in Los Angeles, his brother was threatened with arrest when he went to file a complaint at an LAPD precinct station.[24]

Accepting a complaint also involves officially recording it and assigning it a complaint number. Recording and numbering complaints ensures accountability. In Seattle, for example, the Justice Department found that many complaints were brought to precinct stations but not forwarded to police headquarters, and thus never officially recorded and entered into the complaint database.[25] Not recording complaints is the same as "unfounding" a report of a crime. The incident vanishes from the record, and with respect to complaints it allows a department to claim that it receives few citizen complaints. The Justice Department concluded that the Seattle Police Department's policies on the classification of and findings regarding citizen complaints were "so complex that they damage [the department's] credibility and undermine public confidence."[26]

Once a complaint has been accepted, it has to be classified and assigned to an investigator. Complaints are generally classified by level of seriousness. San Jose uses three categories: Conduct Complaints involve allegations that an officer or officers violated one or more departmental rules, and are investigated by internal affairs; Policy Complaints involve a complaint against the policies or procedures of the police department and are not directed against an officer; and Misconduct Concerns involve minor issues about an officer that would not result in discipline.[27] The New York City Citizen Complaint Review Board uses four categories of complaints: Force, Abuse of Authority, Discourtesy, and Offensive Language (commonly abbreviated as FADO).[28]

The practice of dividing complaints into serious and less serious categories, as San Jose does, raises an important issue because some departments assign less serious complaints to precinct stations to be investigated, reserving only the more serious complaints for internal affairs. In theory, this practice has some justification, if used properly. Minor complaints are the least likely to be sustained, and internal affairs can concentrate its resources of the serious complaints that involve greater harm and are more likely to be sustained. Unfortunately, the practice has been abused by some departments. One practice has involved putting a genuine excessive force complaint in a lower category, thereby reducing the number of officially reported force complaints. (This maneuver is the equivalent of downgrading an aggravated assault to a misdemeanor to lower the official Index Crime rate.) A Justice Department investigation of the Seattle Police Department found two serious problems with the receipt and recording of complains. First, over 60 percent of the complaints received by the department's Office of Professional Accountability were referred "to the officer's supervisors at the precinct level for handling as PIRs [Preliminary Investigative Review] or SRs [Supervisory Review]—neither of which can result in formal findings or any discipline." Second, as already mentioned, the department's Office of Professional Accountability does not track complaints that are made to officers, or at precinct stations, or at City Hall. The result is that both categories of complaints are lost, and neither recorded nor investigated.[29]

Best practices today dictate that all complaints be officially recorded, regardless of the seriousness or merits of the allegation, with an official complaint number. These data will provide a complete picture of the number of incidents where someone sought to record his or her dissatisfaction with some aspect of police service. Once formally recorded, complaints can then be screened and classified appropriately. Information requests, matters pertaining to another agency, or utterly frivolous claims can be placed in appropriate categories.

Improper classification of complaints is a recurring problem. In one of its first important actions in 1993, the San Jose Independent Police Auditor found that the San Jose Police Department was improperly classifying some serious complaints. As a result of the IPA's recommendation, the number of Class I complaints rose significantly the following year (and then declined in 1995 following another change in classification procedures designed to streamline the process).[30]

The Issue of Withdrawn Complaints

In many cases, the complainant does not continue to pursue a complaint and it is dismissed. The complainant may lose interest in the complaint, or decide not to cooperate any further with the investigation, or cannot be located. In New York City, over half (55 percent) of all complaints in 2011 were administratively "truncated": complainants withdrew in 8.1 percent; were uncooperative in 36 percent; were unavailable in 9.7 percent; and could not be identified in 1 percent.[31] The reasons for a complainant withdrawing, refusing to cooperate, or not returning phone calls are complex. The complainant may feel satisfied merely by registering the initial complaint. Or he or she might have decided that it is not worth the time and effort. Finally, he or she might feel alienated by the initial contact with the complaint investigator. In New York City it could be a simple matter of convenience. While the overwhelming number of complaints are filed by telephone, most interviews are conducted at the CCRB headquarters, which is located in lower Manhattan and involves a long subway journey for complainants in Brooklyn, Queens, and the Bronx.[32]

The reasons for complainant withdrawal have important implications for evaluating a complaint process. There is nothing the agency can do if a complainant has genuinely lost interest. But if the reason involved the conduct of the investigator or some other aspect of the complaint process, those are problems that can and should be corrected. The San Jose Independent Police Auditor emphasizes that "the manner and tone used in in taking complaints is critical in instilling confidence in the objectivity and integrity of the IA and IPA offices. The objective is to instill credibility and demonstrate responsiveness to assure citizens that their grievances (real or imagined) are welcomed and will be taken seriously. Be sensitive to the message you send through your body language."[33]

Police Officer Cooperation With Investigations

For decades, experts on police misconduct have argued that the greatest single obstacle to investigating alleged misconduct incidents and achieving accountability is the refusal of other officers to cooperate with investigations. This includes investigations related to citizen complaints, internal police department investigations, and criminal investigations by prosecutors. The so-called code of silence involves four distinct actions: not reporting misconduct by other officers, falsely claiming not to have seen the events in question, actively lying to investigators, and colluding with other officers to create a cover story.[34]

Only fairly recently have police departments begun to develop policies and programs to overcome the code of silence. One promising development is that an increasing number of police departments have adopted formal policies explicitly stating that officers have a duty to report misconduct by other officers. Some departments have adopted policies requiring officers to cooperate fully and truthfully with investigations. The ordinance creating the Boise Community Ombudsman requires that "officers/employees shall, as a condition of their employment, truthfully and completely answer all questions specifically directed and related to the scope of employment and operations of Boise City that may be asked of them by any investigator or supervisor acting on behalf of the Office of the Community Ombudsman."[35] The Seattle Police Department Police Manual (Title 5) specifies that officers are required to cooperate with internal affairs investigations. They sign a form, however, indicating that their statements are "involuntary."[36]

Departmental Cooperation With Citizen Review Agencies

In cities and counties where an external citizen oversight agency investigates citizen complaints, the police or sheriff's departments are required to cooperate with investigations as a matter of law. Yet some have either passively or aggressively failed to cooperate fully. In 2001, for example, the San Francisco Office of Citizen Complaints (OCC) encountered 99 incidents of officers failing to cooperate with investigations as required by law. These cases were forwarded to the San Francisco Police Department, which sustained only 39 of them, and only 7 of those resulted in the officer receiving a written reprimand.[37]

The same report by the San Francisco OCC found a number of flagrant instances of the police department deliberately stalling or interfering with OCC investigations. These practices included changing policies on the release of documents without notifying the OCC, thereby creating delays; failing to respond to legitimate requests for documents; withholding documents in some cases for more than a year; refusing to provide photographs of officers and mug shots of complainants; and delaying release of documents even after the department has agreed to release them.[38] Systematic noncooperation or obstruction of this sort undermines the investigations of complaints and the entire process of accountability.

Interviews at Convenient and Comfortable Locations

One of the reasons complainants do not pursue complaints is that the necessary interviews are a time-consuming process. For citizens this requires taking time off from job or family. Police officers, on the other hand, are officially on duty and being paid when being interviewed by internal affairs. The lack of a convenient and comfortable location is also likely to discourage complainants. As we already noted, the New York City CCRB offices are inconvenient for most New York City residents.

Police headquarters, meanwhile, is an intimidating environment for many citizens, particularly someone who has had a bad experience with the police. Some agencies have taken the obvious steps to overcome this problem. The Washington, D.C., OPC, for example, has staff vehicles that allow its investigators to visit incident scenes and meet complainants and witnesses at convenient locations. The New Jersey consent decree, meanwhile, requires the State Police to

> arrange a convenient time and place, including by telephone (or TDD), to interview civilians for misconduct investigations [and] reasonably accommodate civilians' circumstances to facilitate the progress of an investigation. This may include holding an interview at a location other than a State office or at a time other than regular business hours.[39]

Ensuring Thorough and Fair Investigations

A perceived lack of thoroughness and fairness in complaint investigations is one of the long-standing criticisms of police internal affairs procedures.[40] Interestingly, both complainants and police officers express much dissatisfaction with the complaint process, with both sides perceiving the process as unfair in most surveys. In a survey sponsored by the Denver Independent Monitor, only 26.5 percent of complainants in 2007 felt the complaint investigator was objective, and only 32.5 percent of the officers subject to a complaint investigation felt that internal affairs was "unbiased."[41]

Perceptions of thoroughness and fairness are inevitably highly subjective. With respect to citizen complaints, they undoubtedly involve preconceived attitudes about the police on the part of complainants, and about complainants on the part of police officers. Despite this problem, there are certain complaint investigation procedures that are likely to enhance thoroughness and fairness and the perception of both. Figure 4.2 displays a checklist developed by the San Jose Independent Police Auditor to ensure thorough investigations. Unfortunately, many police departments and citizen review agencies have failed to develop formal investigation procedures.

The Justice Department found in 2011, for example, that in the New Orleans Police Department internal affairs "interviews [we]re not guided by a policy or practice to be consistent and thorough." Additionally, there was a lack of resources, inadequate training for investigators, a failure to follow existing policies, incomplete investigations, and conclusions not supported by the evidence.[42]

> Were all the identified witnesses interviewed? If not, why? The Auditor may send a request to conduct the missed interviews or have IA explain what efforts were made to interview these witnesses.
>
> What efforts were made by the IA investigators to find additional witnesses?
>
> Was a neighborhood canvas conducted? Were leads from the complainant or other witnesses developed?
>
> Did the investigation include any photographs or diagrams?
>
> Was the IA investigator objective in writing the final comprehensive report?
>
> Were consistencies and inconsistencies between civilian witnesses pointed out? Were consistencies and inconsistencies between police officers also pointed out?
>
> Were the facts as represented in the IA reports consistent with the contents of the taped interviews?

Source: From San Jose, Independent Police Auditor, *Policy and Procedures.*

Locating and Interviewing Witnesses

Failure to locate and interview witnesses is a problem that is likely to ensure that a complaint will not be sustained. Failure to make an effort to determine whether there are any witnesses to an incident is a sign of an unprofessional complaint investigation process. Witnesses are crucial, since many complaint incidents are "he said/he said" situations with neither forensic evidence (e.g., medical reports) nor witnesses. The Justice Department report on New Orleans pointed out that "whether a police agency conducts a complete search for witnesses is indicative of the police agency's dedication to determining the truth of misconduct allegations." Its investigation found "not only a failure to canvass for witnesses but a failure to interview even known, highly relevant witnesses."[43] A report on the complaint process in Albuquerque, for example, found a use of force case where several potential witnesses to the incident were not interviewed. In some other cases "witnesses were either not asked the right questions or not asked any questions at all."[44] The 2001 Los Angeles consent decree directs the department to take active steps by "canvassing the scene to locate witnesses where appropriate, with the burden for such collection on the LAPD, [and] not the complainant."[45]

Avoiding Conflicts of Interest

Complaint investigations raise potential conflicts of interest that can lead to bias and/or the perception of bias. An internal affairs investigator may know or be a friend or former colleague of the officer being investigated. Conflicts of interest can also arise in a citizen complaint agency. The civilian investigator may be related to, know, or be a friend of the complainant.

The San Jose Independent Police Auditor addressed this issue with a policy stating that "in order to avoid bias, IA investigators are required to advise the Unit Commander of conflicts due to prior friendships, frequent interaction or adverse contacts with the complainant."[46] The consent decree with the New Jersey State Police adopted a similar policy stating that "the State shall prohibit any state trooper who has a conflict of interest related to a pending misconduct investigation from participating in any way in the conduct or review of that investigation."[47]

Prohibiting Hostile or Leading Questions

Complaint investigations are biased if investigators ask either hostile or leading questions of persons being interviewed. A hostile question to a complainant would be one that is accusatory regarding the complainant's actions or background, or disrespectful with respect to the person's clothing, grooming, or social status. A leading question to a police officer, by contrast, guides that person toward an answer likely to support not sustaining the complaint. An internal affairs interviewer, for example, might ask, "Didn't the complainant . . . ?" Similarly, a civilian interviewer might ask the complainant, "Didn't the officer . . . ?" A former director of the Portland, Oregon, police auditor's office noticed cases where a police officer would hesitate when faced with a difficult question and the internal affairs investigators would suggest an exculpatory answer.[48] The Cincinnati Memorandum of Agreement prohibits investigators from "improperly asking officers or other witnesses leading questions that improperly suggest legal justifications for the officer's conduct when such questions are contrary to appropriate law enforcement techniques."[49]

Probing Inconsistencies

When being interviewed, both complainants and police officers may provide inconsistent answers to certain questions, saying something that contradicts what he or she said earlier. A police officer may say something in the interview that contradicts his or her incident report. A number of audits of complaint investigations have found police internal affairs investigators failing to probe inconsistencies in statements by officers. In some cases the statements by a witness officer may contradict what the subject officer said. Audits have also found internal affairs investigators accepting at face value patently ludicrous statements by officers, for example, regarding how the complainant received a bruise. The San Jose IPA Policy and Procedures addresses this issue by requiring that "inconsistent statements of material issues should be analyzed. This analysis should be applied to both citizen and police witnesses/subject officer's statements."[50]

Judging the Credibility of Officers and Complainants

A particularly serious pattern of bias in complaint investigations has been the practice of automatically giving credence to the officer's testimony and discrediting the statements of the complainant. The Office of Independent Review (OIR) in the Los Angeles Sheriff's Department, for example, found that a "good guy" principle favoring police officers was inappropriately used to mitigate discipline in some internal investigations.[51]

A manual, *Investigating Workplace Harassment: How to Be Fair, Thorough, and Legal,* published by the Society for Human Resource Management (SHRM), warns that "determining the truth from two or more conflicting stories can be a very difficult task." Citizen complaints against police officers always involve conflicting versions of the incident. They are typically "he said/he said" situations, with no witnesses or at least no independent witnesses (that is, no witness police officer or friend of the complainant). The SHRM further advises that, despite what many people think, it is very difficult to make credibility determinations on the basis of peoples' demeanor. The truthful witness may exhibit great nervousness, whereas someone lying may exude extreme confidence and composure.[52] For this reason, corroborating evidence is extremely important, which in turn heightens the importance of locating and interviewing potential witnesses and gathering medical evidence where the complainant was injured.

Police internal investigations have traditionally given an automatic preference to the statements of the officer over those of the complainant or witnesses. This has occurred in some cases despite the fact that the officer's statement is filled with inconsistencies or simply not believable. The Cincinnati consent decree requires that "there will be no automatic preference for an officer's statement over a non-officer's statement, nor will [investigators] completely disregard a witness's statement merely because the witness has some connection to the complainant."[53] The Los Angeles consent decree contains a similar requirement.[54]

Investigating Collateral Misconduct

In the course of some complaint investigations, investigators may discover additional officer misconduct that is not part of the formal complaint. The complainant may allege excessive force without realizing that the officer also violated two other department policies. These additional acts of misconduct are referred to as *collateral misconduct* or, colloquially, misconduct "outside the four corners" of the formal complaint. Many agencies simply ignore collateral misconduct, claiming they are only responsible for investigating what the complainant alleged. Ignoring collateral misconduct is a way of protecting officers and the department, and also of limiting the investigative workload.

Comparing data from the San Francisco Office of Citizen Complaints (OCC) and the New York City Civilian Complaint Review Board is revealing on this issue. The average number of OCC allegations per complaint rose from 1.88–2.81 between 1989 and 1996 to an average of 4.29–4.78 between 1997 and 2000. This increase may have been a direct result of an increase in the staffing in the OCC in 1997 (see below) and the leadership of Mary Dunlap, appointed director of the OCC in 1997. By comparison, the New York City CCRB, which has historically had staffing problems, reported only 1.6 allegations per complaint in the first half of 2003 (Table 4.1). The net result is the San Francisco OCC is investigating far more allegations of officer misconduct than is the NYC CCRB.[55]

Following the lead of the OCC, the Los Angeles consent decree specifies that if an investigator believes that misconduct may have occurred "other than that alleged by the complainant, the alleged victim of misconduct, or the triggering item or report, the investigating officer must notify a supervisor, and an additional Complaint Form 1.28 investigation of the additional misconduct issue shall be conducted."[56]

An Accountability Measure: Recording and Reviewing Interviews

An important new technique for ensuring the quality of complaint investigations is the practice of recording all interviews with officers, complainants, and witnesses.[57] The recordings can then be reviewed by either supervisors or an external oversight agency to identify inadequacies that

Table 4.1   Collateral Misconduct, San Francisco OCC and New York City CCRB

	Complaints Received	Total Allegations	Allegations per Complaint
San Francisco OCC, 2001	999	4,321	4.3
New York City CCRB, 2002	4,512	7,216	1.6

Sources: San Francisco, Office of Citizen Complaints, 2001 Annual Report (San Francisco: Office of Citizen Complaints, 2002); New York City Civilian Complaint Review Board, Status Report, January–June 2003 (New York: Civilian Complaint Review Board, 2003).

need to be corrected. This might involve additional investigation of the case in question, staff training to improve interview techniques, or even removal of the investigator from the internal affairs unit or the citizen complaint agency. The recordings can also be used for personnel evaluations of investigators, including recommendations for transfer or termination.

Auditing and Reopening Investigations

Auditing complaint investigations is a basic quality control strategy. The San Jose IPA has this function as one of its principal functions. It has the authority to observe complaint investigations interviews (but not ask questions), review both tapes and case files, and request further investigation where it finds it needed. It is mandated to review all use of force complaints and 20 percent of all other complaints. In 2011 the IPA agreed with the internal affairs investigation in 63 percent of all cases, agreed with IA in another 19 percent after requesting and receiving additional information, expressed concerns in 13 percent (but the concerns were not serious enough to formally disagree with the investigation), and dis-agreed with 6 percent of all cases.[58]

Disposition of Complaints

Citizen complaint investigations end with a final disposition in one of four categories. The standard disposition categories are:

Unfounded. There is no evidence that the alleged misconduct occurred;

Not Sustained. The alleged misconduct may have occurred, but there is not suf-ficient evidence to resolve the question of responsibility;

Sustained. The officer committed the alleged misconduct;

Exonerated. The officer's conduct was proper.

A complaint investigation typically generates a formal investigative report summarizing the facts of the case. The quality of investigative reports is a recurring problem. Important facts may be omitted as a result of either sloppiness or deliberate omission. Without a complete and accurate investigation report, the head of internal affairs and/or the chief of police do not have a basis for a proper disposition of the complaint. In one of her first actions in 1993, Teresa Guererro-Daley, the San Jose Independent Police Auditor, found that the log in complaint investigation files "contained only scant, handwritten notes that were very difficult to read or audit." As a result, some complaints were improperly placed in a less serious category. On her recommendation, a standard form was developed, and all informa-tion was typed and entered into a central database.[59]

As we will see in both Chapters Five and Six, incomplete and inaccu-rate complaint incident reports have been a problem with regard to the operations of the early intervention system in the Los Angeles Sheriff's Department (the PPI). Both the Special Counsel and the Office of Independent Review have played an important role in auditing the early intervention system, identifying problems, and recommending improvements.[60]

The disposition of complaints should be made by some official other than the investigator to ensure that it is an objective assessment of the evidence. If the investigator makes the disposition decision there will be an inevitable tendency to shape the investigation toward a predeter-mined result.[61]

A recurring problem with complaint dispositions is that some are not rationally related to the facts in the investigation report. The monitor in Pittsburgh, for example, found "illogical leaps to unfound cases" in 8 of 32 cases that were examined. Several cases alleging improper handcuffing and excessive force, for example, were unfounded because the complainants were "found or pled guilty to an arrestable offense."[62]

Standards for Weighing the Evidence

Traditionally, police internal affairs units and even some citizen review agencies did not have formal standards for weighing the evidence in a complaint investigation report. The lack of a clear standard allows inconsistent and arbitrary dispositions. The emerging best practice is to use a *preponderance of the evidence* standard, which is defined as meaning that "it is more likely than not that the alleged action occurred." The citizen complaint process is not a criminal process, and it is generally believed that the *proof beyond a reasonable doubt* standard is too high and would result in no complaints being sustained. Some complaint procedures do, however, use the *clear and convincing evidence* standard. The preponderance of the evidence standard is used by the New York City CCRB, other citizen complaint review agencies, and was required by the consent decrees over the New Jersey State Police and the Los Angeles Police Department.[63]

Feedback to Complainants and Officers

Lack of feedback about the status of complaints is a major problem among both complainants and police officers. At best, complainants generally receive a form letter indicating the final disposition of their complaint but with little explanatory detail. Complainants are often alienated by the combined impact of delays in the completion of investigations, the lack of notice about the delays, and the lack of explanation about the disposition. Police officers are often not treated much better, receiving no updates about the status of an investigation or a letter about the final disposition. This only creates morale problems among the rank and file.

The Washington, D.C., Office of Police Complaints places the disposition of complaint investigations on its website. Philip Eure, OPC director, explains that this process will help both citizens and officers "better understand how the process works and how other complaints have been resolved."[64] The information on the website includes the complaint number, the complaint category, and the complaint examiner's disposition. In the interests of privacy, the names of the complainant and the officer or officers, and the details of the incident, are omitted. The available information is limited, but it does provide the public with data on the percentage of complaints sustained and the percentage sustained in each complaint category.

Staffing and Managing the Complaint Investigation Process

Staffing and Resources

It should go without saying that a complaint review procedure needs sufficient staff and resources to function effectively. Lack of appropriate staffing, however, has been a chronic problem for both internal affairs units and citizen oversight agencies. In a critical report on the New York City CCRB, the New York Civil Liberties Union (NYCLU) found that "virtually all investigator hires were entry-level employees, who were overwhelmed by a large case back log and a manual record-keeping system."[65] The police auditor in Portland, Oregon, found that the excessive delays in investigating complaints by the police department were largely the result of a lack of sufficient investigators in the internal affairs units.[66]

There are no recognized standards regarding the appropriate number of investigators given the size of a police department. Both the CALEA accreditation standards and the IACP concept paper on investigating misconduct are silent on this issue.[67] In addition, there is no research on how much investigative effort is required to investigate complaints that would provide the basis for a rational standard. Common sense suggests that a meaningful analysis of complaints would employ a triage approach, separating the very complex cases (very serious allegations, multiple officers, complex fact pattern), the common complaints (serious allegations, one officer, simple fact pattern), and least difficult cases (less serious allegations, one officer, unclear fact pattern and little evidence).

Lack of sufficient staff in internal affairs units is one of the major causes of a lack of timely disposition of complaints (see the discussion of this important issue below). The San Francisco Office of Citizen Complaints is unique in having a formal standard for staffing. A 1997 ordinance, enacted by referendum, requires the OCC to have one complaint investigator for every 150 sworn officers in the San Francisco Police Department.

In 2011 the OCC had 16 staff investigators, with average case loads of 23 complaint cases.[68]

Although internal affairs is a critical unit in a police department, with a major impact on standards of integrity and accountability, there do not appear to be any standards for selection of IA officers. Historically, officers have avoided the assignment because they dislike the job of investigating fellow officers. In many departments, IA officers have the nickname of "head hunters" among rank-and-file officers. In the absence of any research on the subject, we don't know if police chiefs check the discipline records of IA candidates, have a set of informal standards they use, or generally assign personal friends to the unit. Again, in the absence of any research on the subject, it is believed that many departments assign officers with criminal investigation experience to internal affairs. But as we discuss later, investigating citizen complaints against an officer is very different than investigating a criminal complaint against a citizen.

In the end, who a chief assigns to internal affairs is a major determinant of a department's commitment to accountability. A chief who assigns an IA commander he or she trusts, and then gives clear direction about thoroughly investigating any and all complaints, will have a significant impact on the quality of IA investigations and by extension officer conduct on the street. A chief who assigns an old buddy, and gives no clear direction about being tough on misconduct, will likely allow misconduct on the street to continue.

An Investigation Policy and Procedure Manual

Maintaining a professional complaint review process requires a comprehensive policy and procedure manual that includes, among other things, specific directives addressing the various issues previously covered in this chapter (e.g., locating and interviewing witnesses, not asking leading questions, judging witness credibility, etc.). After sitting in on more than 100 police officer interviews, the San Jose Independent Police Auditor observed that "the quality of interviews differs with each investigator." She then developed a standard format to ensure consistency and thoroughness.[69]

Although there has been no systematic survey of the subject, anecdotal evidence suggests that police internal affairs units have not developed comprehensive sets of policies and procedures. Recently, however, several of the better-managed citizen oversight agencies have developed good sets of policies and procedures, and much of the material presented in this chapter is taken from them. These local agency standards, however, have never been codified and adopted by any professional association as recommended standards.

Training for Investigators

A policy and procedure manual, in turn, becomes the basis for investigator training. Lack of consistency among investigators is a problem. The Department of Justice letter to the Portland, Maine, police department, for example, found that the sergeant assigned part time to complaint investigations "had no prior investigative training before being assigned to the Internal Affairs Unit," and that "the lieutenants and Shift Commanders charged with conducting intake and investigating informal complaints have not received any sort of training or guidance on complaint investigation."[70] In truth, there has been very little research on police internal affairs units, and we have only anecdotal evidence on this and many other issues.

The Special Nature of Citizen Complaints Against Police Officers

The police have traditionally assumed that experience and training in criminal investigation adequately prepares officers for assignment to internal affairs. This view, however, fails to take into account the fact that investigating a citizen complaint against a fellow officer is a very different kind of task. It calls for not making prejudgments about the credibility of either the complainant or one's fellow officer, even though one is a peer employee.

Jayson Wechter, a staff investigator with the San Francisco OCC, explains the special nature of investigating complaints against police officers. He speaks from a wide experience as an investigator for prosecutors, public defenders, and attorneys handling various kinds of civil suits. Complaints against police officers are different because the police are different. They occupy a special place in society, with the awesome power to take people's lives and their liberty. And in this country, popular culture has surrounded police officers with a special aura. Prosecutors long ago learned that it is extremely difficult to obtain judgments against police officers, for the simple reason that judges and juries almost automatically defer to their authority.[71]

Complaint investigators are influenced by the same aura of police authority. In passing, it is worth noting that in some mediation agencies, some mediators decline to accept cases involving complaints against police officers because they realize they are favorably inclined toward officers, whereas some other mediators decline because they realize they have deep-seated biases against officers.[72] Police officers, for their part, are skilled at manipulating this aura to their advantage. And in many cases the complainant is not a model citizen. Complaint investigators need to learn the habit of challenging this authority, albeit in a neutral manner. In short, special training is needed to prepare investigators for the very special task of investigating complaints against police officers.

Despite the special nature of citizen complaints, police departments typically do not provide special training for officers assigned to internal affairs. In San Jose, "officers do not receive training at the Police Academy to prepare them for assignments in IA." The IPA pointed out in 2011 that other assignments in the department also "fail to provide these officers with any experience in conducting internal investigations on fellow officers," and they are trained only after being assigned to IA.[73]

Timely Investigations

The failure to complete complaint investigations in a timely fashion is a pervasive national problem. The Oakland monitor in 2004 found "systemic delays at nearly every stage of the process."[74] To invoke an old cliché, justice delayed is justice denied, in this case for both complainants and the police officers who are the subject of complaints. Moreover, some citizen oversight agencies have been as guilty of unacceptable delays as have been police internal affairs units. The old Washington, D.C., CCRB, which was abolished in 1997, took as long as three years to complete some investigations.[75]

When the San Jose IPA began operating in 1993, it found that about 25 percent of all cases took longer than a year to complete; in addition, some complaints were not even classified for 6 months. To correct this problem, the IPA established a set of formal timelines for the different states of the process: classifying and assigning cases to an investigator (30 days), completing investigations of Class I complaints (180 days), and 365 days for completing all other investigations, as indicated in Figure 4.3.[76] Despite this change and continuous monitoring of the complaints process over

Figure 4.3   Timelines for Complaint Investigations Evaluating the Complaint
Process

30 Days	Classification of all complaints
180 Days	Complete investigations of all Class I Use of Force Complaints
365 Days	Complete investigations of all other complaints

Source: From *IPA 2003 Report: A Comprehensive Ten Year Overview,* by San Jose Independent Police Auditor, 2004, San Jose, CA: Independent Police Auditor, p. 25.

nearly two decades, problems with timeliness remained years later. In 2011 internal affairs closed 26 percent of all cases more than 300 days after the complaints were initially filed. The IPA argued, as noted above, that a lack of a sufficient number of investigators in IA was a major cause of the lack of timeliness.[77]

The citizen complaint process is designed to hold officers accountable for their conduct. Unfortunately, insufficient attention has been given to holding complaint procedures themselves accountable for their performance. Part of the problem is that, as already mentioned, there are no professional standards for complaint procedures, and thus no standards by which to measure them.

Evaluating the Complaint Investigation Process

Despite the importance of complaint investigations, including both internal affairs units and citizen oversight agencies, there is little meaningful research on their effectiveness. The public debate has focused very narrowly on whether external citizen complaint review is more effective than internal affairs investigations, and the measure has been the sustain rate.[78] As we argue below, the sustain rate is a very problematic measure. A more serious problem is that complaint procedures have multiple goals, and they have not been taken into account in the discussions about effectiveness.

Complaint review procedures have multiple goals, which include (1) conducting thorough and fair investigations of complaints (both internal and external), (2) deterring future police misconduct by ensuring discipline in cases of proven misconduct, (3) providing a satisfactory avenue for individual citizens to seek redress for their grievances against the police, (4) ensuring fair treatment of officers accused of misconduct, (5) enhancing public confidence in the police by providing a professional complaint review process, and (6) ensuring that alleged misconduct is properly investigated and proven misconduct is punished. Each of these goals is complex and would require a sophisticated methodology. Evaluating a single complaint review process on several measures would be a very difficult undertaking. And because of the great variations in the structure of processes of both internal affairs units and citizen review agencies, meaningful comparative studies are also very difficult.

The Sustain Rate as an Invalid Performance Indicator

The sustain rate, defined as the percentage of complaints resolved in complainants' favor, has always been used in public discussions as a performance measure of complaint procedures. Unfortunately, it is neither a valid nor a reliable measure for several reasons. First, as we have indicated, it is only one of the many goals of complaint review procedures. Second, complaint data are very problematic. Research has consistently established that people file complaints in a very low percentage of incidents where they feel they have reason to complain about the police. Additionally, because of differences in the openness and accessibility of complaint procedures among police departments and citizen review agencies, the complaint rate (i.e., complaints per 100 officers) varies considerably. As a result the complaint rate is an imperfect measure of the level of police misconduct. (And, we should note, this is why early intervention systems that rely solely or even primarily on citizen complaints will not produce a complete picture of officers' conduct. This issue is discussed in detail in Chapter Five.) All of these factors affect the denominator in the sustain rate. With respect to the numerator, the number of complaints sustained, official data among agencies are not comparable, as some report complaints sustained and others report allegations sustained. Agencies that have a more open and accessible complaint procedure will have a larger denominator, which is likely to depress the percentage sustained. Such agencies will, as a result, appear to be doing a relatively poor job when in fact their openness and accessibility means they are doing a better job. Conversely, agencies that are less open and accessible will have a lower denominator and as a result likely to have a higher sustain rate.[79]

In the end, there are so many problems with complaint data, and the variations in complaint procedures and data reporting procedures, that the sustain rate is simply not a useful measure of the effectiveness of citizen complaint procedures.

Surveying Complainants and Officers

A number of studies have investigated the perceptions of both complainants and police officers about the complaint investigation process. They have consistently found that both groups express high levels of dissatisfaction, and these findings hold true for both internal affairs units and citizen oversight agencies. Interestingly, both citizens and officers feel that complaint procedures are biased against them. It is safe to conclude, therefore, that in general, citizen complaint review procedures have failed with respect to the goal of providing a satisfactory experience for complainants and officers.

Studies by the Denver Office of the Independent Monitor provide valuable insights into experiences and perceptions of the complaint process. A 2006 survey of citizens and officers who had been through the complaint process was conducted before the monitor's office was established. Only about one-third of citizens felt they understood the complaint process, compared with about half of the officers. Forty-one percent of the complainants, moreover, felt that the police department had in some way attempted to discourage them from filing a complaint. About two-thirds of the officers felt that internal affairs was biased against them, while 90 percent of the complainants felt it was biased in favor of the police. Over 80 percent of complainants were dissatisfied with the outcome of their complaints, while about 35 percent of officers were dissatisfied with the outcome. A follow-up study two years later found that the monitor had had a positive effect on perceptions and experiences with the complaint process. Familiarity with the complaint process increased significantly among complainants. Both complainants and officers were more satisfied with the objectivity, politeness, and respectfulness of internal affairs. There was some increase in perceptions of citizens that internal affairs was fair (from 15 percent to 17.3 percent), and a greater increase among officers (from 24.3 percent to 32.5 percent).[80]

Conclusion

Citizen complaints against police officers are an important aspect of police accountability. Citizens have a right to express their dissatisfaction with any government agency, and receive a thorough and fair hearing of their complaint. Complaints, meanwhile, are a valuable form of information for police management, an indicator of a problem or problems that need to be corrected. For this reason, they are incorporated into all early intervention systems designed to identify officers with recurring performance problems (see Chapter Five). Until fairly recently, citizen complaint procedures have failed to serve these needs. A few citizen oversight agencies have developed meaningful standards for ensuring thorough and fair investigations, and an increasing number of police departments have established more open and accessible complaint procedures. The major challenge for the future involves developing national standards for complaint procedures reflecting the issues discussed in this chapter.

Notes

1 President's Commission on Law Enforcement and Administration of Justice, *The Challenge of Crime in a Free Society* (New York: Avon Books, 1967). National Advisory Commission on Civil Disorders, *Report* (New York: Bantam Books, 1968).

2 James G. Kolts, *The Los Angeles Sheriff's Department* (Los Angeles: Sheriff's Department, 1992), 100. Available at http://www.parc.info.

3 Department of Justice, *Investigation of the Seattle Police Department* (December 16, 2011).

4 New York City, Civilian Complaint Review Board, *Statistical Appendices, Jan— Dec 2011*, (New York: Civilian Complaint Review Board, 2012), Table 1A.

5 The variations among citizen oversight agencies are discussed in Samuel Walker, *Police Accountability: The Role of Citizen Oversight* (Belmont, CA: Wadsworth, 2001).

6 Darrel W. Stephens, *Police Discipline: A Case for Change* (Cambridge, MA: Kennedy School of Government, 2011).

7 http://mpdc.dc.gov/node/212832.

8 Department of Justice, *Principles for Promoting Police Integrity* (Washington, DC: Department of Justice, 2001).

9 Jeff Rojek, Geoffrey P. Alpert, and Hayden P. Smith, "Examining Officer and Citizen Accounts of Police Use-of-Force Incidents," *Crime and Delinquency* 58 (no. 2, 2012): 301–27.

10 Commission on Accreditation for Law Enforcement Agencies, Standards for Law Enforcement Agencies, 4th ed. (Fairfax, VA: CALEA, 1999), chap. 52, 1.

11 International Association of Chiefs of Police, *Investigation of Employee Misconduct. Concepts and Issues Paper*, rev. ed. (Gaithersburg, MD: IACP, July 2001).

12 Debra Livingston, "Police Reform and the Department of Justice: An Essay on Accountability," *Buffalo Criminal Law Review* 2 (1999): 843.

13 *United States v. New Jersey*, Consent Decree (December 30, 1999), Par. 59. Available at http://www.usdoj.gov/crt/split.

14 Denver, Office of the Independent Monitor, *Appendices 2012 Annual Report* (Denver: Office of the Independent Monitor, 2013).

15 http://policecomplaints.dc.gov/.

16 Hervey Juris and Peter Feuille, *Police Unionism* (Lexington, MA: Lexington Books, 1977).

17 *United States v. Cincinnati*, Memorandum of Agreement (April 12, 2002), Par. 36. Available at http://www.usdoj.gov/crt/split.

18 *United States v. New Jersey*, Consent Decree (1999), Par. 59. Available at http://www.usdoj.gov/crt/split.

19 *United States v. the City of Los Angeles*, Consent Decree (June 15, 2001), Par. 74. Available at http://www.usdoj.gov/crt/split.

20 New York City, Civilian Complaint Review Board, *Statistical Appendices, Jan—Dec 2011*, Table 7A.

21 *United States v. the City of Los Angeles*, Consent Decree, Par. 74(b).

22 Washington, DC, Office of Police Complaints, *Annual Report 2012* (Washington, DC: Office of Police Complaints, 2013).

23 Boise Community Ombudsman, *Policies and Procedures* (January 1, 2001), 6. Available at http://www.boiseombudsman.org.

24 Lou Cannon, *Official Negligence: How Rodney King and the Riots Changed Los Angeles and the LAPD* (New York: Times Books, 1987).

25 Department of Justice, *Investigation of the Seattle Police Department*.

26 Department of Justice, *Investigation of the Seattle Police Department*, 5.

27 San Jose, Independent Police Auditor, *2012 Year End Report*, 32.

28 New York City, Civilian Complaint Review Board, *Statistical Appendices, Jan—Dec 2011* (2012).

29 Department of Justice, *Investigation of the Seattle Police Department* (December 16, 2011), Appendix D, 1–2.

30 San Jose Independent Police Auditor, *Year End Report, 1993–1994* (San Jose: IPA, 1995). San Jose Independent Police Auditor, *1995 Year End Report* (San Jose: IPA, 1996). Available at http://www.sanjoseca.gov/ipa/.

31 New York City, Civilian Complaint Review Board, *Statistical Appendices, Jan—Dec 2011*, Table 24A.

32 New York City, Civilian Complaint Review Board, *2011 Annual Report* (New York: Civilian Complaint Review Board, 2012).

33 San Jose, Independent Police Auditor, *Policy and Procedures.* Copy in author's files.

34 The original academic study that identified the code of silence is William A. Westley, *Violence and the Police* (Cambridge: MIT Press, 1970), based on a 1950 study of the Gary, Indiana, Police Department. A recent and more thorough report is David Weisburd and others, *The Abuse of Authority: A National Study of Police Officers' Attitudes* (Washington, DC: The Police Foundation, 2001).

35 Boise Community Ombudsman, *Policies and Procedures,* 9, 2.08. "Truthfulness and Cooperation." Available at http://www.boiseombudsman.org.

36 Seattle Police Department, *Police Manual,* Title 5.002, "Public and Internal Complaint Process" (January 23, 2012).

37 San Francisco Office of Citizen Complaints, *Response to the Board of Supervisors Regarding SFPD's Patterns of Withholding Information Requested for OCC Investigations* (April 23, 2003). Available at http://www.ci.sf.ca .us/occ/. The San Francisco City Charter mandates that the Police Department provide the OCC full and prompt cooperation. Sec. 4.127 states, "In carrying out its objectives, the Office of Citizen Complaints shall receive prompt and full cooperation and assistance from all departments, officers and employees of the City and County. The director may also request and the Chief of Police shall require the testimony or attendance of any member of the Police Department."

38 San Francisco Office of Citizen Complaints, *Response to the Board of Supervisors Regarding SFPD's Patterns of Withholding Information Requested for OCC Investigations.*

39 *United States v. New Jersey,* Consent Decree, Par. 77.

40 National Commission on Civil Disorders, *Report* (New York: Bantam Books, 1968).

41 Joseph De Angelis, *Assessing the Impact of the Office of the Independent Monitor on Complainant and Officer Satisfaction* (Denver, Office of the Independent Monitor, 2008).

42 Department of Justice, *Investigation of the New Orleans Police Department* (2011), 91.

43 Department of Justice, *Investigation of the New Orleans Police Department,* 90.

44 Richard Jerome, *Police Oversight Project—City of Albuquerque* (Los Angeles: Police Assessment Resource Center, 2002), 34–35. Available at http:// www.parc.info.

45 *United States v. City of Los Angeles,* Consent Decree.

46 San Jose, Independent Police Auditor, *Policy and Procedures.* Copy in author's files.

47 *United States v. New Jersey,* Consent Decree, Par. 75.

48   Author interview with Lisa Botsko, former director, Portland Internal Investigations Advisory Committee.

49   *United States v. City of Cincinnati,* Memorandum of Agreement, Par. 41.

50   San Jose, Independent Police Auditor, *Policy and Procedures.*

51   Los Angeles Sheriff's Department, Office of Independent Review, *Second Annual Report 2003* (Los Angeles: Sheriff's Department, 2003), 77–8. Available at http://www.laoir.com.

52   Amy Oppenheimer and Craig Pratt, *Investigating Workplace Harassment: How to Be Fair, Thorough, and Legal* (Alexandria, VA: Society for Human Resource Management, 2003), 110–11.

53   *United States v. Cincinnati,* Memorandum of Agreement, Par. 41.

54   *United States v. the City of Los Angeles,* Consent Decree, Par. 84. Available at http://www.lapdonline.org.

55   San Francisco Office of Citizen Complaints, *Year 2001 Annual Report,* 6, available online at http://www.ci.sf.ca.us/occ/. "During 2001, OCC identified an average of 4.67 allegations per civilian complaint (4,250 allegations in 911 complaints filed, excluding merged, voided and no finding cases). In 2001, as in the four previous years, by the measure of average number of allegations identified, OCC maintained the previously documented level of improvement in completeness of its analysis of complaints." New York City Civilian Complaint Review Board, *Status Report, January–June 2003,* 9.

56   *United States v. the City of Los Angeles,* Consent Decree, Par. 82.

57   Boise Community Ombudsman, *Policies and Procedures,* 9. "2.09 Tape Recordings. a. The complete interview of an officer/employee accused of a Class I violation shall be recorded and a copy may be obtained by the officer/employee under investigation upon request. The officer/employee may also bring his/her own recording device, if he/she wishes. The cost of taping and any mechanical devices used by the officer/employee shall be borne by the officer/employee." http://www.boiseombudsman.org.

58   San Jose Independent Police Auditor, *2011 Year End Report,* 40.

59   San Jose Independent Police Auditor, *1994 Year-End Report,* 16.

60   Merrick Bobb, *16th Semiannual Report* (Los Angeles: Police Assessment Resource Center, 2003), 43–59. Los Angeles Sheriff's Department, Office of Internal Review, *Tenth Annual Report* (Los Angeles: Los Angeles Sheriff's Department, 2012), 106.

61   "A Model Citizen Complaint Procedure," in Walker, *Police Accountability: The Role of Citizen Oversight,* Appendix, 188–97.

62   Pittsburgh, *Auditor's Eighteenth Quarterly Report. Quarter Ending February 16, 2002,* 26.

63   Oppenheimer and Pratt, *Investigating Workplace Harassment: How to Be Fair, Thorough, and Legal,* 108. *United States v. New Jersey,* Consent Decree, Par. 81. "The State shall make findings based on a 'preponderance of the evidence' standard."

64 Washington, DC, Office of Police Complaints, "Decisions," http://police complaints.dc.gov/page/complaint-examiner-decisions. Eure: Washington, DC, Office of Complaint Review, Press Release, August 5, 2003. Available at http://policecomplaints.dc.gov/.

65 New York Civil Liberties Union, *Five Years of Civilian Review: A Mandate Unfulfilled* (New York: NYCLU, 1998).

66 Portland, Police Internal Investigations Auditing Committee, *Fourth Quarter Monitoring Report 1997* (Portland, PIIAC, 1998), 11.

67 Commission on Accreditation for Law Enforcement Agencies, *Standards for Law Enforcement Agencies*, 4th ed. (Fairfax, VA: CALEA, 1998).

68 San Francisco, Office of Citizen Complaints, *2011 Annual Report* (San Francisco: Office of Citizen Complaints, 2012), 1–2.

69 San Jose Independent Police Auditor, *1995 Year End Report*, 21–2.

70 U.S. Department of Justice, *Investigation of the Portland, Maine, Police Department. Letter to Mr. Gary Wood, Corporation Counsel,* March 21, 2003.

71 Jayson Wechter, *Investigating Police Misconduct Is Different* (Omaha: University of Nebraska at Omaha, 2004). Available at http://samuel walker.net/.

72 Samuel Walker, Carol Archbold, and Leigh Herbst, *Mediating Citizen Complaints Against Police Officers: A Guide for Police and Community Leaders* (Washington, DC; Department of Justice, 2002). Available at http://www .cops.usdoj.gov.

73 San Jose, Independent Police Auditor, *2011 Year End Report*, 56.

74 Oakland Police Department, *Negotiated Settlement Agreement Second Semi-annual Report*, vii.

75 ACLU—National Capital Area, *Analysis of the District of Columbia's Civilian Complaint Review Board and Recommendations for its Replacement* (Washington: ACLU–National Capital Area, 1995).

76 San Jose, Independent Police Auditor, *Policy and Procedures.* Copy in author's files.

77 San Jose, Independent Police Auditor, *2011 Year End Report*, 40–41, 56.

78 Walker, *Police Accountability.*

79 The issues surrounding the sustain rate are discussed at length in Walker, *Police Accountability: The Role of Citizen Oversight*, 120–2, 134–5.

80 Joseph De Angelis and Aaron Kupchik, *Measuring Complainant and Officer Satisfaction With the Denver Police Complaint Process: Results From the Baseline Survey* (Denver: Office of the Independent Monitor, 2006). Joseph De Angelis, *Assessing the Impact of the Office of the Independent Monitor on Complainant and Officer Satisfaction* (Denver: Office of the Independent Monitor, 2008).

FIVE

Early Intervention Systems

A New Approach to Police Accountability

The dirty little secret in policing has always been that in every department a few officers repeatedly engage in misconduct. A cliché repeated by a many chiefs is that "5 percent of my officers cause 90 percent of my problems."[1] The other parts of this secret are that other officers in the department know who they are and that departments rarely did anything to correct their conduct. That tradition began to change about 25 years ago with the development of early intervention systems (EISs), which are now recognized as the most powerful police accountability tool. Figure 5.1 presents a short description of the role and value of early intervention systems by the International Association of Chiefs of Police (IACP).

An EIS is a computerized database of police officer performance that allows supervisors and commanders to identify those officers with a pattern of problematic performance, such as use of force incidents, citizen complaints, or other indicators, and to then undertake an intervention designed to correct an officer's conduct. An EIS may include as few as five or as many as 25 indicators. Interventions may involve counseling, retraining, or other options. An EIS is separate from a department's formal discipline system and is designed to act early, before an officer is engaged in a serious incident, and prevent future misconduct.[2]

Figure 5.1   The IACP on Early Intervention Systems

When carefully designed and implemented, early intervention systems can benefit individual officers, police departments, and the community. Increasingly being integrated into broader personnel assessment or risk management systems, early intervention management strategies provide a means of identifying officers whose current performance indicates there may be more serious problems in the future. Effective intervention at an early stage avoids potential problems for the officers themselves, their department, and the community. At the individual level, early intervention can save officers from citizen complaints and/or excessive-force incidents and the resulting internal affairs investigations. It saves them from acquiring reputations as problem officers that may block promotion or choice assignments, and ultimately may save their careers. For the department, citizen complaints and excessive-force allegations involve time-consuming and costly investigations, along with negative reactions in the community. For the community, effective intervention can prevent the injuries and insults that arise from officer misconduct.

Source: International Association of Chiefs of Police, *Protecting Civil Rights: A Leadership Guide for State, Local, and Tribal Law Enforcement* (Alexandria, VA: IACP, 2006), p. 49.

While simple in concept, an EIS is extremely complicated to develop and operate. The major questions involve choosing the number of indicators in the system, the "thresholds" that will be used to identify officers for intervention, determining the proper intervention for each officer, monitoring the performance of officers who have been through intervention, and ensuring that the EIS continues to operate properly over time. This chapter discusses the major issues and challenges related to making an EIS successful.

The Background and Development of an EIS

Early intervention systems grew out of the recognition that a few officers (typically estimated at about 5 percent of the force) are responsible for a disproportionate number of any police department's problems, and in the 1970s in response to growing recognition of the need to address police use of force problems. Herman Goldstein in 1977 was the first police expert to discuss the possibility of "Identifying Officers with a Propensity for Wrongdoing" and taking administrative action to improve their performance.[3] Several departments, including Oakland, New York City, and Kansas City, experimented with programs to identify officers involved in frequent shooting or use of force incidents, but none of those programs lasted very long (and in fact may not have progressed beyond the talking stage).[4] The 1981 U.S. Civil Rights Commission report, *Who Is Guarding the Guardians?*, provided the first documentation of the concentration of problematic performance among a few officers. As Table 5.1 indicates, in the Houston Police Department, one officer had received a total of 12 complaints and two others had 11 complaints over a 2-year period. By comparison, 298 officers received only 2 complaints. The officers who had received 5 or more complaints during this period represented only 12

Table 5.1   Citizen Complaints, Houston Police Officers, 1977–1979

Number of Complaints	Number of Officers
2	298
3	136
4	70
5	33
6	18
7	8
8	6
9	1
10	0
11	2
12	1
	573 Total

Source: From *Who Is Guarding the Guardians? A Report on Police Practices* (p. 166), by the U.S. Commission on Civil Rights, 1981, Washington, DC: Government Printing Office.

percent of all officers receiving complaints, but they accounted for 41 percent of all the complaints. In response to its Houston data, the Civil Rights Commission recommended that "a system should be devised in each department to assist officials in early identification of violence-prone officers." [5] The same pattern of a small number of officers receiving a disproportionate number of all citizen complaints persists today. In 2011, the Justice Department found that in Seattle 4 percent of the officers who ever used force were responsible for 18 percent of all reported force incidents.[6]

Events in the Miami, Florida, metropolitan area in the early 1980s led to the first EIS programs known to have survived. The Miami-Dade Employee Identification System developed in response to a series of racial incidents in the late 1970s and early 1980s. The most controversial incident involved the fatal beating of Arthur McDuffie, an African American insurance agent, by Miami-Dade officers, and a riot that erupted in May 1980 after four officers were acquitted of criminal charges for his death.[7] In response, a local ordinance directed the Miami-Dade Police Department to develop an employee profile system (EPS) with detailed information on each employee, and the EPS became the basis for an EIS. At about the same time, the Miami Police Department also developed an EIS in response to racial conflict with the community.

During the 1980s, other police departments across the country followed the Miami-Dade example. A major turning point occurred with the highly publicized beating of Rodney King by Los Angeles police officers in March 1991. The Christopher Commission, appointed to investigate the King incident, identified 44 "problem officers" with extremely high rates of complaints in the department.[8] The Commission pointed out that these 44 officers were "readily identifiable" through existing departmental records, but the LAPD did not use these records to address the officers' performance problems, nor did it incorporate the information into its regular performance evaluations or promotion decisions.[9] A year later, the Kolts Commission, appointed to investigate the Los Angeles County Sheriff's Department (LASD), found a similar group of 62 "problem officers" in the department and recommended the development of an EIS.[10] The LASD's Personnel Performance Index (PPI) became fully operational in 1997 and soon became widely regarded as the best EIS in the country.

Becoming a Best Practice in Policing

By the late 1990s, EIS emerged as a recommended "best practice" in policing. The Department of Justice recommended that police departments develop EISs in its 2001 report, *Principles for Promoting Police Integrity*, and the Civil Rights Division has incorporated them into all of the consent decrees and memoranda of agreement in pattern or practice suits it has brought.[11] A Vera Institute evaluation of the implementation of the Pittsburgh consent decree called the department's early intervention system "the centerpiece of the Police Bureau's reforms in response to the consent decree."[12] In 2001, the Commission on Accreditation for Law Enforcement Agencies (CALEA) adopted a new standard requiring all large agencies to have an EIS.[13] CALEA Standard 35.1.15 reads:

> A comprehensive Personnel Early Warning System is an essential component of good discipline in a well-managed law enforcement agency. The early identification of potential problem employees and a menu of remedial actions can increase agency accountability and offer employees a better opportunity to meet the agency's values and mission statement.

Basic Considerations of an EIS

Centerpiece of the New Accountability

Early intervention systems originated as a procedure for identifying those few officers with apparent patterns of serious misconduct. Fairly quickly, however, they evolved to become a comprehensive accountability system incorporating the elements of the new accountability described in Chapter One. They are a data-driven process that when used properly can be a crucial element of supervision. By incorporating officer reports on critical incidents, citizen complaints, and other indicators, they can be used to analyze patterns of officer conduct and identify problems that might need to be addressed through changes in policy, training, or supervision. Figure 5.2 provides two examples based on the authors' research illustrating how an EIS can address certain performance problems. A 1989 report by the International Association of Chiefs of Police (IACP) explained that an EIS is "a proactive management tool useful for identifying a wide range of problems [and] *not just a system to focus on problem officers.*"[14]

Figure 5.2 EIS in Action: Two Case Studies

Department A. In one large police department a female officer was flagged by the EIS because of a high number of use of force incidents. The counseling session with the officer revealed that she had a great fear of being struck in the face, and as a consequence was not properly taking control of encounters with citizens. After losing control over the person or persons, she would then use force to reassert control of the situation. Her supervisor referred her to the training unit, where she was instructed in tactics that would allow her to protect herself while maintaining control of encounters that had the potential for conflict. As a result, her use of force incidents declined dramatically.[15]

Department B. In another large department, a patrol officer was identified by the EIS system because of a series of use of force incidents. During the intervention session the officer's supervisor discovered that he was having severe personal financial problems. The supervisor recommended professional financial consulting; the officer followed this advice, and his performance improved significantly.[16]

A San Diego Police Department technical assistance report on creating an EIS listed the number of different problems in a department that an EIS can address. In addition to the violation of the rights of individual citizens in specific incidents, an EIS can address problematic officer behavior that "(a) Erodes public confidence; (b) Contributes to loss of services due to suspensions and transfers; (c) Contributes to costly liability issues; (d) Contributes to employee attrition rates due to terminations and resignations; [and] (e) Increases employee injury and accident rates."[17]

Introducing an EIS

An EIS cannot be simply plugged into a department that lacks basic accountability procedures. It requires a reasonably comprehensive and well-functioning critical incident reporting system (see Chapter Three). Missing, incomplete, or inaccurate reports on use of force, vehicle pursuits, and other incidents undermine the effectiveness of an EIS by not providing a full picture of officers' performance. A department must also have an open and accessible citizen complaint system that receives, properly records, and investigates thoroughly all potential citizen complaints (Chapter Four). As we explained in Chapter

Four, even unsustained citizen complaints are important "management information" about officers' performance. The effectiveness of an EIS is enhanced when it presents as complete a picture as possible of officers' performance, including such indicators as sick leave use, filing of resisting arrest charges, and involvement in civil suits against the department. Finally, a department that does not have an up-to-date information technology system will have trouble developing an efficient and effective EIS.

In short, an EIS is not a free-standing tool that can significantly change a department by itself. It often requires major improvements in (and in some cases even the creation of) other policies and procedures in a department. One of the reasons some departments have had difficulty in complying with federal consent decrees and memoranda of agreement is that they have been required to make major reforms related to policies and data systems while at the same time implementing an EIS.

A Note on Terminology

Just as the nature and purposes of EISs have evolved over time, the terminology has also changed. Initially, they were known as *early warning systems*, but experts began to recognize that the term had a negative connotation, suggesting that the system is primarily oriented toward discipline. EIS evolved in the direction of comprehensive personnel assessment systems that examine more than just use of force issues. The Los Angeles Sheriff's Department calls its system the *Personnel Performance Index* (PPI), the Phoenix Police Department calls its system the *Personnel Assessment System* (PAS), while in Cincinnati it is known as the *Risk Management System* (RMS). As we discuss in Chapter Seven, an EIS has a risk management function and can be included in a comprehensive risk management program.

This book also does not use the term *problem police officers* and instead uses the term *officers with performance problems*. The former term labels officers (as in, "bad cops") and suggests that their performance cannot change. The term *officers with performance problems* focuses on certain behavior, without labeling an officer, and conveys the message that performance can improve. As the IACP explains, an "effective early intervention identifies potentially problematic behaviors in individual officers rather than identifying and removing problematic officers."[18]

Early Intervention and the Formal Discipline System

Early intervention systems are separate from a police department's formal discipline system. Internal affairs investigations are reactive, undertaken in response to allegations of officer misconduct in a citizen complaint or a supervisor's report. (The exception to this rule involves proactive investigations of officers arising from rumors about serious misconduct such as corruption.)[19] Internal affairs investigations are directed toward discipline, where misconduct is confirmed. Disciplinary actions are entered into an officer's official personnel record.

EISs, on the other hand, are proactive and directed toward corrective action rather than discipline. A review of an officer's EIS file focuses on a broad range of officer conduct, seeking to identify patterns of problematic performance that interventions are designed to correct. Being subject to an EIS intervention, moreover, is not entered into an officer's official personnel file. Interventions are often informal and flexible in order to address the officer's behavior, ranging from informal counseling by a supervisor to referral to professional counseling for family problems or substance abuse. An important aspect of an EIS is the capacity to establish relationships among many performance categories. A pattern of use of force incidents and a high rate of sick leave time, for example, may suggest that an officer is under stress due to off-the-job problems.

From Punishment to Behavior Change

EISs are part of a significant shift in thinking about police personnel management away from traditional discipline and toward changing the behavior of officers. Police departments have long been characterized as punishment-oriented bureaucracies, with innumerable rules and regulations that can be used to punish an officer, but with few procedures for either rewarding good conduct or helping officers with problems.[20] Robin Engel's research on police supervisors found that "traditional" supervisors "give more instruction to subordinates and are less likely to reward and more likely to punish patrol officers. The traditional supervisor's ultimate concern is to control subordinate behavior."[21] Apart from employee assistance programs (EAP) for substance abuse or family problems, and stress reduction programs, police departments have done relatively little in a formal way to correct problem behavior.[22]

The informal and flexible nature of EISs, moreover, facilitates addressing personal problems that are often the underlying cause of a police officer's on-the-job performance issues. The San Diego Police Department technical assistance report, for example, explained that "our immediate interest was in the causes of unexplained deterioration in performance and in mitigating or preempting the need for discipline." It found that "mistake-based problematic behaviors" generally occur "early in an employee's career while judgment and attitude-based problematic behaviors" more often occurred later in an officer's career. Experienced officers are more likely to be affected by "age, diet, finance, and family issues," along with "the physiological symptoms of chronic stress illness that affect performance."[23] Interventions that involve professional counseling for family problems, stress, or substance abuse are a more appropriate response to these issues than traditional discipline.

Another contribution of an EIS database is that it can pinpoint specific performance problems underlying a pattern of sustained citizen complaint or excessive force incidents. Because EIS data are incident-specific, they can identify specific problems related to racial attitudes, anger management, or the need for tactical training in particular citizen encounters such as traffic stops.

Finally, and perhaps most important, an EIS database provides a documented picture of an officer's performance and any problems that exist. Critics of traditional police performance assessment systems have noted that they utilize general categories and subjective assessments such as "works well with people" or "demonstrates initiative."[24] Traditional performance evaluations, moreover, also tend to be heavily influenced by officers' reputations, which may not reflect actual performance. EISs, however, can identify specific areas of performance that need correcting, such as a pattern of citizen complaints alleging rudeness, and develop a response tailored to that problem. The IACP points out that "early intervention offers the added advantage of augmenting supervisors' direct interactions and observations based on reference to an objective set of performance indicators."[25]

EISs Do Not Predict Future Behavior

Contrary to what some people believe, EISs are not systems for *predicting* officer performance. In the past there were a number of attempts to develop methodologies for predicting officer performance based on background characteristics such as education, work experience, military experience, and so on. In the 1970s some experts believed that it would be possible to screen job applicants and determine which ones were unsuited for police work. None of these efforts proved to be successful.[26] An EIS, by contrast, is a retrospective system that documents actual on-the-job performance. It makes no claim of predicting what an officer's performance will be in the immediate future.

The Components of an EIS

An EIS consists of four basic components: performance indicators, the identification and selection process, intervention, and post-intervention monitoring.

Performance Indicators

The performance indicators are those officer activities and personnel information that are officially recorded by the department and entered into the EIS database. There is no consensus of opinion among experts about the best number of performance indicators to be included in an EIS. The Pittsburgh Performance Assessment and Review System (PARS) uses 18 performance indicators, while the Phoenix PAS utilizes 24 indicators. Other departments use as few as five indicators. Large systems can be characterized as *comprehensive personnel assessment systems.* They collect a very wide range of data and have the capacity to address a wide range of issues, such as identifying top-performing officers or investigating racial profiling. These systems require both a sophisticated technological infra-structure and an enormous amount of administrative oversight.[27] Other systems collect as few as five performance indicators data and as a conse-quence have more limited capabilities in terms of assessing an officer's performance.

Experts on EISs agree that a system should *not* rely on just one indicator, as many of the first EISs did and some still do. Using only one indicator does not provide a broad picture of an officer's performance. The initial Minneapolis early warning system, for example, used only citizen com-plaints,[28] and Boston was doing the same as recently as 2012.[29] By them-selves, citizen complaints provide a very limited picture of an officer's performance, in part because only a very small percentage of citizens who feel they have some reason to complain actually file a complaint.[30]

Figure 5.3 lists the 20 indicators mandated by the consent decree covering the Oakland, California, police department.[31] In addition to use of force reports and citizen complaints, Oakland also includes sick leave usage (Item #17). Many police commanders believe that frequent use of sick leave is an indicator of possible personal problems, such as substance abuse. Resisting arrest charges filed by an officer (Item #13), meanwhile, are seen by many experts as a device by which officers cover their own use of force by charging the citizen with an offense that would justify the use of force.[32] Criminal suspects do resist arrest and even the best officers will file resisting arrest charges, but an EIS can identify a pattern where an officer is filing a much higher rate of such charges than peer officers, and where there are other indicators of potential problems.

The number of performance indicators in an EIS involves a trade-off between effectiveness and efficiency. A larger number of indicators increases the capability of the system to analyze the full scope of an officer's performance and identify a variety of different problems. At the same time, however, a larger system imposes a very heavy administrative burden on the department involving data entry and overall system management. As discussed later, the Los Angeles Sheriff's Department PPI system, widely regarded as one of the best systems, encountered serious problems with data entry, in large part because of the sheer size of the department and the resulting PPI workload.[33] A smaller EIS with fewer indicators is easier to create and maintain, but it is more limited in its capacity to assess officer performance.

Identification and Selection of Officers

The identification and selection of officers for intervention is an extremely complex process. The "thresholds problem," as it is often called, turns on the question, "How many problematic indicators and over what period of time should cause an officer to be chosen for intervention?" There is no simple answer to this question, and a rigid formula is not considered to be satisfactory.

In some early EISs, identification and selection was a single, nondiscretionary decision. In the early Minneapolis system, for example, any officer receiving three complaints in a 12-month period was automatically referred to intervention.[34] Most experts today, however, argue that this approach is too rigid and creates a number of problems. First, as we have already argued, using only one performance indicator fails to capture the

Figure 5.3   EIS Requirements in the Oakland (CA) Consent Decree

1. All uses of force required to be reported by OPD.

2. OC spray canister check-out log (see Section V, paragraph D).

3. All police-canine deployments.

4. All officer-involved shootings and firearms discharges, both on duty and off duty.

5. All on-duty vehicle pursuits, traffic accidents, and traffic violations.

6. All citizen complaints, whether made to OPD or CPRB.

7. All civil suits and/or tort claims related to members' and employees' employment at OPD, or which contain allegations that rise to the level of a *Manual of Rules* violation.

8. Reports of a financial claim as described in Section VI, paragraph G (3).

9. All in-custody deaths and injuries.

10. The results of adjudications of all investigations related to items (1) through (9), above, and a record of all tentative and final decisions or recommendations regarding discipline, including actual discipline imposed or nondisciplinary action.

11. Commendations and awards.

12. All criminal arrests of and charges against OPD members and employees.

13. All charges of resisting or obstructing a police officer (Penal Code §§69 and 148), assault on a police officer (Penal Code §243(b) (c)), or assault-with-a-deadly-weapon on a police officer (Penal Code §245(b) (c)).

14. Assignment and rank history for each member/employee.

15. Training history for each member/employee.

16. Line-of-duty injuries.

17. Sick leave usage, particularly one-day sick leaves.

18. Report Review Notices or Case Evaluation Reports for the reporting member/employee and the approving supervisor.

19. Criminal cases dropped due to concerns with member veracity, improper searches, false arrests, etc.

20. Other supervisory observations or concerns.

Source: From *Allen v. City of Oakland,* Consent Decree (2003). The settlement agreement is available at http://www.oaklandpolice.com.

full range of an officer's performance. Second, a rigid formula of three complaints in a 12-month period (or three use of force reports in a given period) does not take into account the nature and context of these incidents. There could be very legitimate reasons why an officer received that many complaints during a given reporting period. It could be the result of a rash of gang-related activity in the neighborhood that involved the officer in a number of difficult arrests that required the use of force. Third, a single department-wide formula (e.g., three complaints in a 12-month period) fails to take into account the enormous differences in officers' work environments. An officer working in a high-crime precinct will inevitably use force more often and receive more complaints than an officer working in a low-crime area. An officer in a low-crime area who receives two complaints will not be identified by the system but in fact may have serious performance problems.

The Justice Department faulted the Seattle Police Department in 2011 because the thresholds in its EIS were too high. The EIS was "triggered" when an officer "participates in seven uses of force, or receives three OPA complaints, in a period of six months." As a result, the EIS fails to identify officers with frequent uses of force that did not meet the very high level of seven in six months. Nor did it appear that other performance indicators were used to identify potential performance problems in the Seattle EIS.[35]

The emerging best practice for EISs is to use a *two-stage process* for identifying and selecting officers for intervention. The first stage, *identification,* relies on the EIS database to identify officers who have a relatively high number of problematic performance indicators, such as use of force reports, citizen complaints, and other indicators. From this list, certain officers are *selected* for intervention. As the discussion that follows clearly indicates, this two-stage process is extremely complex and labor intensive, involving considerable effort in the selection stage. The alternative, however, is a rigid numerical formula that is likely to both identify officers who do not need intervention (false positives) and fail to identify some officers who do (false negatives).

It is generally believed that a system of peer group officer comparisons is the best system for identifying officers for possible intervention. The Cincinnati Risk Management System (ordered by the Memorandum of Agreement with the Justice Department) includes data on the "average level of activity for each data category by individual officer and by all officers in a unit."[36] Given the wide variation in crime and disorder in different parts of a metropolitan area, it is both reasonable and fair to assess officers on the basis of their peers working in the same or similar environments. It is reasonable, for example, to assume that officers working high-crime areas or shifts are more likely to generate use of force reports and citizen complaints than officers working low-crime areas or times of day.[37]

A special commission on use of force in Spokane, Washington, offered the sound recommendation that EIS thresholds should be "set at an appropriate level so as to initiate relevant and effective intervention (i.e., not so high that intervention never occurs or occurs too late)." It decided that the standard should be thresholds that "capture approximately 3–5% of the line officer population."[38] The 3–5 percent standard undoubtedly reflects the old complaint by police chiefs, cited at the beginning of this chapter, that about 5 percent of a department's officers cause 90 percent of its problems. If the system captures many more than that, the resulting workload will overwhelm the system. A lower threshold raises the possibility of not identifying some officers in need of intervention.

In a two-stage process, officers who have been initially identified are then subject to a performance review that involves both quantitative and qualitative analyses. The review may well discover legitimate explanations for an officer's high number of use of force reports in a given period. Perhaps there has been an upsurge in gang activity or some other criminal activity that led to more use of force reports. This point highlights an extremely important principle with EIS systems: *The numbers in an EIS database do not speak for themselves.* The mere fact that an officer received three citizen complaints and uses force four times in one period means nothing without a closer review of the incidents, crime in the area, and the officer's overall record. In short, an officer is not "guilty" of anything simply because of relatively high numbers and being initially identified by the EIS.

The weakness of mere numbers in an EIS also operates with regard to low numbers. An officer working a low-crime residential neighborhood might have low number of citizen complaints or use of force reports, but they might be high given the characteristics of the neighborhood and in comparison with other officers working that area. This issue illustrates the importance of a peer group analysis in an EIS.

The Los Angeles Sheriff's Department's PPI illustrates a two-stage process in operation. First, it identifies officers who have been involved in a disproportionate number of "risk" incidents, or on the basis of a supervisor's referral. (Note that the PPI allows for supervisors' discretion independent of the EIS numbers.) They are then screened by the Performance Review Committee (PRC), which consists of rotating panels of three commanders that meet twice a month. The PRC solicits the opinion of the officer's captain and assigns a lieutenant to prepare a detailed Employee Profile Report (EPR; known informally as a "Blue Book"). The EPR becomes the basis for a PRC decision about whether or not to refer the officer to intervention, known in the LASD as Performance Review. Between 1996 and 2002, a total of 1,213 employees were identified by the PPI system, but only 235 (or 19 percent) were placed on Performance Review. When an officer is placed on Performance Review, a Performance Plan is prepared, which might include such intervention strategies as counseling, retraining, reassignment, or a more thorough fitness for duty evaluation.[39]

As should be evident, the two-stage process in the LASD's PPI is both highly labor intensive and discretionary. The process does not rely simply on numbers (the performance indicators) but engages supervisors in an assessment of an officer's performance in the context of his or her peer officers, the context of the work environment, and any other relevant factors that might affect performance. This process imposes a considerable administrative burden in terms of the time and effort required to analyze the data and assess all of the relevant factors. The decisions involved call for judgment, opening the door for possible favoritism or bias. Avoiding those problems is an additional EIS management problem.[40]

Box 5.1 illustrates how an EIS peer group analysis can apply to the contentious issue of racial profiling, while Box 5.2 illustrates how a peer group analysis and a two-stage process operates with respect to five hypothetical cases.

BOX 5.1   SPECIAL APPLICATION: EIS AND RACIAL PROFILING

An EIS has special relevance for addressing the extremely complex issue of racial profiling. It is the consensus of opinion among experts on the subject that official data on traffic enforcement do not automatically indicate an illegal practice of discrimination based on race, ethnicity, or color.[41] Disparities in stops could be the result of a number of different factors, including driving behavior or the condition of the vehicle. Existing data sets are simply not specific enough, and officer reports of "erratic driving" are almost impossible to prove or disprove after the fact.[42]

(Continued)

(Continued)

An EIS offers a way out of the dilemma (although it might not be satisfactory to all community activists). A peer group analysis of traffic stops can identify an officer assigned to a precinct or district who is stopping drivers of color at a disproportionate rate relative to other officers. These data do not indicate guilt of discrimination, but they can serve as the basis for a supervisor's inquiry. The supervisor can go over the data with the officer, point out the disparity, counsel an officer about the disparity, discuss the matter, and explain the possible problems that could arise from stopping too many drivers of color. If the officer is stopping a very large number of drivers of color, the supervisor can emphasize the many responsibilities of patrol officers and the need to balance activities.[43]

A study of traffic stops by the Washington State Police illustrates how the process can work. The study examined the traffic stops of 16 Washington State Patrol troopers assigned to South Seattle during 2003 to 2005 for the purpose of determining racial patterns in stops. A peer group analysis compared the performance of all 16 officers. The study found no "conclusive evidence" that troopers used race as a factor in stops, searches, and drunk driving arrests. Nonetheless, it identified significant variations among the troopers in their use of race, and a few troopers were identified as "potential problem troopers." In particular, "troopers 541 and 401 may have used race as a factor to stop a higher share of minority motorists as compared to their similarly situated peers." The study recommended that law enforcement agencies "strongly consider incorporating traffic enforcement racial profiling analyses" into their EIS for the purpose of identifying potential problem officers.

Source: Adapted from Brent D. Fulton, *Incorporating Traffic Enforcement Racial Profiling Analyses Into Police Department Early Intervention Systems* (Santa Monica, CA: Rand Corporation, 2007), 81, 102.

BOX 5.2   HYPOTHETICAL EXAMPLES OF HOW A PEER OFFICER COMPARISON APPROACH CAN BE USED

Officer A

Indicators. Officer A had five use of force reports during one reporting period. Relative to other officers in the same unit, this was a very low figure, but his performance record indicated that he made only eight arrests during this period.

Analysis. Officer A used force in more than half of the arrests he made. The ratio of force to arrests is cause for departmental concern and probable intervention.

Discussion. Officer A represents the classic officer with a use of force problem. An intervention counseling session will seek to determine if the cause is improper tactics that can be corrected through training, or personal problems that require professional counseling.

Officer B

Indicators. Officer B had no citizen complaints or use of force reports for the reporting period. The performance data, however, also indicates that he also had made no arrests, no traffic stops, and no field stops. Further examination of his records indicate that he was working the maximum number of hours permitted for off-duty employment.

Analysis. Officer B is devoting all his energy to his off-duty employment rather than fulfilling his responsibilities to the department and will be referred for intervention.

Discussion. In the intervention counseling session the officer will be advised of this problem and instructed to engage in an acceptable level of basic police work.

Officer C

Indicators. A female driver filed a citizen complaint against Officer C alleging an inappropriate sexual advance during a traffic stop. An examination of the officer's EI file indicated a very high number of traffic stops involving females relative to peer officers.

Analysis. Officer C appears to be abusing his law enforcement powers to harass female drivers and will be referred for intervention.

Discussion. In the intervention counseling session, Officer C will be presented with the data, advised that his behavior is inappropriate, and informed that he will be subject to intense supervision for the next 6 months.

Officer D

Indicators. Officer D makes a high number of arrests relative to his peer officers who work in a high-crime area, yet he receives few citizen complaints compared with his peers.

(Continued)

(Continued)

Analysis. Officer D is an exemplary officer, engaging active crime-fighting work and conducting himself in a professional manner.

Discussion. The officer will be advised by his supervisor that his performance is exemplary and that a letter of commendation to this effect will be placed in his file.

Officer E

Indicators. Officer E makes roughly the same number of traffic stops as peer officers working the same precinct, a neighborhood with a significant Latino population, but stops a far higher percentage of Latino drivers than the other officers (about 60 percent of all stops, compared with about 40 percent for other officers).

Analysis. The officer's traffic stop data suggests possible bias against Latino drivers and will be referred for intervention.

Discussion. Officer E will be presented with these data at the intervention counseling session. He will be offered an opportunity to explain the disparity. If he fails to present a reasonable explanation, he will be advised of the apparent pattern of bias and informed that his performance will be subject to intense supervision over the next 6 months.

The experience of the Pittsburgh Police Department with a federal consent decree illustrates how an EIS operates on a routine basis. The consent decree directed supervisors "to use the PARS [Performance Assessment and Review System] on a quarterly basis to assess allegations of racial bias for patterns or irregularities."[44] These indicators include:

- Notation on the Supervisor's Daily Activity Report (SDAR) of any indication of racial or gender bias on the part of a given officer;
- A complaint by a supervisor of racial or gender bias against an officer;
- A peer complaint of racial or gender bias;
- An OMI [Office of Municipal Investigations] complaint of racial or gender bias;
- Filing of a lawsuit, in which the officer is named, contending racial or gender bias;

- Any indication during a normal review of routine police reports (offense reports, arrest reports, search and seizure reports, subject resistance reports, etc.) that an officer shows potential racial or gender bias;
- Comments made by an officer indicating racial or gender bias; or
- A non-OMI complaint of gender or racial bias.

The court-appointed monitor in Pittsburgh found that supervisors were in fact conducting the required reviews and "during the week of February 4, 2002 identified one officer with at least one of these 'trigger' events."[45] Used on a regular basis, this kind of performance review would not only spot potential racial or ethnic bias very quickly but would also communicate to officers that their performance is being closely monitored. The result would probably be improvement in all types of officer activity and not just with respect to racial or ethnic bias. Whether or not such improvements in fact occur is a question that can be addressed by a properly designed evaluation.

Intervention

The intervention phase of EIS consists of counseling, retraining, or other actions for officers who have been selected. In most EISs an officer's immediate supervisor does the counseling, which typically involves a discussion of the officer's performance problems and is intended to lead to some agreement about how the officer might correct these problems. Possible outcomes include advisement from the supervisor, referral to training over particular tactics, or a recommendation that the officer seek professional counseling. Where remedial training is involved, it is handled by the department training unit. The training might involve a reinstruction on tactics for traffic stops or on handcuffing suspects who resist. In some departments, the counseling session involves other command officers meeting as a committee; some systems use a written performance improvement plan with specific goals. Independent of EIS, the Los Angeles Sheriff's Department has experimented with innovative forms of discipline, such as education-based discipline, that could easily be incorporated into an EIS intervention program.[46]

Some programs conducted interventions through a class with a number of officers. Group sessions have a number of problems, however. It is difficult to schedule a class with a number of officers, which often results in a delay in holding the classes. Group sessions, moreover, are not able to concentrate on the specific problems of individual officers. The first New Orleans police department EIS in the 1990s included group classes, and while some time was set aside for private counseling with each officer the amount of time was limited and the other officers waited idly during other officers' sessions.[47] A more serious problem is that bringing together officers who have been identified as having performance problems leads to group solidarity and the officers embracing the label of "problem officers." Officers in the New Orleans group classes, in fact, called it the "bad boy's class." The result is that the process reinforces the officers' problematic behavior.[48]

For individualized intervention, some departments provide a specific list of alternative actions that the supervisor can choose from. In the Miami-Dade Police Department, the "Action Alternatives" include referral to the departmental Psychological Services Program or participation in the Stress Abatement Program. Another alternative is a determination that "no problem exists" and that no formal action is necessary.[49] But in many programs, particularly those that were created in the early years without much planning, the interventions are left entirely to the discretion of the immediate supervisor, with no specific list of alternative actions.

Although the intervention stage is the critical component of an EIS, it has received the least attention from EIS experts (with most of the attention focusing on the "thresholds"). Intervention is critical to the impact of an EIS because it is where the department delivers the "treatment" designed to improve an officer's performance. As we explain in more detail shortly, an EIS dramatically changes the role of sergeants. It appears, however, that most departments have instituted EISs with little or no training for supervisors regarding their responsibilities in interventions. As we discussed in Chapter Four, departments generally provide no special training for investigating citizen complaints. Just as investigating citizen complaints is significantly different than routine criminal investigations, the responsibilities of intervention in an EIS are different than traditional supervision and discipline. Nor do there appear to be procedures for holding them accountable for properly conducting interventions.[50]

Inadequate training of sergeants for interventions can result in a number of problems. Sergeants may tell officers not to worry about the intervention and that the whole system is just "bullshit." Such a message would completely undermine the purpose of the EIS and breed cynicism about the department's entire accountability effort. Less flagrant but also serious is a situation in which a sergeant sincerely tries but fails to help an officer understand and change his or her performance.

Interventions require certain skills in human relations that all sergeants may not have and for which they are not specifically trained. The sergeant has to firmly but fairly point out the performance problems in an empathetic and nondisciplinary way.[51] Traditional training for supervisors emphasizes the formal and legalistic aspects of discipline: applying the department's discipline code, avoiding grievances and lawsuits, and so forth. In an intervention session a sergeant is expected to coach rather than discipline, for the purpose of helping the officer improve his or her performance. This requires discussing performance deficiencies in a nonthreatening way and suggesting means of improvement.

To date there has been little discussion of what action to take when interventions fail to improve an officer's performance and an officer is identified a second (or possibly a third) time by the EIS. Some EISs include termination as a possible response to identified officers. A convenient alternative is to transfer the officer to an assignment in which he or she will have little contact with the public, and no contact in potentially volatile situations or where use of force might occur (e.g., an internal desk job).

Post-Intervention Monitoring

Following an intervention, the department monitors the officer's performance for a specified period of time. Post-intervention monitoring efforts vary in terms of their formality. Many departments simply keep an officer on the EIS list until a certain period of time has passed (e.g., two quarters) without a significant number of problematic indicators. The Pittsburgh PAS system requires sergeants to observe officers by conducting "roll-bys" on a regular basis.[52]

Impacts of an EIS

The impact of an EIS on a department goes much further than providing a new tool for monitoring and correcting officer behavior. An EIS transforms important aspects of a police department in ways that the creators of EISs never anticipated.

Transforming the Role of Supervisors

EISs create a special set of challenges for sergeants. In particular, a Police Executive Research Forum *Guide for Front-Line Supervisors* in an EIS found that the challenges are especially difficult in departments "that did not have a strong system of accountability already in place."[53] An EIS requires supervisors to assume a new role and to perform new tasks. This aspect of the impact of EISs was not recognized when EISs first appeared but are now recognized as a critical issue. The Vera Institute evaluation of the Pittsburgh consent decree concluded that the PARS system had "a sweeping change in the duties of the lowest level supervisors."[54] One consequence was that sergeants were spending less time on the street and relatively more time at a desk, staring at a computer screen reviewing data and looking for patterns of conduct. Sergeants complained about the change, but that reaction is to be expected when a major transformation occurs in any tradition-bound job.

EISs change the role of supervisors in several ways. The PERF *Guide for Front-Line Supervisors* called this "one of the biggest changes in the role of supervisors."[55] First, the database gives them systematic data on the performance of the officers under their command. This forces sergeants to become *data analysts* with an emphasis on identification of patterns of conduct. It is also a radical departure from the traditional reliance on unsystematic impressions when doing personnel appraisals, often affected by particularly salient incidents such as a major arrest by an officer.

Second, in systems such as the Pittsburgh PARS, in which sergeants are required to access the system's database on a daily basis, it creates a new standard of intensive supervision. Pittsburgh sergeants are also expected to conduct roll-bys of officers who have been identified by the system. Finally, where the system records sergeants' log-ins (as in Pittsburgh), higher-ranking command officers can hold them accountable for their role in the EIS. The court-appointed monitor in Pittsburgh found that sergeants were in fact performing these new duties, with the result that officers with identified problems, and even some supervisors, were being selected for monitoring.[56]

Third, an EIS provides specific direction for a sergeant's role with respect to supervision. Robin Engel's study of supervisory styles in two large urban departments is particularly illuminating with regard to the role of sergeants. She found that some sergeants do not act as supervisors at all; some see their role as protecting their officers from higher command, whereas some others act as patrol officers themselves, directly engaging in police work. Even among those who do act as supervisors, many are able to act only in a strict disciplinary fashion: enforcing the letter of department rules (that is, playing it "by the book").[57] If Engel's findings are representative of sergeants across the country, the introduction of an EIS potentially has a significant impact on most American police sergeants, forcing them to change their daily habits and how they define themselves as supervisors. The PERF guide for supervisors concluded that "learning how to engage officers about their performance problems" is "perhaps one of the most difficult adjustments" that supervisors have to make in an EIS.[58]

Fourth, an EIS can transform supervision by allowing supervisors to check the past performance histories of officers newly assigned to them. With regular shift changes, sergeants often find themselves responsible for officers about whom they know nothing. As one commander reports, "There is a lot of movement of personnel, so supervisors often do not know the histories of their officers. The EWS report brings them up to speed in a much more timely fashion."[59] Even in a medium-sized department, in which officers' reputations are often known to others, an officer's reputation may not accurately reflect his or her overall performance. The Los Angeles consent decree requires that "when an officer transfers into a new division or area, the Commanding Officer (CO) shall promptly require the watch commander or supervisor to review the transferred officer's TEAMS I [Training Evaluation and Management System] record."[60]

The San Jose Police Department has taken EISs to a new level by developing a Supervisor's Intervention Program (SIP) that addresses the performance of supervisors as well as rank-and-file officers. Whenever the team of officers under a supervisor's command receives three or more citizen complaints within a 6-month period, the supervisor is required to meet with his or her chain of command and the head of Internal Affairs.

Changing the Organizational Culture

An EIS also has the potential for changing the culture of a department as a whole with respect to accountability. Virtually all police scholars, police managers, community activists, and outside observers talk about the culture of policing, often referring to the police officer subculture. Despite the recognition that it is important, there is relatively little research on the police subculture.[61] This is not the occasion for a full discussion of the subject, but suffice it to say that the culture of a police organization involves the ideas, values, and habits that shape everyday policing. It includes what is expected and what is tolerated in routine interactions with citizens. The problem in unprofessional departments is that inappropriate behavior is pervasive and tolerated.

To the extent that an EIS involves a serious effort to correct performance problems, it has the potential for altering both the formal and informal norms of the organization. At this point in the development of EISs we can only speculate on their impact on the culture of police organizations. There have been no studies of this issue, and measuring the impact would be extremely difficult. Even in the best of circumstances, changes resulting from an EIS would be slow and subtle and not evident for some time. Measuring changes in officer use of force would be difficult because implementation of the EIS would probably be accompanied by changes in use of force reporting, making the official data not comparable over time.

EISs and Other Police Reforms

EISs are closely related to several other important recent innovations in American policing. The following section discusses these parallels.

EISs and Problem-Oriented Policing

For all practical purposes, EISs are a form of problem-oriented policing (POP). As initially formulated by Herman Goldstein, POP is a process through which police departments disaggregate crime and disorder into specific problems, such as residential burglaries or graffiti, and develop narrowly tailored responses appropriate to each one.[62] In an EIS, officers with performance problems are "the problem." Both POP and an EIS are data driven and rely on systematic data: on crime and disorder in POP, and officer performance in an EIS.

POP uses the SARA model of Scanning, Analysis, Response, and Assessment to identify and address problems. See Figure 5.4 for the application to EIS. Scanning involves a process of determining specific problems. Analysis involves determining the underlying causes of each problem. Response involves developing a plan to deal with the problem.

Figure 5.4   Applying the SARA Model to an EIS

SCANNING

Review performance data in the EIS database

Identify officers with apparent performance problems

ANALYSIS

Performance evaluation of officers identified in the scanning phase

Select officers for intervention

RESPONSE

Intervention: counseling, retraining, etc.

ASSESSMENT

Post-intervention review of performance of officers subject to intervention

And finally, Assessment involves determining whether the response was effective. In an EIS, the scanning process involves reviewing the database and identifying and selecting officers with performance problems. Analysis involves determining the exact nature of each officer's performance problem. Response involves the intervention, and Assessment involves post-intervention monitoring and determining whether the intervention was successful.

EISs and COMPSTAT

EISs are also very similar to the purpose and processes of COMPSTAT programs. One of the most important innovations in policing in recent years, COMPSTAT involves the collection and analysis of systematic data on crime and disorder for the purpose of identifying patterns and then developing appropriate responses in terms of police strategies and tactics. At the same time, it is designed to heighten the accountability of precinct commanders by pinpointing the problems under their command, requiring them to develop the responses, and regularly assessing the effectiveness of their actions.[63]

In a similar way, an EIS provides systematic data on officer performance and requires their supervisors to take the appropriate corrective action. Whereas COMPSTAT looks outward from the department, defining the problem as crime and disorder, EISs look inward, defining the problem as officers with recurring performance problems. The similarity between EISs and COMPSTAT was recognized in the VERA evaluation of the Pittsburgh PARS (its EIS) when it described one key element as modeled after COMPSTAT. The Quarterly COMPSTAR (the term used in Pittsburgh) meetings in Pittsburgh involve a review of officers who have been identified by the PARS. Area commanders make presentations about any officers under their command who have been identified and conclude with a recommendation regarding formal intervention. After a discussion, the chief of police makes a final decision on what course of action to take.[64]

EISs and Risk Management

An EIS is essentially a risk management system. The concept of risk management, which is well developed in the private sector and in medicine, is a process for reducing an organization's exposure to financial loss due to litigation. It involves data collection and analysis to identify the areas of financial risk, to examine the underlying causes of these problems, and then to correct those problems through improved policies, procedures, and training.[65] We discuss risk management in detail in Chapter Seven.

The Effectiveness of EISs

Despite the fact that EISs are widely regarded as an extremely important police accountability tool, there has been surprisingly little research on their effectiveness. Evaluating their effectiveness is complicated by the fact that EISs have multiple dimensions. They have to (1) correctly identify officers with performance problems (and not incorrectly identify officers who do not need corrective intervention); (2) deliver interventions that effectively correct officers' performance problems; (3) interact effectively with other accountability procedures in the department; (4) reduce the overall number of incidents that involve mistreatment of citizens, violations of department policy, or criminal law violations; and as a consequence (5) improve community trust and build legitimacy.

The NIJ Evaluation of Three EISs

An NIJ study of EISs in three police departments found significant reductions in use of force and citizen complaints among officers following intervention. First, the study found that in both Minneapolis and Miami-Dade, the EIS successfully identified officers whose performance records were significantly worse than those of peer officers who had been hired in the same years. In Miami-Dade, officers selected by the department's EIS averaged twice as many use of force reports per year as a comparison group of non-EIS officers, and were almost three times as likely to have ever been suspended. In Minneapolis, officers selected by the early warning system averaged twice as many complaints as their non-EIS peers and were three times as likely to have been suspended.[66]

The successful identification of officers whose disciplinary records are significantly worse than their peers is an important finding. There has been some concern among police officials that an EIS may identify active and productive officers, who, because of their arrest activity, are more likely to use force and receive complaints than less-active officers, and as a consequence deter them from active police work. The term "de-policing" has been used to describe a reduction in effort by police officers because of fear that they will be identified and punished by new accountability measures. The Vera Institute evaluation of the consent decree in Pittsburgh, which included the introduction of an EIS, found no evidence of reduced police activity.[67] A Harvard University study of the Los Angeles Police Department under a consent decree, which included implementing an EIS along with other accountability measures, meanwhile, also found no evidence of de-policing.[68]

The NIJ study found that in both Miami-Dade and Minneapolis, the EIS systems had a positive impact on officers' performance. In Minneapolis, the average number of complaints per year received by EIS officers fell from 1.9 prior to intervention to 0.65 following intervention. In Miami, 27 of the 28 EIS officers had at least one use of force report; following intervention only 14 had a use of force report. Twenty of the 28 officers had four or more complaints prior to intervention, whereas only 9 of the 28 had four or more complaints following intervention.

The nature of the New Orleans Professional Policing Enhancement Program (PPEP) program did not permit a quantitative analysis of EIS outcomes, but it did permit a valuable direct observation of the training class for problem officers. Observation of the class found that officers responded in very different ways to various units of the curriculum and teaching methodologies. Most of the officers expressed open hostility to the PPEP program at some point, referring to it as "politeness school," or "bad boys' class." They were visibly disengaged from units that involved lectures, and in particular lectures about general topics such as the role of the police, stress management, and substance abuse in American society.[69]

At the same time, however, the officers were actively engaged in the course unit that asked them to critique case studies drawn from the department's files. They were clearly knowledgeable about proper police tactics in difficult situations, able to critique what the officers involved did wrong, and noticeably proud of their own expertise. This engagement and sense of professionalism in this component of the class was exhibited by the same officers who had earlier voiced extreme hostility to the PPEP program.[70]

Officers in the PPEP classes were given an opportunity to complete a written evaluation of the class. A total of 26 evaluations from all the classes that had been offered were available for analysis. While the number is small, the responses were very revealing. The officers gave the PPEP classes extremely positively ratings. On a scale of 1–10, they gave it an average rating of 7.0. When the four officers who gave it the lowest possible rating (1) are omitted, the average rating rises to 8.1. These responses are extremely significant in light of the fact that the officers in the observed class openly disparaged the PPEP program. Narrative comments on the evaluation forms also included highly favorable assessments of the class. All of the officers made at least one positive comment about the class. Comments included favorable references to the verbal judo, complaint reduction, and stress reduction components. About three-quarters of the officers also made negative comments, but all were related to the PPEP program in general or the police department and its leadership, and not about the content of the PPEP class itself.[71]

In short, the New Orleans evidence strongly suggests that, despite their openly expressed hostility to the PPEP program at certain moments, officers generally appreciated efforts to help them improve their performance. This finding is consistent with the lack of active opposition to EISs reported by police managers in the PERF survey discussed below.

The Los Angeles Sheriff's Department's PPI System

After becoming fully operational in 1997, the PPI system in the Los Angeles Sheriff's Department was widely regarded as arguably the best EIS in the country. LASD representatives were invited to give presentations about the system at national conferences sponsored by the U.S. Department of Justice and other organizations. Early reports by the Special Counsel to the Los Angeles Sheriff's Department indicate positive outcomes for the PPI system. Among officers subject to Performance Review (PR), the rate of officer-involved shootings dropped from an average of .50 per month before PR to zero following PR. Use of force incidents dropped from an average of 7.11 per month before PR to .98 per month after PR. Finally, personnel complaints dropped from an average of 3.86 to .74 in the same time periods.[72] These are very substantial improvements in police performance, with enormous implications for police-community relations.

In addition, 11 percent of all officers placed on Performance Review left the department within a short period of time. This included 10 retirements, six discharges, one resignation, and one departure for unknown reasons.[73] It is not unreasonable to believe that the PPI influenced these decisions, sending a strong message to the officers that their performance did not meet department expectations and that they might expect future disciplinary problems. It is reasonable to argue that in this respect the PPI had a deterrent effect on misconduct. These departures not only saved the department the immediate expense of conducting a full 2-year performance review but also undoubtedly reduced the risk of future serious misconduct by one or more of these officers.

A Longitudinal Study With Intriguing Results

A longitudinal study of an EIS program in one northeast U.S. police department yielded intriguing results that raise important questions about how to evaluate the impact of EISs and other accountability reforms. The study examined 11 Officer-Civilian Interaction (OCI) School classes over a period of nine years, with pre- and post-OCI School data on complaints, uses of force, and arrests among officers subject to the OCI School and control groups of officers. In each class, both OCI officers and controls experienced declines in all categories of conduct.

Interestingly, the declines were greatest in the initial group of classes and less so in later years. In short, the study found an overall improvement in the conduct of police officers over the course of a decade, but cautioned that "these changes should not be attributed to the OCI School intervention." The authors went on to speculate that the positive changes "may reflect to at least some degree the success of the larger organizational system in regulating officers' behavior," of which the EIS is only one part. This interpretation is rich in its implications and deserves some discussion.[74]

Measuring the impact of an EIS is difficult and may be impossible in a department that is experiencing a number of changes simultaneously. Policing is a complex enterprise and an officer's behavior is affected by many factors simultaneously: changes in the community environment, changes in critical incident policies, reassignment of sergeants, changes in inservice training, changes in internal affairs, the assignment of new commanders, and most important the appointment of a new police chief with different commitments and goals than the previous chief. Beginning with the latter, we can say that a new accountability-minded chief will make many of the other changes. All will in various ways affect officer performance on the street. If we assume that the new chief introduces an EIS along with reorganizing internal affairs, revising certain critical incident policies, and strengthening annual inservice training, how can an evaluation isolate the specific effect of the EIS apart from the other changes? True, it is possible to isolate pre- and post-EIS intervention on those few officers subject to it, but it is highly likely that the other changes will effect change in the conduct of other officers in the same direction. This effect is what the authors of the study just cited seem to suggest. An evaluation of the impact of a consent decree, which has many dimensions, poses similar difficulties.

The Experiences and Perceptions of Police Managers With an EIS

In 2002, the University of Nebraska at Omaha, in collaboration with the Police Executive Research Forum (PERF), conducted a national survey of PERF members regarding their perceptions and experiences with EISs. A total of 135 managers responded to the survey, about 40 percent of whom had experience with an EIS. The responses from more than 50 police managers with direct experience with an EIS represent the most comprehensive assessment of how early intervention systems are operating.[75] The findings were both very positive and surprising in certain important respects.

Police managers overwhelmingly reported that their EIS had some positive impact on the quality of on-the-street police service. Almost half (49 percent) reported a positive impact and 28 percent reported a mixed impact, for a combined total of 77 percent. Perhaps even more important, no manager reported a negative impact on the quality of police service. Some skeptics have suggested that the heightened scrutiny of performance in an EIS might cause "de-policing," where officers reduce their activity level to avoid potential citizen complaints or use of force incidents.[76] No manager in the survey, however, reported that the EIS caused officers to back off and reduce their activity level.

Managers in the survey reported that their EIS had enhanced supervision in their department. Many offered specific examples. One explained that "sergeants have been able to evaluate the strengths and weaknesses of their squad even before meeting with them; they are able to develop a proactive strategy to address personnel and leadership issues." Another explained that it encouraged proactive supervision: "Supervisors pay more attention to what is going on, document all activities more thoroughly, and talk with officers when things might look like a problem." A third added that the "program provides a way for the department to provide nondisciplinary direction and training before the officer becomes a liability to citizens, the department, and him/herself." One manager in the survey confirmed the capability of an EIS to help supervisors familiarize themselves with newly assigned officers, explaining that "there is a lot of movement of personnel, so supervisors often do not know the histories of their officers. The EWS report brings them up to speed in a much more timely fashion."[77]

Several managers commented that the database facilitated a new style of supervision. One, for example, commented that the EIS is "a useful tool to involve supervisors and lieutenants in a nontraditional model of problem solving. It has served to enhance their management skills and help round out their people-interaction skills."[78] The comments by other managers amplified this point, as some explained that the database allows supervisors to talk to officers about specific performance problems and to avoid generalities that might otherwise be dismissed by officers. Finally, by providing systematic data on all officers, managers felt the EIS enhanced fairness. One commented that it "levels the playing field. No one can be accused of playing favorites."

The most surprising finding in the PERF study was the managers' perception of rank-and-file officers' response to their EIS. Contrary to the expectations of many people, the managers did not report significant opposition from rank-and-file officers or from police unions.[79] The negative reactions that did exist primarily involved an initial fear of the unknown and lack of knowledge about the EIS. One manager commented that "the system was met with much cynicism and distrust when first introduced. [But] experience and education has reduced those attitudes." Another observed that "most [officers] no longer believe this system is out to 'get' them, but rather to assist them." Only 16 percent of managers reported any serious opposition from police unions, and there is no record (either from the survey or any other source) of a police union succeeding in blocking the operation of an EIS once it is in place (although in some instances, the union has insisted that development of an EIS is a bargaining issue).[80]

A comment by one manager suggests one possible explanation about the lack of strong rank-and-file resistance. This manager observed that "nothing hurts morale like no action being taken against problem officers." An EIS shows "that problem people can be dealt with." Insofar as an EIS does identify officers with performance problems and leads to some corrective action, other officers will develop a more positive attitude about the department and its commitment to professional standards. And as mentioned earlier, part of the folklore of the police subculture is that peer officers do in fact know who the problem officers are. A contributing factor to officer cynicism is the perception that bad officers are not punished and good performance not rewarded. In this respect, a properly functioning EIS may contribute significantly to the morale of the better officers.

Police managers reported that the major problems with an EIS involved failures in planning and implementation, but not with the basic concept of an EIS. One manager commented that "while the system was crafted appropriately, it was not explained to the officers or the first line supervisors to the extent necessary to make it an understandable and viable system."[81] Along the same lines, another manager complained that department leaders "did not explain the purpose of the program well." Finally, a number of managers felt that the department did not follow through in terms of fully using the potential of their EIS. According to one, "the program does not hold a prominent place in the organization. As a result, no results are provided to commanders as to its effectiveness or benefits." The following section examines some of problems in follow-through that have occurred in some EISs.

In the end, the significant aspect of the PERF survey is the overwhelmingly positive perceptions of police managers toward EISs. There is no evidence that managers question the basic concept of EISs or have found that they are dysfunctional when operating as planned. The PERF survey, of course, involved police managers. To date there has been no equivalent survey of rank-and-file officers or of sergeants regarding their experiences and perceptions of EIS.

Implementing and Managing an EIS

Although EISs have enormous potential as an accountability tool, they are also extremely complex and difficult to both implement and manage. As the Police Executive Research Forum *Guide for Law Enforcement Chief Executives* on EISs makes clear, the chief executive is ultimately responsible for the creation and continuing maintenance of an effective EIS.[82]

In some instances, departments had not in fact implemented the EIS they claimed to have. In its 2002 *Annual Report,* the Pennsylvania State Police described a functioning early intervention system. But when a sexual abuse scandal erupted in 2003, media inquiries revealed that the EIS was still only in the process of being developed.[83] In other cases, the EISs were woefully inadequate by recognized standards. The Miami (Florida) Police Department established one of the first EISs in the early 1980s. A serious corruption and brutality scandal in 2000, however, raised serious questions about whether the system was functioning effectively. Eleven officers were indicted on federal criminal charges, and several were eventually convicted. Some of the officers had substantial histories of misconduct that should have been detected by an EIS. A U.S. Department of Justice investigation concluded that "it is clear that the MPD recognizes that its EWS needs to be improved, and we understand that significant changes to the EWS are contemplated."[84] The system was undermined by a pattern of under-reporting of use of force incidents and a practice of discouraging citizens from filing complaints.

An evaluation of the Albuquerque Police Department by the Police Assessment Resource Center (PARC) found a number of problems with its EIS. The system was managed by a single part-time volunteer. There was already a backlog in entering use of force reports in this relatively new system. In addition, the system functioned through a single computer located in Internal Affairs. As a result, "access to the information in the early warning system is not readily available to APD commanders and managers, except through requests for reports to the volunteer." Moreover, no one in the police department had been trained either to assist or take over from the volunteer in the event of his unavailability or departure. In operation, it was not clear whether commanders met with all officers identified by the EIS, and they did not document what actions they took with regard to those officers.[85]

The Saga of TEAMS II in the Los Angeles Police Department

The saga of the TEAMS (Training Evaluation and Management System) in the Los Angeles Police Department (LAPD) is a disturbing story of a long delay in implementing an EIS. The story is especially disturbing because the LAPD was under intensive public scrutiny following the 1991 beating of Rodney King and the subsequent Christopher Commission report on the department. The Christopher Commission identified a group of 44 officers that had particularly serious performance records and recommended the creation of an EIS to address the problem.[86] Implementation of the TEAMS dragged on for over a decade before finally being completed.

A 1996 report to the Los Angeles Police Commission by Merrick Bobb reported that the LAPD did not then have an operational EIS as recommended by the Christopher Commission and that the TEAMS was "weak and inadequate."[87] The Los Angeles Police Commission then sought and received a $175,000 federal grant to facilitate the implementation of an expanded TEAMS, to be called TEAMS II. In the wake of the 1999 Rampart scandal, however, a subsequent Police Commission report found that TEAMS II was not operational. In fact, the city had not even drawn on the federal grant awarded to implement the system. Finally, in 2001 the Department of Justice initiated a pattern or practice suit against the LAPD. The resulting consent decree directed the department to complete the implementation of TEAMS II. TEAMS II, however, proved to be one of the major reasons the consent decree was not implemented within the 5-year time frame. It was finally fully operational in 2009.[88]

The TEAMS I and II story is particularly disturbing with respect to the possibilities of achieving meaningful accountability measures in a large police department. The ominous implications of the story, in fact, apply not just to EISs but to the full range of related policies and procedures, such as use of force reporting systems, citizen complaint procedures, the review of misconduct reports, and so on.

The Case of the Los Angeles Sheriff's Department's PPI System

As noted earlier, the PPI in the Los Angeles Sheriff's Department has been widely regarded as one of the best EISs in the country. Merrick Bobb, Special Counsel to the LASD and the most knowledgeable outside expert on the department, described it as "without question, the most carefully constructed and powerful management tool for control of police misconduct currently available in the United States."[89] Nonetheless, in early 2003 Bobb published a report identifying serious problems with the management of the PPI. First, crucial performance data were not being entered into the system, and reports that were being sent to it "are often sloppy and error-ridden.[90] Because it relates to the role of external oversight, the original report on the PPI and follow-up reports are covered in detail in Chapter Six. As that discussion makes clear, an EIS is an extremely complex operation that requires continuous management attention.

Conclusion

Early intervention systems are the centerpiece of the new accountability. Properly designed and implemented, EISs have the potential for identifying officers with recurring performance problems and correcting their conduct through well-designed intervention. EISs also have the potential for transforming the culture of a police department and helping to instill new standards of accountability. In Chapter One we discussed the PTSR (Policy, Training, Supervision, Review) framework for the new police accountability. EISs are an important part of both supervision and review. It is a sophisticated mechanism for close supervision of officers, offering a full picture of officers' performance and permitting a comparison with peer officers. An EIS is also part of the review process, as the data permit an analysis of patterns of officer conduct over time and across different geographic units of the department. Properly used, EIS data can also assist the policy and training components of the PTSR framework by identifying department-wide issues that might require changes in formal policy and officer training. Experience to date, however, clearly indicates that EISs are extremely complex mechanisms that are difficult to implement and possibly even harder to maintain over time. They do not operate automatically and require an enormous investment of resources, particularly in terms of management attention. There is evidence that EISs are indeed effective, but the full story of this important innovation remains to be written.

Notes

1   Comments, police chiefs, Justice Department Conference, *Strengthening Police Community Relationships,* June 9–10, 1999.

2   Samuel Walker, *Early Intervention Systems for Law Enforcement Agencies: A Planning and Management Guide* (Washington, DC: Department of Justice, 2003).

3   Herman Goldstein, *Policing a Free Society* (Cambridge, MA: Ballinger, 1977), 171. Goldstein cited an experimental (but short-lived) program by Hans Toch in the 1970s in which peer officers counseled Oakland, California, police officers with records of use of force incidents. Hans Toch, James Douglas Grant, and Raymond T. Galvin, *Agents of Change: A Study in Police Reform* (New York: Wiley, 1975).

4   Toch et al., *Agents of Change.*

5   U.S. Commission on Civil Rights, *Who Is Guarding the Guardians?* (Washington, DC: Commission on Civil Rights, 1981), 81–86.

6   U.S. Department of Justice, *Investigation of the Seattle Police Department* (December 16, 2011), 21.

7   Bruce Porter, *The Miami Riot of 1980* (Lexington, MA: Lexington Books, 1984). U.S. Commission on Civil Rights, *Confronting Racial Isolation in Miami* (Washington, DC: Government Printing Office, 1982).

8   Christopher Commission, *Report of the Independent Commission on the Los Angeles Police Department* (Los Angeles: The Christopher Commission, 1991). Available at http://www.parc.info.

9   Ibid., 40–8.

10   James G. Kolts, *The Los Angeles County Sheriff's Department* (Los Angeles: County of Los Angeles, 1992). Available at http://www.parc.info.

11 U.S. Department of Justice, *Principles for Promoting Police Integrity* (Washington, DC: U.S. Department of Justice, 2001). Available at http://www.ncjrs.org, NCJ 186189. Samuel Walker and Morgan Macdonald, "An Alternative Remedy for Police Misconduct: A Model State Pattern or Practice Statute," *George Mason University Civil Rights Law Review* 19 (Summer 2009): 479–552.

12 Robert C. Davis, Christopher W. Ortiz, Nicole J. Henderson, Joel Miller, and Michelle K. Massie, *Turning Necessity Into Virtue: Pittsburgh's Experience With a Federal Consent Decree* (New York: Vera Institute, 2002), 45–7. Available at http://www.ncjrs.org, NCJ 200251.

13 Commission on Accreditation for Law Enforcement Agencies, *Standards for Law Enforcement Agencies*, 4th ed., Standard 35.1.15, "Personnel Early Warning System" (2001).

14 International Association of Chiefs of Police, *Protecting Civil Rights: A Leadership Guide for State, Local, and Tribal Law Enforcement* (Washington, DC: IACP, 2006), chap. 3, "Developing an Early Intervention Strategy."

15 Comment, Commander in charge of the EIS in an unnamed police department. Early Intervention Systems, State of the Art Conference, Phoenix, AZ, January 2003.

16 Ibid.

17 San Diego Police Department, *Enhancing Cultures of Integrity: Building Law Enforcement Early Intervention Systems Technical Assistance Guide* (Washington, DC: Department of Justice, 2011).

18 International Association of Chiefs of Police, *Protecting Civil Rights*, 53.

19 International Association of Chiefs of Police, *Building Integrity and Reducing Drug Corruption in Police Departments* (Arlington, VA: IACP, 1989).

20 Herman Goldstein, *Police Corruption* (Washington, DC: The Police Foundation, 1975). Albert J. Reiss, *The Police and the Public* (New Haven: Yale University Press, 1971).

21 Robin Shepard Engel, *How Police Supervisory Styles Influence Patrol Officer Behavior* (Washington, DC; Department of Justice, 2003).

22 Peter Finn and Julie Esselman Tomz, *Developing a Law Enforcement Stress Program for Officers and Their Families* (Washington: Government Printing Office, 1997), 23–26. Available at http://www.ncjrs.org, NCJ163175.

23 San Diego Police Department, *Enhancing Cultures of Integrity: Building Law Enforcement Early Intervention Systems. Technical Assistance Guide* (Washington, DC: Department of Justice, 2011).

24 Frank Landy, *Performance Appraisal in Police Departments* (Washington, DC: The Police Foundation, 1977).

25 International Association of Chiefs of Police, *Protecting Civil Rights*, 58.

26 Gary Stix, "Bad Apple Picker: Can a Neural Network Help Find Problem Cops?" *Scientific American* (December 1994): 44–5. Bernard Cohen and Jan

M. Chaiken, *Police Background Characteristics and Performance* (Lexington, MA: Lexington Books, 1973).

27 A good description of these two systems is available in Special Counsel Merrick J. Bobb, *16th Semiannual Report* (Los Angeles: Special Counsel, 2003), 68–72. Available at http://www.parc.info.

28 Samuel Walker, Geoffrey P. Alpert, and Dennis J. Kenney, *Early Warning Systems: Responding to the Problem Police Officer* (Washington, DC: Department of Justice, 2001).

29 "The Boston Police Department May Be Paying the Price for Letting a Program to Help Troubled Cops Lapse," *Commonwealth Magazine*, January 15, 2013.

30 Samuel Walker, *Police Accountability: The Role of Citizen Oversight* (Belmont: Wadsworth, 2001), 121–35.

31 *Allen v. City of Oakland* (2003). The consent decree is available at http://www.oaklandpolice.com.

32 Christy Lopez, *Disorderly (mis)Conduct: The Problem with 'Contempt of Cop' Arrests*, Issue Brief (Washington, DC: American Constitution Society, 2010).

33 Merrick Bobb, *16th Semiannual Report* (Los Angeles: Police Assessment Research Center, 2003).

34 Walker, Alpert, and Kenney, *Early Warning Systems: Responding to the Problem Police Officer.*

35 U.S. Department of Justice, *Investigation of the Seattle Police Department*, 23.

36 *United States v. Cincinnati*, Memorandum of Agreement, Sec. IA (A), http://www.usdoj.gov/crt/split.

37 Peer group analysis is discussed in Lorie A. Fridell et al., *By the Numbers: Analyzing Race Data* (Washington, DC: Police Executive Research Forum, 2004), 143–59.

38 City of Spokane, *Draft Report of the City of Spokane Use of Force Commission* (Spokane: City of Spokane, 2012), 24.

39 Merrick J. Bobb, *16th Semiannual Report* (Los Angeles: Police Assessment Research Center, 2003), 39, 42. Available at http://www.parc.info.

40 The administrative burdens are evident from the reports on the PPI in the Los Angeles Sheriff's Department. Bobb, *16th Semiannual Report*. Michael J. Gennaco, Office of Independent Review, *Tenth Annual Report* (Los Angeles: Los Angeles Sheriff's Department, 2012), 106 [and earlier reports].

41 Fridell et al., *By the Numbers.*

42 The comprehensive discussion of traffic stop data sets and the problems in interpreting each one is in Fridell et al., *By the Numbers.*

43 Peer group analysis or "internal benchmarking" is discussed in Fridell et al., *By the Numbers*, chap. 7, 143–59.

44 *United States v. Pittsburgh*, Consent Decree, Paragraph 20-b, http://www.usdoj.gov/crt/split.

45 Pittsburgh Police Bureau, *Auditor's Eighteenth Quarterly Report, Quarter Ending February 16, 2002*, 18.

46 Michael J. Gennaco, Office of Independent Review, *Seventh Annual Report* (Los Angeles: Los Angeles Sheriff's Department, 2009), 25–34.

47 Author Walker, personal observations. Walker, Alpert, and Kenney, *Early Warning Systems: Responding to the Problem Police Officer*.

48 Ibid.

49 Miami-Dade Police Department, Employee Identification System. Excerpts in Walker, *Early Identification Systems for Law Enforcement Agencies*, Appendix C.

50 This topic was the subject of a working conference cosponsored by the Austin, TX, Police Department and this author, March 3, 2004.

51 Discussion, Early Intervention System State of the Art Conference, Phoenix, AZ, February 2003.

52 Davis et al., *Turning Necessity Into Virtue.*

53 Samuel Walker, Stacy Osnick Milligan, and Anna Berk, *Strategies for Intervening With Officers Through Early Intervention Systems: A Guide for Front-line Supervisors* (Washington, DC: Police Executive Research Forum, 2006), 17.

54 Davis et al., *Turning Necessity Into Virtue.*

55 Walker et al., *Strategies for Intervening With Officers Through Early Intervention Systems*, 21.

56 Pittsburgh Police Bureau, *Monitor's Eighteenth Quarterly Report, Quarter Ending February 16, 2002*, 21.

57 Robin Sheppard Engel, *How Police Supervisory Styles Influence Patrol Officer Behavior* (Washington, DC: U.S. Department of Justice, 2003). Available at http://www.ncjrs.org, NCJ 194078.

58 Walker et al., *Strategies for Intervening With Officers Through Early Intervention Systems*, 28.

59 These quotes and a full discussion of the survey are from Walker, *Early Intervention Systems for Law Enforcement Agencies*, chap. 4.

60 Los Angeles Police Department, *10th Quarterly Report of the Independent Monitor*, 10. Par. 51c. Available at http://www.lapdonline.org.

61 Steve Herbert, "Police Subculture Revisited," *Criminology* 36 (no. 2, 1998): 343–369.

62 Herman Goldstein, "Improving Policing: A Problem-Oriented Approach," *Crime and Delinquency* 25 (1979): 236–58. Michael S. Scott, *Problem-Oriented Policing: Reflections on the First 20 Years* (Washington, DC: U.S. Department of Justice, 2000). Available at http://www.ncjrs.org.

63 James J. Willis, Stephen D. Mastrofski, David Weisburd, and Rosann Greenspan, *Compstat and Organizational Change in the Lowell Police Department* (Washington, DC: The Police Foundation, 2004).

64 Davis et al., *Turning Necessity Into Virtue*, 45–7.

65 Carol Archbold, *Police Accountability, Risk Management, and Legal Advising* (New York: LFB Scholarly Publishing, 2004). Michel Crouhy, Dan Galai, and Robert Mark, *Risk Management* (New York: McGraw-Hill, 2001).

66 Walker, Alpert, and Kenney, *Early Warning Systems: Responding to the Problem Police Officer.*

67 Davis et al., *Turning Necessity Into Virtue.*

68 Christopher Stone et al., *Policing Los Angeles Under a Consent Decree: The Dynamics of Change at the LAPD* (Cambridge: Harvard University, 2009).

69 Walker, Alpert, and Kenney, *Early Warning Systems: Responding to the Problem Police Officer.*

70 Direct observation by author Walker. Walker, Alpert, and Kenney, *Early Warning Systems: Responding to the Problem Police Officer.*

71 Walker, Alpert, and Kenney, *Early Warning Systems: Responding to the Problem Police Officer.*

72 Special Counsel Merrick J. Bobb, *15th Semiannual Report* (Los Angeles: Police Assessment Research Center, 2002), 68. Available at http://www.parc.info.

73 Ibid., 64.

74 Robert E. Worden, Moonsun Kim, Christopher J. Harris, Mary Anne Pratte, Shelagh E. Dorn, and Shelly S. Hyland, "Intervention With Problem Officers: An Outcome Evaluation of an EIS Intervention," *Criminal Justice and Behavior* 40 (2013), 409–37.

75 The survey is reported in detail in Walker, *Early Intervention Systems for Law Enforcement Agencies,* chap. 4.

76 See the discussion of de-policing in Stone et al., *Policing Los Angeles Under a Consent Decree,* and in Davis et al., *Turning Necessity Into Virtue.*

77 Walker, *Early Intervention Systems for Law Enforcement Agencies,* 78.

78 Ibid.

79 In Seattle, the police union originally demanded that the EIS be subject to collective bargaining or meet and confer procedure, which substantially delayed its implementation. Author interviews with Seattle officials.

80 Walker, *Early Intervention Systems for Law Enforcement Agencies,* 81.

81 Ibid., 80.

82 Samuel Walker, Stacy Osnick Milligan, and Anna Berke, *Supervision and Intervention Within Early Intervention Systems: A Guide for Law Enforcement Chief Executives* (Washington, DC: Police Executive Research Forum, 2005).

83 Pennsylvania State Police, *Annual Report* (2002), 19.

84 U.S. Department of Justice, *Investigation of the Miami Police Department, Letter to Alejandro Vilarello,* March 19, 2003, 19. Available at http://www.usdoj.gov.crt.split.

85 Richard Jerome, *Police Oversight Project. City of Albuquerque* (Los Angeles: Police Assessment Resource Center, 2002), 80–81. Available at http://www.parc.info.

86 The chronology of events is very well documented in Los Angeles Police Commission, *Report of the Rampart Independent Review Panel* (Los Angeles: Los Angeles Police Commission, 2000), 136–62 and Appendix B, 217–19. Available at http://www.lapdonline.org. Christopher Commission, *Report of the Independent Commission on the Los Angeles Police Department* (Los Angeles: City of Los Angeles, 1991). Available at http://www.parc .info.

87 Merrick Bobb, *Five Years Later: A Report to the Los Angeles Police Commission* (Los Angeles: Police Assessment Research Center, 1996). Available at http://www.parc.info.

88 *United States v. the City of Los Angeles,* Consent Decree (2000). The consent decree is available at http://www.usdoj.gov/crt/split.

89 Merrick J. Bobb, *11th Semiannual Report* (Los Angeles: Police Assessment Research Center, 1999), 55. Available at http://www.parc.info.

90 Bobb, *16th Semiannual Report,* 44, 49.

SIX

External and Internal Review

Review: Becoming a Learning Organization

Review of police operations, including policies, training, and supervision, is the fourth component of the PTSR framework described in Chapter One. Police history, and even the recent history of police accountability measures, tells us that many important innovations in policing have simply faded away.[1] Ensuring that accountability innovations function as intended and do not wither away is one of the functions of the review process. Review can be done by external and/or internal procedures.

The bulk of the discussion of external review in this chapter covers police auditors, which are a form of external citizen oversight of the police. Internal review, in the sense used in this book, originated with the Firearms Discharge Review Board (FDRB), which was part of the pioneering 1972 New York City Police Department policy on deadly force.[2] Similar review procedures for officer-involved shootings are now fairly common in American policing, and the practice of reviewing critical incidents has grown and expanded in recent years. Review is an important part of the way a police department becomes a learning organization, as we discussed in Chapter One. Most important, it is a process by which a department examines particular incidents or patterns of incidents to determine whether there is anything that can be learned in order to change policy, training, or supervision.

Both internal and external review have organizational change as their overall goal. Mike Gennaco, head of the Office of Independent Review (OIR) in the Los Angeles Sheriff's Department, explains the strategy guiding his office:

> an oversight body *must look beyond the particular cases of misconduct to systemic issues implicating policy and training* [emphasis added]. [The] OIR endeavors to use individual cases to identify ambiguities in policy, laxity in enforcement, and deficiencies in training. Whenever policies and practices can be reformed to eliminate potential civil rights violations and future liability, it will directly benefit the people of Los Angeles County.[3]

Police Auditors as External Review

External citizen oversight of the police has been one of the principal demands of civil rights activists since the 1960s. This demand has usually been for a civilian review board, an independent agency that would investigate citizen complaints against the police. In the 1990s, a new form of citizen oversight emerged: the police auditor.[4] This chapter argues that the police auditor is more likely to be an effective form of citizen oversight than the traditional civilian review board (see the discussion in Chapter Four) because as a part of a comprehensive PTSR framework it has greater potential for changing the police organization and making long-term improvements in a police department.

Police auditors have two special capabilities that enhance their ability to promote organizational change. First, as full-time government officials they have the authority to probe deeply into departmental policies and procedures with an eye toward correcting them and reducing future misconduct. They have the authority to gather information about a police department that neither the news media nor academic scholars have (unless, of course, they have special permission as part of a research project). Second, as permanent agencies they can follow up on issues and determine whether or not prior recommendations for change have been implemented. The capacity for sustained follow-up addresses not only the historic limitation of blue-ribbon commissions (as discussed in Chapter Two),[5] but also one of the most serious problems in police accountability: how to ensure the implementation of recommended reforms and sustain reform over the long term.

The police auditor originated in 1993 with the creation of the San Jose Independent Police Auditor (IPA), the Special Counsel to the Los Angeles Sheriff's Department, and the Seattle Police Auditor.[6] The Washington, D.C., Office of Police Complaints (OPC) and the New York City Civilian Complaint Review Board (CCRB) engage in police auditor *functions* even though they are primarily citizen complaint review agencies. The Washington OPC, for example, has made a number of policy recommendations to the police department.[7] Thus, it is important to distinguish between the formal structure of police auditors and the auditing function.

When they first appeared, police auditors were a political compromise, designed to satisfy community activists with some form of citizen oversight of the police, but as an alternative to a citizen review board, which police unions have bitterly opposed.[8] Even after being established, some police auditors have suffered from a lack of political support, and a few no longer exist. The Philadelphia Integrity and Accountability Office (IAO), created as part of the settlement of a civil suit against the police department, was allowed to lapse. The mayor of Omaha fired the Public Safety Auditor in 2006 and she has not been replaced, even though the ordinance creating the officer is still in effect.[9]

Police auditors should not be confused with court-appointed *monitors*, which are part of the settlements of federal pattern or practice suits against police departments. As the term is used in this book, a police monitor is an agent of the court, its investigating authority is limited to the specific terms of the consent decree, and it has a fixed life span as set by the consent decree or memorandum of agreement, which is typically five years.[10] Police auditors, on the other hand, are permanent agencies, free to continue their work indefinitely, and are not limited in terms of the issues they can investigate.[11]

Authority and Structure

The authority and structure of existing police auditors differ in certain respects.[12] Most are established by ordinance, as is the case with the San Jose Independent Police Auditor (IPA) and the Denver Office of the Independent Monitor (OIM). Both are municipal agencies independent of the police department. The Special Counsel (SC) to the Los Angeles Sheriff's Department (LASD) exists by authority of a contract with the

County of Los Angeles Board of Supervisors. The Office of Independent Review (OIR) for the sheriff's department, however, is an internal unit within the sheriff's department. Although not independent in a formal sense, the OIR has been given broad freedom of action by the sheriff through its first decade of operation. It is remarkable that the LASD has two forms of oversight, and this indicates that in a law enforcement agency of 8,000 sworn officers there is enough business to keep two well-staffed agencies busy. The Seattle Office of Professional Accountability (OPA) was created as a hybrid outsider–insider office. It is a part of the Seattle Police Department but must be staffed by a non-sworn person with the equivalent rank of assistant police chief.

Functions and Activities

Police auditors perform several different functions, although not all auditors perform all of them.

Auditing the Complaint Process

Most police auditors audit or monitor the police department's citizen complaint process. This includes reviewing the procedures by which the department publicizes the complaint process, receives complaints, and records and classifies complaints, as well as reviewing patterns of complaints. The Denver Office of the Independent Monitor, for example, monitors the Denver police complaint process with respect to patterns in citizen complaints and discipline. Particularly important, it tracks data on the timeliness of the disposition of citizen complaints. Long delays in the process have been a pervasive national problem. In 2010, for example, it recommended changing the role of the Disciplinary Review Board was accepted, recommended changes to ensure consistency in data being entered in the police department's internal affairs database, and obtained policy changes to prevent police officers stopped for drunk driving from receiving preferential treatment.[13]

Auditing Police Operations

Most police auditors also audit basic police operations, and it is in this capacity that they have the greatest potential for enhancing police accountability. The Special Counsel to the Los Angeles Sheriff's

Department has, for example, audited civil suits against the department, use of force trends, the canine unit, foot pursuits by officers, and many other issues. The Denver Office of the Independent Monitor, meanwhile, has worked with the Denver Police Department on its Crisis Intervention Team, its policy on handling people with "excited delirium," the reporting and tracking of use of force incidents, and others.[14]

Policy Review

The audits of the complaint process and of police operations described above led to recommendations for changes in police policy. *Policy review,* as it is called, is potentially the most important accountability function that any citizen oversight agency can perform because it is directed toward organizational change that hopefully will prevent future misconduct.[15] Policy review is the primary function of the Special Counsel to the LASD, and it has made innumerable policy recommendations since 1993. The Washington, D.C., Office of Police Complaints has made far fewer, but policy review is only one of its official functions. Between its creation in 1993 and 2011, the San Jose Independent Police Auditor made a total of 150 recommendations, over 70 percent of which were accepted by the San Jose Police Department.[16]

Policy recommendations are not binding on the police chief or the sheriff. For that reason, critics argue that the auditor model is "toothless." To put the issue in perspective, the recommendations of citizen complaint review agencies (see Chapter Four) regarding the disposition of complaints are also not binding. Policy review has other important values, however. The detailed reports that accompany police recommendations provide openness and transparency, and inform the public about the details of police operations, providing the basis for an informed debate over controversial issues. Too often, public controversies are uninformed by facts and consist of little more than angry charges and counter charges in the media. LASD Special Counsel Merrick Bobb explains that

> The dialogue between us [the LASD Special Counsel] and the Department has been primarily an exchange of views about cause and effect—we tend to emphasize the degree of management control and the LASD emphasizes the danger of the environment in which Century deputies operate. At least, that is true of the *public* dialogue between us. Our private dialogue has been different and more earnest in tone, with the focus mainly on efforts by management at Century and in the Department as a whole to reduce force used by deputies at the station.[17]

As permanent institutions, police auditors are a major improvement over the traditional blue-ribbon commission in terms of following up on important issues. As we noted in Chapter Two, blue-ribbon commissions dissolve after delivering their final report. They have no capacity to monitor whether their recommendations were implemented. Police auditors, on the other hand, can revisit an issue several times. The Special Counsel to the LASD, for example, not only tracks civil suits on a regular basis but has done follow-up reports on innumerable issues. Later in this chapter we will illustrate the value of follow-up reports in the cases of the LASD Century Station, a troubled precinct station, and on the operations of the LASD's early intervention system.

Community Outreach

One of the long-standing criticisms of American police departments has been that they are closed bureaucracies that provide little information about their activities and are hostile toward critics and citizen complainants in particular. The community outreach function of police auditors is designed to overcome this problem. Outreach activities include meeting with community groups, particularly those with historic problems with the police; providing information about how to file a complaint; and listening to community concerns about the police department, and in particular about police conduct issues that need to be addressed. Because the auditor's office is independent of the police department, it has greater credibility with community groups than do representatives of the police department.

The San Jose Independent Police Auditor in 2011 conducted 96 events related to people of color, immigrants, and agencies that serve those communities; 65 events related to teenagers; and activities related to homeless people and people with mental health issues. The IPA also issued a revised version of its booklet on police relations with juveniles, *A Student's Guide to Police Practices,* with detailed advice to young people on their responsibilities in dealing with police officers.[18] The Seattle OPA sponsored a similar booklet, *Respect: Voices and Choices,* published in eight languages other than English.[19]

Contributing to Transparency

As we have already indicated, police auditors contribute to greater openness and transparency for the police departments they serve. The historic closed and secretive nature of American police organizations has been a combination of two factors: the inherent nature of all bureaucracies to be self-protective in the face of outside inquiry, and the unique tradition of the police subculture. Community policing, it should be noted, is designed to overcome this problem. Until relatively recently, it has often been difficult for outsiders, including even responsible public officials, to obtain information on police operations.

Police auditors contribute to greater openness and transparency in several ways. The community outreach activities described above are one important activity. All police auditors issue public reports that provide varying degrees of detail about the police department they are responsible for. The reports of both the LASD Special Counsel and the OIR are notable for their wealth of detail about the operations of the Sheriff's Department, its problems, and what action is being taken to correct those problems. The Denver Office of the Independent Monitor annually reports on policy issues that are being investigated, along with updates on previous policy issues. The Boise Community Ombudsman has issued a series of detailed reports on controversial incidents (e.g., shootings, sexual assault investigations) that separate the facts from the rumors and misunderstandings, and include recommendations for changes in police operations where appropriate.[20] The OIR in the LASD has also issued special reports on particularly controversial incidents.[21] The reports of the New York City Civilian Complaint Review Board (CCRB), by comparison, contain abundant statistics about citizen complaints, but apart from occasional policy review reports provide little information about police operations that are of great concern to the community.[22]

Case Study: A New Standard in Openness on Police Discipline

Police disciplinary procedures have historically been secret. Either as a matter of practice or police officers' union contract, departments have not disclosed whether or not an officer in a certain incident was disciplined or the nature of the discipline imposed. This secrecy contrasts sharply with the openness of discipline in other professions. The disbarment or suspension of an attorney is generally public information across the country, and the public is informed about the act that led to the disciplinary action, and in the case of suspension the length of time involved. Similar data is not publicly available, and as a consequence it is not possible for the public or researchers to know what the "going rate" of punishment, for example, for a charge of excessive force that did not result in injury.[23]

The lack of openness or transparency with regard to discipline has long been a source of discontent among local civil rights activists who charge that their police department does not punish officers for serious misconduct. Police department secrecy only contributes to this perception of the police and undermines trust and legitimacy.

The most notable exception to this rule is the LASD Office of Independent Review, which regularly publishes data on disciplinary actions. The OIR's *Tenth Annual Report* provides detailed information of sworn and non-sworn personnel who had left the department facing either criminal charges or discipline for violating department policy. Twelve deputies left facing criminal charges (6 resigned, 5 were discharged, and 1 was discharged but reinstated). The nature of the criminal charge was listed for each officer. The report provides the same information for 26 deputies who left the department for violations of department policy. In addition, the report provided lengthy, detailed narrative descriptions of three of these cases, summarizing the alleged misconduct, the OIR recommendation, the result of the LASD's internal investigation, the disciplinary actions taken, and other information.[24] The regular OIR reports of this nature are the most detailed picture we have of the disciplinary process in any law enforcement agency.

Case Studies of Police Auditors in Action

The Special Counsel to the Los Angeles Sheriff's Department

The Special Counsel to the Los Angeles Sheriff's Department is arguably the most successful citizen oversight agency in the United States. Over the course of 20 years, it has established a very creditable record of investigating a wide range of issues related to police accountability, identifying problems that need correcting, making recommendations for change, and then monitoring the implementation of those recommendations. Perhaps most important, the Special Counsel's office is one citizen oversight agency that has been able to present some evidence of its effectiveness.[25]

The Special Counsel operates as an independent agency under a series of fixed-term contracts with the Los Angeles County Board of Supervisors. He hires his own staff, conducts investigations, and publishes semiannual reports. By mid-2013, it had issued 31 semiannual reports, which collectively provide a more detailed picture of LASD operations than is available about any other law enforcement agency in the United States. Merrick Bobb, who began his career in police oversight on the staff of the Christopher Commission, has served as the Special Counsel since its inception, and was also the founder and director of the Police Assessment Resource Center (PARC), a private, nonprofit organization that has emerged as an important organization in the field of police accountability.

The original mandate of the Special Counsel was to reduce the costs of civil litigation over misconduct by the Sheriff's Department, which had been identified by the 1992 Kolts investigation as a serious problem.[26] Bobb has taken a very broad interpretation of the Special Counsel's mandate and addressed a wide range of issues within the LASD that might impact civil litigation, directly or indirectly.

The Case of the Century Station

The Special Counsel's reports on the LASD's Century Station is one of the best examples of the contribution a police auditor can make in terms of investigating a problem, making recommendations for change, and then revisiting the issue to assess whether the recommendations were implemented and the status of the original problem. At the time of the initial investigation, the Century Station was a troubled precinct in the LASD. The area, in impoverished South Central Los Angeles, was marked by high levels of violent crime, and a very high number of officer-involved shooting compared with other LASD stations (3 times as many as any other station in 1995 and 1996).[27]

The Special Counsel's 1998 report concluded that the high number of officer-involved shootings was not the result of a few bad officers or an inevitable product of the high-crime rate in the neighborhood. Instead, the shooting problem was more the result of serious management deficiencies that could be corrected. The problems included the concentration of young and inexperienced officers assigned to the station; the youth and inexperience of many sergeants; and a ratio of sergeants to officers of 1 to 20 or even 25, which far exceeded the LASD's own recommended standard of 1 to 8. The LASD also imposed a very heavy training burden on the station, with as many as 30 new officers assigned to it at any one time. At times, new officers were being trained by officers with fewer than two years of experience of their own. The station suffered from a high turnover of officers at all ranks, in part because of the bad reputation of the station and the feeling of so many officers that they would be stigmatized if they remained there too long. Finally, only a few officers spoke Spanish despite the fact that an estimated half of the community's population spoke only Spanish.[28]

The Special Counsel's analysis of officer-involved shootings identified a number of management-related factors. They included the practice of partners splitting up during foot pursuits, with the resulting loss of communication; the number of shootings related to vehicle pursuits and foot pursuits; shootings by trainee officers; and an insufficient number of officers who would be best qualified to be Field Training Officers (FTOs).

The LASD responded to the Special Counsel's report and recommendations by assigning a new commander to the station; having lieutenants spend more time in the field, responding to serious force incidents; and having supervisors make greater use of positive reinforcement toward officer behavior rather than punitive discipline. The result was a dramatic decline in officer-involved shootings, from 14 in 1997 to 1 in 1999 and 4 in 2000. But when the Special Counsel revisited the Century Station in 2002 it found that many of the old problems had reappeared. Officer-involved shootings returned to their old high levels, with 12 in 2001, in part because the LASD had failed to maintain many of the important reforms.[29] "The captains and other supervisors responsible for the improvements in the Century Station," moreover, "had moved on," and their replacements did not maintain the same level of attention to shootings.[30]

Two important lessons emerge from the Century Station experience. The first is that external oversight can make a significant difference in policing, with the time, resources, and outsiders' perspective to study a problem; identify the underlying causes; and make recommendations for change. As explained in Chapter One, this process is analogous to the SARA model used in problem-oriented policing. The second lesson is how fragile reforms can be in policing. Improvements were undermined not by evil intent but by a combination of neglect, a failure of top commanders to ensure continuity, and to a certain extent the silent operation of traditional personnel procedures. The erosion of reforms in the Century Station probably offers a general lesson for all police departments. Perhaps the most important lesson is the role the Special Counsel can play, through its institutionalized auditing function, to monitor important accountability-related reforms and ensure that they are maintained.

Monitoring the LASD's Early Intervention System

The fragility of significant reforms and the consequent need for continuous oversight are also evident in the Special Counsel's reports on the LASD's early intervention system. The Personnel Performance Index (PPI), noted in Chapter Five, was widely recognized as perhaps the best EIS in the country, and cited as a model for other departments to emulate.

In 2003 the Special Counsel found that the PPI was not operating effectively. Officer performance data were not being entered in a timely fashion (with delays often as long as 6 months), some citizen complaint data were not entered into the system, many reports were incomplete or contained errors (more than half of the incident reports submitted were being rejected for reasons of quality), and some commanders were not even aware of the capabilities of the PPI. Some, in fact, did not even know about its existence, and one even created a small tracking system on his precinct computer.[31]

The Special Counsel's report was extremely embarrassing to the LASD and, presumably, provoked actions to bring the PPI back up to its full potential. A follow-up report found that by 2004 the error rate in incident reports had been reduced to 10 percent. The percentage of use of force report packages without the required synopses fell from 52 percent in 1999 to zero in 2003. Some additional personnel were assigned to help reduce the backlog in entering data. The Special Counsel praised these "commendable improvements" but concluded that the LASD still "falls short" of using the PPI as intended.[32] The LASD Office of Independent Review (discussed below) reviewed aspects of the PPI several years later and found that continuing monitoring was necessary. In 2011, for example, it found that use of force and citizen complaint reports (referred to as "packages") were as much as 11 months late in being entered into the PPI. OIR recommendations regarding staffing issues and the development of an electronic data system succeeded in eliminating the backlog.[33]

The Special Counsel reports on the LASD PPI system dramatize the critical role of institutionalized review in policing. An early intervention system is a critical element of the new police accountability, yet the LASD had allowed the system to decline in several very important respects. These problems occurred not through bad intent, but were the result of problems that are almost inherent in a large police department: the sheer enormity of the task of entering accurate data into the PPI in a timely fashion and budget problems that reduced the number of data entry personnel.

In passing, it is worth pointing out that the delays and quality problems with the report packages for the PPI have enormous implications for all early intervention systems. As we noted in Chapter Five, EISs are extremely complex administrative tools. Maintaining timeliness and quality are major challenges for police departments that regularly face budget problems and where administrative tasks typically take second place to the always politically important demands of keeping police officers on the street.[34]

The LASD Office of Independent Review

In 2001, LASD Sheriff Lee Baca took the extraordinary step of creating the Office of Independent Review (OIR), giving the LASD a second auditor, paralleling the work of the Special Counsel. With a staff of several attorneys, the OIR has much the same mandate as the Special Counsel: to examine the LASD's policies and procedures, make recommendations for change, and make public reports about its findings.[35] As discussed earlier, the OIR's reports on discipline cases set a new standard of openness for this generally secretive subject.

The OIR's methodology often involves beginning with a specific incident, such as a citizen complaint, a lawsuit, or controversial occurrence. OIR staff review the quality of the LASD's internal investigations for thoroughness and fairness, and look for policy failures that need correcting. By the end of its second year, the OIR had reviewed more than 300 cases.[36] The review of individual cases often leads to larger policy issues that need to be addressed. In one of the first important investigations, the OIR began with a false arrest suit involving an officer assigned to the LASD's community policing program. It found that officers in the program essentially operated with minimal day-to-day supervision and no clear policy about surveillance of citizens. Many officers named in the lawsuit had never been trained in proper surveillance techniques, and officers would gather in a fast-food store parking lot and decide what to do that night. As a result of the OIR's report, the LASD developed a new policy on surveillance and provided training for the community policing unit officers, conducted in part by OIR staff.[37]

Reflecting on its initial experiences, the OIR explained that it "has been present long enough to have seen internal investigations go through the entire cycle, from inception through the decision-making and grievance process." As a result, the staff "has begun to learn the challenges and influential circumstances that can affect outcomes differently at the different stages. In particular, OIR has created checks to ensure that the principled decisions are not undermined by last-minute developments or hasty settlements that are reached behind closed doors."[38] In addition to identifying problems and undertaking investigations, the OIR "rolls out" to individual force incidents. An OIR attorney is on call at all times and receives immediate notification of major force incidents. Upon arriving at the scene, the OIR attorney seeks to determine as quickly as possible whether the incident involves potential problems that merit further attention.[39]

In passing, we should note that roll outs to critical incidents are practiced by a number of police departments and external review agencies, including the Los Angeles Police Department, the Denver Office of the Independent Monitor, and the Boise Ombudsman. Having an independent set of eyes and ears at the scene of an officer-involved shooting, to gather facts immediately and to prevent officers from "huddling" to create a common story about the incident, is an important accountability procedure.

In another important finding, the OIR also discovered that in a number of misconduct cases the LASD did not follow through and actually implement the disciplinary action it had decided on. The department had a practice of reaching "settlement agreements" in cases that called for some discipline short of termination. These agreements with the employee often include a requirement of remedial action such as alcohol counseling, anger management, leadership school, retraining, and so on. The OIR discovered, however, that the LASD had no effective system for ensuring officer compliance with the agreed-on terms. An audit of 19 randomly selected settlement agreements found that 9 had either no compliance with the required remedial action or no documentation of compliance.[40]

In an interesting development, the OIR in 2011 extended its auditing activities to the Los Angeles County Probation Department. Its activities included addressing hiring standards, employee misconduct, disciplinary practices, and other issues.[41] This development suggested that the practice of police auditing served as a useful model for correctional agencies.

Summary: The Los Angeles Sheriff's Department

To sum up the activity of the Special Counsel and the Office of Independent Review, no other law enforcement agency in the United

States is subject to such close scrutiny by outside investigators as is the LASD. What is particularly significant is that both auditors have found serious problems in a variety of different aspects of the department's operations and, more seriously, the recurring problem of the department's failure to follow through on actions and programs it has undertaken. This latter point highlights the need for continuing external oversight.

It is necessary, however, to comment on the situation with the Los Angeles County Jail, which is the responsibility of the LASD. After many years of problems, the conditions in the jail reached crisis proportions in 2012. Both the Special Counsel and the OIR have investigated and written reports on the jail over the years.[42] Readers can properly ask why their oversight has not corrected the problems. This book responds that, given the size of the jail population (the largest in the country) and the pervasive substance abuse and mental health problems among jail inmates, together with the antiquated central jail facility, the Los Angeles jail is probably unmanageable. A resolution of the recurring problems probably requires new facilities and a significant commitment of resources to substance abuse and mental health treatment programs by the county.

The San Jose Independent Police Auditor

The San Jose Independent Police Auditor (IPA) is an independent municipal agency with three major responsibilities: to receive citizen complaints, to monitor complaint investigations, and to promote public awareness of the complaint process.

With respect to the citizen complaint process, the IPA has the power to disagree with the findings of police internal investigations. Disagreements are rare, however. In 2011 the IPA disagreed with the findings in 6 percent of the cases it audited; agreed with 19 percent of the cases after requesting and receiving additional information; closed 13 percent of the cases with concerns (which it deemed not serious enough to warrant disagreement); and agreed with 63 percent of the cases.[43] Critics of police auditors are certainly likely to see the 6 percent disagreement rate as a sign that the IPA does a weak job of auditing internal affairs. We can argue, however, that the disagreement rate does not fully account for the full impact of the auditor. The mere fact of an outside auditor unquestionably puts pressure on internal affairs to maintain the quality of investigations. This is reinforced when the auditor asks for additional information. The "closed with concern" category means that in some cases the quality approaches but does not quite cross the line into unacceptable. These thoughts are mere conjecture, of course, based on common sense. It is possible that a sophisticated evaluation, probably using qualitative as well as quantitative methods, could at some point in the future provide a better evaluation of the impact of the IPA auditing process.

Policy Review

The policy review activities of the IPA represent its most important achievements. Between 1993 and 2011, the IPA made a total of 150 policy recommendations to the San Jose Police Department. In 2011 it conducted an audit of the 109 recommendations issued between 1993 and 2009 and found that 85, or 78 percent, had been adopted. The audit identified certain recurring themes in the recommendations over the years. The most important concerned "Internal Affairs Policies," and included such issues as changes in the way complaints are classified, standardized definitions of complaint categories, a new and more private room for interviewing complainants and witnesses, and procedures to eliminate bias in investigations. The second most common theme involved "Professionalism and Community Relations," and included such issues as an "on-lookers" policy explicitly stating that citizens have a right to observe police actions, and closer supervision of strip searches of persons arrested for misdemeanor crimes. Officer "Use of Force" was the third recurring theme, and included a procedure to reduce wrist injuries from being handcuffed.[44]

While the strip search policy undoubtedly strikes most people as an obviously important issue, the significance of many of the recommendations may not be immediately apparent. Many appear to be very minor and insignificant "housekeeping" items. But therein lies their importance. Small issues such as having a receptionist and providing access to rest rooms for complainants loom very large in the eyes of citizens with grievances against the police. Sustained attention to such issues not only enhances public satisfaction and trust but also prevents small issues from developing into larger problems. A seemingly minor handcuff injury, for example, could prove to be a major medical issue for some people. Perhaps even more important than particular recommendations, the process of sustained oversight by an external agency socializes the police department into the habit of answering to outsiders on a regular basis.

Updating Previous Issues

As is the case with the Special Counsel to the LASD, the San Jose IPA has the capacity to revisit issues and publicly report on the status of prior recommendations. The *2001 Year End Report*, for example, devoted 10 pages to "Updates on Prior Issues."[45] On the issue of police officials providing prompt and accurate information about where citizens could file complaints, calls to three different SJPD phone numbers yielded inaccurate or only partly accurate responses. Consequently, the IPA recommended a training program for all SJPD officials about the complaint process. With respect to shootings of citizens, the IPA reported that the SJPD had implemented the prior recommendation to enhance officer training and to provide officers with a wider range of less than lethal force options. The IPA noted that the number of shooting incidents had declined, perhaps as a result of these changes.

Community Outreach

The IPA also engages in an extensive program of community outreach. The *2001 Year End Report* devotes nine pages to community outreach, describing presentations to community groups, particularly youth groups, new police officers, and national associations. In 2002 the IPA published a very readable booklet for young people discussing both their rights and responsibilities when dealing with police officers.[46]

The Boise Ombudsman

The Boise, Idaho, Ombudsman is particularly notable for its detailed follow-up reports on controversial incidents. In one notable case, the police officers responding to sexual assault allegations by two teenage girls engaged in extremely unprofessional and inappropriate behavior. They inappropriately concluded that the girls were lying, threatened to arrest them for perjury, leaked information about the incident to neighbors, and conducted interrogations without a third-party witness in violation of departmental policy. The Ombudsman's report reviewed the facts of the case in detail, identified the specific areas of misconduct, and highlighted areas in which the police department needed to take corrective action.[47] In addition to the specific recommendations for reform, this and other Ombudsman reports serve to clear the air by providing an independent public examination of controversial police cases.

The Ombudsman staff also conducts immediate roll outs to shootings and other critical incidents. As noted in Chapter Three, this practice is now found in several other jurisdictions. The presence of an independent investigator on the scene of an incident is designed to preserve all relevant evidence and prevent blatant cover-ups of officer misconduct.

Recent Blue-Ribbon Commissions

As discussed in Chapter Two, blue-ribbon commissions have a long history in American criminal justice and in policing. While many commissions made extremely important contributions—the 1968 Kerner Commission report on the riots of the 1960s and the 1991 Christopher Commission report on the Los Angeles Police Department following the beating of Rodney King—they also have serious limitations. Most seriously, they have no mechanism for compelling adoption of their recommendations or following up on whether they are adopted. Nonetheless, blue-ribbon commissions still play an important role in certain circumstances.

A good example of a valuable recent blue-ribbon commission is the 2012 Spokane, Washington, Use of Force Commission. A 2006 incident resulted in the 2011 criminal conviction of the officer involved, and in 2012 the City of Spokane settled a civil suit with the victim's family. The controversy surrounding these events over a 6-year period caused the Spokane City Council to create an independent commission to undertake an "expansive" investigation of use of force by the Spokane Police Department.[48]

The Use of Force Commission report delivered in late 2012 embodied the principles and procedures of the new police accountability.[49] The bulk of the report called for a revised mission statement for the department, engagement with the community regarding policy and procedures, improved training for officers regarding use of force, emphasizing de-escalation of potentially violent police-citizen encounters, improving use of force reporting and review, creation of an early intervention system, and many other recommendations.

The most innovative aspect of the report was its call for a "culture audit" of the police department. While most police experts agree that the police subculture is a critical element of policing, and usually an obstacle to accountability, there has been relatively little research on the subject and even fewer discussions of how it might be changed in the interests of accountability. The results of a culture audit, should it be undertaken, could make a significant contribution to the development of police accountability.

In important respects, the Spokane report is an index of decades of progress in police accountability. All of the recommendations reflect policies and procedures that have developed in recent years and are now found in many departments, while the idea of a culture audit breaks new ground.

The Limits of External Review

Police auditors can and have made significant contributions to police accountability. As we have explained, they are an important part of the PTSR framework described in Chapter One. All forms of external review have limitations, however, and we now turn our attention to these issues.

All forms of external review are inherently limited by the simple fact that they are external to the police departments they review. They can investigate, make recommendations, and report to the public, but like blue-ribbon commissions they cannot compel the adoption of their recommendations. For this reason, police auditors and other forms of external review are regarded skeptically by some community activists. Citizen review agencies, as we have already noted, also have no power to compel adoption of the recommendations they make regarding the disposition of the complaints they investigate. Public trust in police auditors is also weakened by the fact that many community activists are focused on particular incidents and want discipline of the officers involved. By comparison, the police auditor role in seeking to change the police organization lacks the emotional appeal of discipline of an officer.

The criticisms of community activists are important because *public perception* is a crucial aspect of police accountability and the legitimacy of the police. It is not sufficient that a police department reduce the number of excessive force incidents; it is also necessary that the department be perceived as doing so.

The positive contributions of police auditors involve a fundamental question of how one defines police accountability. This book rests on the assumption that ultimately accountability is best achieved by heightening the accountability of the chief executive. That is not achieved by taking power away from the police chief or sheriff. It is achieved by providing chief executives with tools and resources that will help them make better decisions in critical situations. The outside perspective provided by a police auditor is one resource. An early intervention system is another resource. State-of-the-art policies on use of force and other critical incidents are another set of basic tools. Weakening the authority of a police chief executive, by transferring power over discipline or policy making to an external authority, is in the view of this book more likely to undermine accountability than to enhance.

Another weakness of police auditors involves limitations on the independence of police auditors. All forms of external review of the police are products of a political process. It is always possible that political forces might undermine the authority of a police auditor. The Omaha police auditor, for example, was fired and not replaced because a report on traffic stops and the underlying problems with the police department's inadequate policies, training, and supervision offended the mayor. The Philadelphia Integrity and Accountability Office was allowed to lapse because of a lack of political support.[50] The Miami-Dade police-citizen review board was abolished because of a budget crisis, but a lack of political support contributed to its demise. The LASD Office of Independent Review could be abolished by any sheriff at any time. The LASD Special Counsel could be abolished by the County Board of Supervisors. In the end, in a democratic society, where public agencies are subject to popular will, there is simply no way around the fact that police oversight agencies may at some point lose their political support.

The Collaborative Reform Process: A Promising New Initiative

The most promising new initiative in police accountability is the Collaborative Reform Process, which produced a lengthy and detailed 2012 report on officer-involved shootings by the Las Vegas Metropolitan Police Department (LVMPD).[51] The unique aspect of the process was the collaboration between a police department under criticism for a pattern or shootings, a new unit of the Justice Department, and a private consulting organization. Several officials at the 2012 PERF conference on Justice Department pattern or practice investigations endorsed the idea of more collaborative alternatives to litigation between the U.S. Justice Department and local police departments.[52]

The Justice Department unit was the Critical Response Technical Assistance Program, a new initiative in the Office of Community Oriented Policing Services (the "COPS Office"). As its name indicates, its function is to provide technical assistance to a law enforcement agency regarding use of force or other issues on a collaborative basis, without litigation. The substantive technical assistance is provided by a private consulting organization. The collaborative approach by a Justice Department unit is an alternative to investigation and litigation by the Civil Rights Division. As is explained below, the substantive findings and recommendations of the Las Vegas collaborative report closely parallel the findings letters, consent decrees, and memoranda of agreement by the Civil Rights Division (improved use of force policies, review of officer-involved shooting incidents, etc.). Thus, the results are essentially the same but without the cost and polarization of a litigation approach.

The Las Vegas collaborative reform process began with a five-part series of stories on officer-involved shootings by the LVMPD that was highly critical of the department. Local activists, led by the Nevada ACLU, criticized the department, made a set of policy recommendations, and asked the Civil Rights Division to investigate the department. The LVMPD adopted some of the recommendations, but in the face of continued criticisms accepted the Justice Department's invitation to participate in the collaborative process. It is not at all clear whether the Civil Rights Division would have chosen to investigate the LVMPD, given the number of requests for action it receives, or if so when that might have occurred. In short, the collaborative reform process was a speedy and, tentatively at any rate, effective response to a problem.

The LVMPD report reviews and critiques the department's use of force policy. Although finding it generally good, the report makes 12 recommendations for improvement, including the addition of a "mission statement that emphasizes the sanctity of human life."[53] The chapter on training includes many of the issues found in Civil Rights Division documents: training related to defensive tactics, the Crisis Intervention Team, conducted energy devices, de-escalation of incidents, and alternative training methods.[54] Two entire chapters are devoted to force incident review and documentation, and they reflect the developing best practices in the new police accountability. It should be noted that the LVMPD had in place three different review procedures for force incidents: the Force Investigation Team (FIT), to investigate possible criminal charges; the Critical Incident Review Team (CIRT), to examine possible changes in policy and training, if needed; and the Use of Force Review Board, to review possible administrative (i.e., noncriminal) charges against officers. While these procedures undoubtedly exceeded those in most police departments, the report found needed improvements in all three and made a series of recommendations to that effect.

Perhaps the most important set of findings and recommendations related to officer tactics in officer-involved shooting incidents, which totaled 57 between 2007 and 2011. The most frequent tactical errors involved radio communications (40 percent of all cases), officer approach to the incident (31 percent), and coordination among officers (31 percent). Tactical errors were significantly more frequent in fatal shootings than nonfatal. Flawed officer approaches, for example, typically involved officer failure to "slow down the action of the incident" by creating a perimeter or defining the situation as a barricade. Radio communications errors included failing to provide updates to dispatch about an evolving incident, "not announcing actions over the radio," and miscommunication with the dispatcher.[55] Four of the five recommendations called for improvements in training, and a fifth involved a new policy.

The findings and recommendations related to tactical errors illustrate several important points that are crucial to the new police accountability. First, they highlight the importance of a systematic review of critical incidents, which in this case uncovered important aspects of officer-involved shootings. Second, they highlight the importance of a data-driven analysis of critical incidents. Third, the errors identified are readily addressed by focused training. It is unreasonable, of course, to think that all questionable officer-involved shootings will ever be eliminated. But it is reasonable to understand how the key elements of the new police accountability can significantly reduce them.

There are some questions surrounding the collaborative reform process model, however. Civil rights activists point out that final reports lack the compulsory element of a consent decree. A police department could simply walk away from the report and refuse to implement its recommendations. That is certainly true, but there are competing considerations. First, as Rachel Harmon and other observers have pointed out, the resources of the Civil Rights Division are extremely limited and it is unreasonable to expect that it could investigate more than a few police departments a year (as the record to date clearly illustrates). Second, the history of the Las Vegas collaborative report indicates community pressures and the potential for Civil Rights Division intervention are strong inducements for a police department to implement any recommended reforms.

The Conditions of Success for External Review

In 2005 all of the then-existing police auditors met in Omaha, Nebraska, for a working conference on the experience of auditing police departments, successes achieved, problems encountered, and the needs for effective auditing. The conference produced a report on the Core Principles for an Effective Auditor's Office, which appears in Figure 6.1.

Assuming a proper vision and direction, a police auditor's office needs sufficient resources to do its job adequately. Many civilian review boards have been starved into failure by a lack of resources. Mike Gennaco, head of the LASD Office of Independent Review, observed that his office's initial success was made possible by "the commitment of significant resources by the [Los Angeles County] Board of Supervisors." The OIR began with a staff of six full-time attorneys, all of whom had backgrounds in civil rights and criminal law.[56]

Closely related to sufficient resources is the cooperation of the chief of police or sheriff. Gennaco reports that he enjoys "unfettered access to LASD materials."[57] Teresa Guererro-Daley has also enjoyed the full cooperation of a succession of chiefs of the San Jose Police Department. By contrast, the New York City CCRB has faced hostility and noncooperation from the NYPD over the course of several decades. The success of the San Francisco OCC has also been hindered by a lack of support from a succession of mayors and often-covert noncooperation from the San Francisco Police Department.

In the end, the issues of support from the political environment and cooperation from police chief executives apply to all forms of attempted police reform. If we have learned anything over the past several decades, it is that meaningful reforms are easily undermined, if only through quiet neglect. Federal courts can order a department to adopt a new use of force policy, but the department itself must implement it. And if the elected officials with direct responsibility for a police department do not carefully monitor implementation it is very likely that nothing will change. The police auditor is a potentially valuable tool for police accountability. Whether that tool will be used and used properly is a question that will be answered by people outside the auditor's office.

Figure 6.1 Core Principles for an Effective Police Auditor's Office

INDEPENDENCE

A police auditor's office must be fully independent of the law enforcement agency under its jurisdiction.

Specific language in the enabling ordinance must indicate that an auditor may be removed from office only for cause and through a clearly defined removal process.

CLEARLY DEFINED SCOPE OF RESPONSIBILITIES

The scope of the responsibilities of a police auditor's office must be clearly defined by ordinance (or contract).

Specific language, for example, must define the auditor's responsibility to audit complaint files, have unfettered access to all relevant records and reports, make policy recommendations, issue public reports, investigate individual critical incidents, and so on.

ADEQUATE RESOURCES

A police auditor's office must have adequate resources to ensure that all duties can be conducted effectively and efficiently.

Adequate resources primarily include full-time professional and clerical staff.

Part-time staff only are not considered adequate.

Volunteer staff are not adequate.

The exact size of an auditor's office staff should be based on a formula reflecting the size of the law enforcement agency under the auditor's jurisdiction, as measured by the number of full-time sworn officers.

UNFETTERED ACCESS

A police auditor must have unfettered access to all documents and data in the law enforcement agency.

This unfettered access must be spelled out in the enabling ordinance.

The only exception to this rule would be files related to an ongoing criminal investigation.

All documents must be provided to the police auditor without charge to the auditor's office.

FULL COOPERATION

A police auditor must have the full cooperation of all employees of the law enforcement agency under its jurisdiction.

All employees, including sworn officers, shall cooperate as a condition of their employment.

With respect to potential self-incrimination, the standards defined in *Garrity v. New Jersey* shall prevail.

SANCTIONS FOR FAILURE TO COOPERATE

The enabling ordinance of an auditor's office must specify sanctions for failure to cooperate with the work of an auditor on the part of any law enforcement agency employee.

PUBLIC REPORTS

A police auditor must issue periodic public reports.

Such public reports shall be issued at least once a year and, ideally, more frequently.

NO PRIOR CENSORSHIP BY THE POLICE DEPARTMENT

Reports by the police auditor shall not be subject to prior censorship by the law enforcement agency.

A police auditor may reject any and all demands by the law enforcement agency to see draft copies of public reports.

COMMUNITY INVOLVEMENT

A police auditor must have the benefit of community involvement and input.

Community involvement and input can best be achieved through an advisory board consisting of members who represent the diverse composition of the local population.

CONFIDENTIALITY AND ANONYMITY

The work of a police auditor must respect the confidentiality of public employees as defined in the applicable state statute.

(Continued)

(Continued)

Violation of confidentiality shall be considered a serious breach of professional standards.

In the interests of enhancing public understanding, a police auditor may report on specific incidents with personal identifiers removed without violating standards of confidentiality.

ACCESS TO THE POLICE CHIEF OR SHERIFF

A police auditor must have direct access to the chief executive of the law enforcement agency under its jurisdiction.

Upon request, a police chief or sheriff must agree to meet with the police auditor.

It is understood that a chief executive may decline to meet in the case of an unreasonable number of such requests. Failure to meet with a police auditor for a period of one year shall be considered unsatisfactory performance on the part of a chief executive and shall be taken into consideration in performance review.

NO RETALIATION

The enabling ordinance of an auditor's office must specify that there shall be no retaliation against the auditor for work done as a part of the auditor's responsibilities, including statements made in public reports.

New Developments in Internal Review

The internal review of critical incidents has developed significantly in recent years, and the best practice today involves a multilayered process with reviews by several different entities. In terms of a serious inquiry into what happened in critical incidents, with an eye toward either discipline or revisions to department policies, internal review originated with the landmark 1972 New York City Police Department deadly force policy. It directed that each firearms discharge would be reviewed by the Firearms Discharge Review Board; reviews were primarily directed toward determining whether the officer complied with the new deadly force policy.[58]

The next important step in the development of internal review involved separate and parallel investigations, with the second review focused on examining incidents to determine if it revealed a need for changes in department policies, training, or supervision. As the Denver Office of the Independent Monitor explained, "do the facts [of the case] indicate any need for additional training or any revision or reformulation of agency policy?"[59] At the 2012 PERF conference on federal pattern or practice litigation, a Los Angeles police official commented that one of the important "legacies" of their consent decree experience was the practice of conducting audits of such police actions as warrant requests, arrests, and so on. If fact, he explained that the LAPD now teaches this process to other departments around the country.[60]

One of the best examples of the separate administrative review was the 2003 Police Assessment Resource Center (PARC) report on officer-involved shootings in the Portland, Oregon, police department, which examined 32 officer-involved shootings and two in-custody deaths between 1997 and mid-2000. The report identified a number of significant deficiencies with the department's existing internal review process. Most seriously, it found "no consistent commitment to meaningful review" of death incidents and no "lessons learned" from these events. The department's procedures focused narrowly on "whether a crime had been committed," to the neglect of "policy and tactical" issues. Thirty-one percent did not receive a "documented internal review at either the unit or executive level," and in another 13 percent the review did not conform to the department's standards. Incident investigations, moreover, were not always thorough nor impartial.[61]

One of the more notable findings of the PARC report was that the lack of meaningful review that looked beyond culpability of the officer(s) in particular incidents was deeply ingrained in the department's culture. It quoted one senior officer who explained that "we are hesitant to be critical . . . we hate to call each other on the carpet," and "People are afraid to ask hard questions." In about 40 percent of the cases, unit commanders did not comply with the department's protocol requiring them to critique the actions of the officers under their command. Many of the incident after-action reports were "cursory and uncritical."[62] The statements can be taken as a critique of the traditional culture of police departments nationally. This aspect of the PARC Portland report, moreover, highlighted the point that the new police accountability involves more than the creation of new bureaucratic procedures, although they are important, but also the development of a new organizational culture willing to ask hard questions about its own operations.

With respect to identifying possible changes in policy, training, supervision, or tactics, the PARC report found that while many incidents unfold very quickly, with little opportunity for consideration of choices about how to respond, in 18 incidents officers had advance information that the situation posed a "serious risk" and, consequently, "time to manage their response effectively." The missed opportunities in 11 incidents included failure to gather important information before acting, failure to assess the possible degree of risk, failure to assemble sufficient police resources before taking action, and failure to use effectively the time they had available. Additionally, communication failures affected 13 of the cases PARC examined. These failures included not alerting other officers to dangers, supervisors not communicating tactical instructions, failure to communicate to other officers tactical decisions that were made, and coordinating police radio traffic. Additionally, supervisors made a number of mistakes in managing developing incident scenes, such as not issuing directives at critical moments, or in some cases not assuming the role of supervisor at all.[63]

The PARC Portland report confirmed the point we discussed in Chapter Three (pp. 66–67) that many critical incidents that pose a high degree of potential risk, including possible loss of life, are fluid events where police officers have some power to shape the outcome. This view is contrary to the popular view of police work in which the police are virtual prisoners of a dangerous environment and have decisions forced on them. The findings and recommendations of the PARC Portland report were confirmed 10 years later in the Collaborative Reform Process report on officer-involved shootings in the Las Vegas Metropolitan Police Department. That report also found that communication problems adversely affected many shooting incidents and that officers did not choose tactical alternatives that might have precluded the use of deadly force.[64]

The internal review of critical incidents for purposes of identifying possible changes in policy, training, or supervision embodies several aspects of the new police accountability described in Chapter One. First and obviously, it involves systematic review of a police department's operations. Second, it is data driven and is enhanced by encompassing not only the largest number of incidents possible but also by incorporating as much detail as possible about each incident. Both the Portland and the Las Vegas reports included information about radio communications, for example. Nonetheless, the Portland report involved only 34 death incidents, indicating that a detailed examination of even a small number of incidents can yield valuable insights. Finally, internal review as described here represents police departments becoming learning organizations, as described by William Geller.[65]

Conclusion

External and internal reviews of the police are crucial parts of the PTSR framework for accountability. It is the part of the process that is best able to address issues of organizational change. As described in this chapter, the best external police auditors have successfully addressed precincts that are most troubled within a department and also the operations of important components of the new accountability. As permanent institutions and with unrestricted mandates, police auditors have enormous potential for thorough and continuing monitoring of key police operations. Additionally, as a result of the experience they acquire, staff members of existing police auditors are an invaluable resource to serve as short-term consultants for reviews of other law enforcement agencies or even as permanent staff for auditors in other jurisdictions.

Important new developments with regard to internal review have also developed. The most important involves the Critical Incident Response Team in the COPS office of the U.S. Justice Department. (The continuation of that office, of course, is contingent on policy decisions by future Attorneys General and federal budget considerations.) The work of that office in the Collaborative Reform Process on the Las Vegas Metropolitan Police Department is widely cited throughout this book because of the quality of its investigation into officer-involved shootings and its recommendations. American policing would be well served if the Critical Incident Response Team office continues as a resource for departments experiencing accountability troubles.

Notes

1 Samuel Walker, "Institutionalizing Police Accountability Reforms: The Problem of Making Police Reforms Endure," *Saint Louis University Public Law Review* 32 (no. 1, 2012): 57–93.

2 James J. Fyfe, "Administrative Interventions on Police Shooting Discretion: An Empirical Examination," *Journal of Criminal Justice* 7 (Winter 1979): 309–23.

3 Los Angeles Sheriff's Department, Office of Independent Review, *First Annual Report 2002* (Los Angeles: Los Angeles Sheriff's Department, 2002), 32. Available at http://www.laoir.com.

4 Samuel Walker, *Police Accountability: The Role of Citizen Oversight* (Belmont, CA: Thomson, 2001).

5 Samuel Walker, "Setting the Standards: The Efforts and Impacts of Blue-Ribbon Commissions on the Police," in *Police Leadership in America: Crisis and Opportunity*, ed. William A. Geller, 354–70 (New York: Praeger, 1985).

6 The Seattle Police Auditor is a separate agency from the Office of Professional Accountability (OPA) that was created in 1999 and is located within the Seattle Police Department but staffed by a non-sworn person. The Police Auditor reviews citizen complaints, while the OPA primarily devotes its efforts to community outreach and policy reform. Brochure, *Civilian Oversight of the Seattle Police Department* (Seattle: OPA, n.d.).

7 The Washington, D.C., Office of Police Complaints' website is http://police complaints.dc.gov/.

8 On the fight over citizen oversight in San Jose, see ACLU of Northern California, *A Campaign of Deception: San Jose's Case Against Civilian Review* (San Francisco: ACLU of Northern California, 1992). Walker, *Police Accountability: The Role of Citizen Oversight*, 38–40.

9 Tristan Bonn, Omaha Public Safety Auditor, *Anatomy of Traffic Stops* (Omaha: City of Omaha, 2006). Available at http://samuelwalker.net.

10 Samuel Walker and Morgan Macdonald, "An Alternative Remedy for Police Misconduct: A Model State Pattern or Practice Statute," *George Mason Civil Rights Law Journal*, 19 (Summer 2009): 479–552.

11 Walker, *Police Accountability*.

12 The ordinances establishing police auditors are generally available on their websites. See the analysis in Walker, *Police Accountability: The Role of Citizen Oversight*.

13 Denver Office of the Independent Monitor, *Annual Report 2012* (Denver: Office of the Independent Monitor, 2013).

14 Denver Office of the Independent Monitor, *Annual Report 2011* (Denver: Office of the Independent Monitor, 2012), Chapter Five.

15 Walker, *Police Accountability*, 93–104.

16 San Jose Independent Police Auditor, *Year End Report 2012* (San Jose: Independent Police Auditor, 2013), 14. Available at http://www.ci.san-jose.ca.us/ipa.

17 Merrick Bobb, *15th Semiannual Report* (Los Angeles: Police Assessment Resource Center, 2002), 14. Available at http://www.parc.info.

18 San Jose, Independent Police Auditor, *2011 Year End Report*, 23–25. San Jose, Independent Police Auditor, *A Student's Guide to Police Practices* (San Jose: Independent Police Auditor, 2002). Available at http://www.ci .san-jose.ca.us/ipa.

19 Seattle Police Department, Office of Professional Accountability, *Respect: Voices and Choices.* Available at http://www.cityofseattle.net/police.

20 See http://www.boiseombudsman.org.

21 See, for example, the April 27, 2010, Office of Independent Review investigation and report on the death of Marlon Martinez while an inmate in the Lost Angeles County Jail. This and other reports are at http://laoir.com/reports/. Other reports are available on the OIR website.

22 The New York Civilian Complaint Review Board website is http://www .nyc.gov/ccrb.

23   The "going rate" is discussed in Samuel Walker, *Sense and Nonsense About Crime, Drugs, and Community: A Policy Guide* (Belmont, CA: Cengage, 2011), 53–74.

24   Los Angeles, Office of Internal Review, *Tenth Annual Report* (Los Angeles: Los Angeles Sheriff's Department, 2012), 111–18.

25   This point is argued in Walker, *Police Accountability*, 149–157, with more extensive material on other citizen oversight agencies. The reports of the Special Counsel are archived at http://www.parc.info.

26   James G. Kolts, *The Los Angeles Sheriff's Department* (Los Angeles: Los Angeles Sheriff's Department, 1992). Available at http://www.parc.info.

27   Merrick Bobb, *9th Semiannual Report* (Los Angeles: Police Assessment Resource Center, 1998), 12. Available at http://www.parc.info.

28   Ibid.

29   Bobb, *15th Semiannual Report*, 9.

30   Ibid., 9.

31   Bobb, *16th Semiannual Report*, 43–59.

32   Bobb, *18th Semiannual Report*, 47–56.

33   Los Angeles Sheriff's Department, Office of Independent Review, *Tenth Annual Report* (Los Angeles: Los Angeles Sheriff's Department, 2012), 106.

34   Police Executive Research Forum, *Is the Economic Downturn Fundamentally Changing How We Police?* (Washington, DC: Police Executive Research Forum, 2010).

35   See the discussion of the creation of the OIR in Office of Independent Review, *First Report* (Los Angeles: Los Angeles Sheriff's Department, 2002), 1–2.

36   Los Angeles Sheriff's Department, Office of Independent Review, *Report of Oversight of Administrative Discipline Cases: October thru December 2003* (Los Angeles: Los Angeles Sheriff's Department, 2004). Available at http://www.laoir.com.

37   Los Angeles Sheriff's Department, Office of Independent Review, *First Report* (Los Angeles: Los Angeles Sheriff's Department), 36–40.

38   Ibid., 2.

39   Ibid., 62–3.

40   Ibid., 63.

41   Los Angeles County, Office of Independent Review, *Second Annual Report, Los Angeles County Probation Department* (Los Angeles: Los Angeles Sheriff's Department, 2013).

42   Merrick Bobb, *31st Semiannual Report* (Los Angeles: Los Angeles Sheriff's Department, 2012). The Special Counsel had reported on the jails in seven previous reports. Los Angeles Sheriff's Department, Office of Internal Review, *Tenth Annual Report* (Los Angeles: Los Angeles Sheriff's Department, 2012). Los Angeles Sheriff's Department, Office of Internal Review, *Violence in the Los Angeles County Jails: A Report on Investigations and Outcomes* (Los Angeles: Los Angeles Sheriff's Department, 2011).

43   San Jose, Independent Police Auditor, *2012 Year End Report* (San Jose: Independent Police Auditor 2013), 40. Available at http://www.ci.san-jose.ca.us/ipa.

44   San Jose Independent Police Auditor, *2011 Year End Report*, 14–15.

45   San Jose Independent Police Auditor, *2001 Year End Report*, 20–30.

46   San Jose Independent Police Auditor, *A Student's Guide to Police Practices* (San Jose: San Jose Independent Police Auditor, 2002).

47   Boise Community Ombudsman, *Public Report: Police Handling of a Reported Rape in Barber Park* (Boise: Community Ombudsman, June 27, 2000). Available at http://www.boiseombudsman.org.

48   City of Spokane, *Draft Report of the City of Spokane Use of Force Commission* (Spokane: City of Spokane, 2012).

49   Ibid., 1–2.

50   See, for example, Philadelphia Police Department, Integrity and Accountability Office, *Use of Force* (Philadelphia: Philadelphia Police Department, 1999).

51   James K. Stewart et al., *The Collaborative Reform Process: A Review of Officer-Involved Shootings in the Las Vegas Metropolitan Police Department* (Washington, DC: Department of Justice, 2012).

52   Police Executive Research Forum, *Civil Rights Investigations of Local Police: Lessons Learned* (Washington, DC: Police Executive Research Forum, 2013), 37.

53   Stewart et al., 61.

54   Ibid., 64–85.

55   Ibid., 44, 49.

56   Los Angeles Sheriff's Department, Office of Internal Review, *First Annual Report 2002* (Los Angeles: Los Angeles Sheriff's Department, 2002), 1.

57   Ibid.

58   Fyfe, "Administrative Interventions on Police Shooting Discretion."

59   Denver Office of the Independent Monitor, *2012 Annual Report* (Denver: Office of the Independent Monitor, 2013), 70.

60   Police Executive Research Forum, *Civil Rights Investigations of Local Police: Lessons Learned*, 30.

61   Police Assessment Resource Center, *The Portland Police Bureau: Officer-Involved Shootings and In-Custody Deaths* (Los Angeles: Police Assessment Resource Center, 2003), 1–2.

62   Ibid., 136–37.

63   Ibid., 170–77.

64   Stewart et al., *The Collaborative Reform Process.*

65   William A. Geller, "Suppose We Were Really Serious About Police Departments Becoming 'Learning Organizations,'?" *National Institute Journal* (December 1997): 2–8.

PART III

Contemporary Issues in Accountability

SEVEN

Risk Management as an Accountability Strategy

Police accountability is based on the idea that police officers and police agencies are held responsible for their actions and decisions. One way to infuse police accountability into police organizations is to implement risk management programs. Risk management requires the monitoring, tracking, and changing of police department policies, procedures, and training to reduce exposure to future risk.

Early intervention systems (EISs), which we discussed in Chapter Five, are a form of risk management. Why then have a separate chapter on this subject? The answer is that risk management is a much broader concept than EISs. Additionally, as this chapter explains, the police can learn much from the experience of risk management from other professions and organizations where it is more developed than in policing.

What Is Risk Management?

Risk management is a tool that is used to identify potential risks and liability problems within organizations. Many organizations adopt risk management to help reduce costs associated with liability claims and litigation, reduce the risk of potential harm to their clients and employees, and as a result, provide higher-quality services.[1] This approach to minimizing exposure to risk has been used in a wide variety of professions including medicine, psychology, and banking/finance.[2]

Regardless of the type of profession, the risk management process consists of five general steps:[3]

1. *Identify risks, frequency of exposure to risks, and the severity of losses resulting from exposure to risks.* Organizational risks and losses are identified when risk managers conduct a historical analysis of organizational loss data (specifically past and pending payouts from lawsuits and liability claims). Most organizational loss comes from physical, human, and financial assets.[4] *Physical assets* include vehicles, buildings, computer equipment, and other technology/equipment. Employees working within organizations are *human assets*. *Financial assets* include any financial resources that are available to organizations that have a direct impact on how they function (this includes annual budgets and external grants). Police organizations possess all three types of assets and are vulnerable to organizational loss as a result of exposure to liability risks. Early intervention systems can be used to identify problem officers, practices, and procedures as they track various types of actions made by officers over an extended period of time (usually more than one year).

2. *Explore methods to manage exposure to identified risks.* This step involves a thorough review of organizational policies, procedures, training, and supervision of employees. This step mirrors the concept of PTSR (Policy, Training, Supervision, and Review) that was presented in other chapters of this book. Many police agencies come up with ideas about changes to policies, procedures, and training by researching what other police agencies across the country do to reduce liability.

3. *Choose an appropriate response to manage exposure to identified risks.* This stage consists of making changes to policies, training, and supervision in order to reduce exposure to identified risks.

4. *Execute the response that was chosen to manage exposure to risks.*

5. *Evaluate the impact that the response has on exposure to identified risks.*

The risk management process is not over after all five steps are completed (see Figure 7.1). This process is ongoing as organizational risks and liabilities change over time. It is the constant review and assessment that is involved in the risk management process that increases accountability of individual police officers and police organizations overall.

Figure 7.1   The Risk Management Process

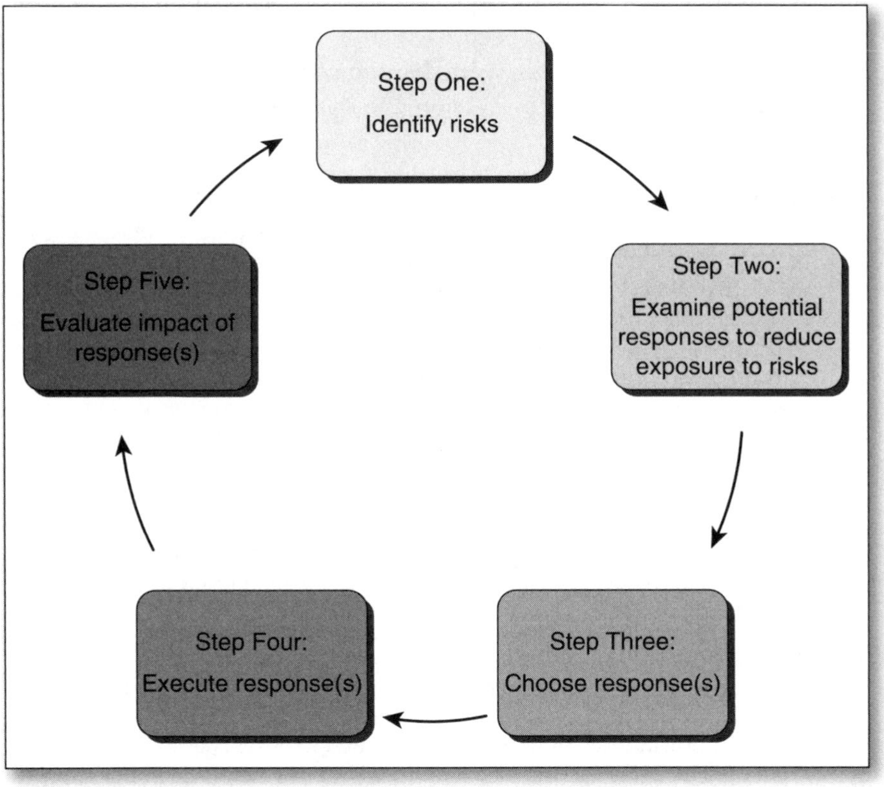

Risk Management, Police Liability, and Accountability

It has been suggested by insurance assessors and other risk management professionals that the use of risk management in police organizations increases safety of police officers and citizens; improves the quality of police service provided to the public; increases accountability for police officers; and improves financial management of the costs associated with liability.[5] Risk management is a sensible choice for police administrators as many duties associated with police work exposes officers and agencies to risk.[6] Officer use of force, vehicular pursuits, and use of canine units are three actions used by the police that can result in serious harm to citizens and exposure to liability for police officers. Officer accountability is important for these formal actions as there is a high level of harm that can result from each of these actions.

Police Officer Use of Force

Egon Bittner pointed out that the authorization of the use of force is an aspect of police work that makes it unique to all other professions.[7] This distinctive aspect of police work also contributes to police officer exposure to high levels of risk, which in turn, can lead to litigation, liability claims, and other types of organizational loss. The use of force also puts citizens at risk for physical harm at the hands of police officers. Improper use of lethal and nonlethal force by police officers during arrests and improper service of due process are two incidents where damages are commonly sought and where settlements are paid out to citizens.[8]

Liability Assessment and Awareness International (LAAW) asserts that liability related to police officer use of force can be managed by close supervision.[9] This group suggests that department policies should be restrictive when identifying situations where use of force is deemed appropriate in order to keep officer behavior under control. By maintaining high standards when reviewing cases of alleged misuse or abuse of force, police executives are able to increase officer accountability.[10]

The suggestions made by LAAW mirror the findings of research conducted on the use of force, which suggests that restrictive policies and enforced mandatory reporting of use of force incidents can harness officer behavior.[11] Some police agencies try to manage officer use of force by adopting policies that include language referencing a use of force continuum. Force continuums identify appropriate levels of force to be used by officers based on the actions of citizens with whom they interact. Some believe that continuums increase officer accountability as it requires them to control the amount of force used when interacting with citizens.[12] Others argue that the use of force continuum may result in more injuries for officers as they may be hesitant to use force in instances where it may be necessary.[13] A recent study by Richard Hough and Kimberly Tatum examined use of force policies from police agencies in the state of Florida. Many (74%) of the police agencies included language referencing a use of force continuum in their use of force policies and officer training programs despite the fact that the state of Florida had backed off of using force continuums in 2006.[14] Hough and Tatum suggest that the sustained use of the continuum reflects its utility within the agencies and may also be a reflection of the agencies' stance on the use of force. Nearly all (92%) of the agencies include mandatory reporting of use of force in their policies. This is an important finding, as mandatory reporting increases officer accountability.

Vehicular Pursuits

Another high-risk incident that can result in organizational loss is the operation of police vehicles engaged in pursuits. Some common issues related to police pursuits include officers exercising discretion that leads to them becoming involved in vehicular pursuits when it is unnecessary, not using emergency lights and equipment properly when police vehicles are parked, the placement of police vehicles during routine traffic stops and investigations of traffic accidents, and the failure to use (or in some cases misuse) police vehicle occupant restraints.[15] In the book *Police Pursuits: What We Know*, Geoffrey Alpert and his colleagues explain how the use of risk management can reduce liability and increase officer accountability when they are faced with the decision to pursue another vehicle. Alpert suggests that police executives scrutinize the history of their organization's losses by reviewing both past and pending lawsuits, and also survey police personnel to measure their knowledge of policies and liability issues associated with the operation of police vehicles.[16] Since the operation of police vehicles is an essential and required part of policing, the identification and management of the risks associated with vehicle operation becomes a necessary task for police executives.

Similar to the research on police officer use of force, the research on police pursuits has found that clarification of pursuit policies, enforced mandatory reporting, adequate supervision, and monitoring of pursuit activities will reduce the frequency of pursuits, as well as injuries and accidents associated with pursuits.[17] Monitoring vehicular pursuits also increases accountability of police officers.

Canine Units (K-9 Units)

Canine units can also be a source of potential liability for police agencies.[18] More police agencies are using canine units today than in the past. Approximately 8,000 canine units were involved in police operations in 2007 compared to 7,500 in 2003.[19] As more police agencies adopt canine units, there will be an increase in the use of canine units when apprehending suspects, and in turn, will increase police agencies' exposure to liability. Some jurisdictions, such as Los Angeles, rely heavily on canine units to help them find and capture fleeing suspects. An increased use of police canine units results in an increase in the number of dog bites. It has been reported "that an average of nearly one person per day is bitten by Los Angeles Police Department canines" and that "more than 900 men, women, and children have been attacked and mauled by these dogs in a three year period."[20]

The increase in complaints about bites from canine units caught the attention of the United States Department of Justice (DOJ) and the International Association of Chiefs of Police (IACP). Both groups proposed that law enforcement agencies adopt a policy of "bark and hold" instead of the traditional "bite and hold" when it comes to the use of canine units.[21] The idea behind this change in policy is that there will be fewer unnecessary bites, which would result in lower liability costs. Ironically, a recent study found that "bite and hold" dogs had lower mean "bite ratios" when compared to "bark and hold" dogs. This finding challenges the presumed impact of the change in policy suggested by the DOJ and the IACP. This example highlights the importance of creating evidence-based policies within police agencies.

There is also research that indicates that minority citizens are bitten by police canine units more often than white citizens because they are used more frequently in diverse neighborhoods.[22] In contrast, a study conducted in a suburb in Montgomery County, Maryland, did not find a racial difference in the use of police canine units.[23] It is important for police executives to implement policies that allow them to track the use of canine units so that a racial disparity in its use does not occur.

Police Accountability After Hours: Managing Off-Duty Conduct of Officers

The public has high expectations of police officers working in their communities when they are both on and off duty. The conduct of police officers while they are not in uniform is difficult for police administrators to manage, as some off-duty behaviors may be unethical but not illegal.[24] Managing off-duty behavior requires a careful balance between individual officers' rights to privacy and maintaining organizational integrity in the eyes of the public. In order to be successful in this balancing act, police administrators need to articulate in written form their expectations of officers' behavior both on and off duty, and then relay this information to every sworn employee working in their organization. This can be accomplished through clearly defined mission statements, codes of conduct, and oaths of office.[25]

Officers can be charged with conduct unbecoming of an officer if their behavior both on and off duty conflicts with organizational policies. This general charge is used in cases where an officer's behavior is viewed as unethical, but it is not specifically identified in any formal organizational policies. This broad charge opens the door for police agencies to be named in lawsuits. Risk management can be useful in proactively handling this type of case by requiring that organizational expectations for on- and off-duty behavior be articulated in written policies and also communicated to all officers working in the organization, along with the corrective actions that will be taken if officers choose to engage in this type of behavior (such as suspension with or without pay, mandatory retraining or additional training, or in some cases termination of employment).

One way that police agencies can inform officers of expectations of conduct when off duty is to identify specific behaviors that will not be tolerated by the organization. For example, some agencies will not tolerate sworn police personnel cursing or making rude comments/remarks to members of the public either on or off duty.[26] In September 2012, two off-duty Bellevue (Washington) police officers were disciplined for cursing at a security guard at a Seahawks game.[27] Cursing is not illegal; however, police administrators know that this kind of behavior reflects poorly on the image of their organization.

Police administrators sometimes face a difficult task when they have to prove that a specific incident or behavior violates a broadly written policy of off-duty behavior. Part of this difficult task is considering whether or not they are violating an officer's First Amendment rights. In March 2012, a New Orleans police officer was suspended for posting comments on a local newspaper website that featured a story about the Trayvon Martin case. The officer posted "Act like a Thug Die like one!" below the article in the online newspaper.[28] When the website's commentator called the posting racist, the officer responded with another post: ". . . come on down to our town with a 'Hoodie' and you can join Martin in HELL and talk about your racist stories!"[29] The officer's wife posted similar comments on the same website. One might argue that although crude and offensive, the officer has just as much of a right to express his opinion as his wife when he is not in uniform. It is cases like this one that demonstrate the importance of having clearly stated expectations of officer conduct both on and off duty.

The use of social media by off-duty police officers has created additional issues regarding rules of conduct. In May 2012, a sergeant in the Greenville (Mississippi) Police Department complained on Facebook that the mayor of Greenville did not send a city representative to the funeral of a deceased officer. The sergeant was fired shortly after the Facebook post on the grounds of insubordination and violation of rules of conduct. The sergeant is suing both the city and police department for violating her right to free speech.[30] This case leads to the question: Should police officers be disciplined or terminated as a result of posts made on Twitter, Facebook, and MySpace when they are not in uniform?

This is an easy question to answer when such posts to social media sites are made using department equipment (computers and department-issued cell/smartphones) while on duty. This was the case in 2011 when a Fort Lauderdale police officer was fired over tweets he posted on Twitter about his superiors within the department and also citizens that he encountered while on duty.[31] Some of his tweets included: "Police officers are not substitute parents. If you were not ready for the responsibility of being a parent u should've used protection. So deal with your own fucking kids and stop calling the police because you're a fucked up parent," "They should tie all women's tubes after they sign up for food stamps," and "Just caught a couple having sex in their car in a church parking lot. The car was shaking so much I thought it would flip."[32] The Fort Lauderdale police department had implemented a social media policy for all employees several months before the tweets were posted by the officer. The policy does not prohibit the use of social media; however, it does place some restrictions on the type of information that employees may post on those sites (either on or off duty).

In an effort to reduce or prevent litigation, risk managers working within police agencies require clarification or adoption of policies for all types of officer behavior (both on and off duty), including the use of social media websites. Many cases involving police officers and social media are currently working their way through the legal system;[33] thus, the courts will play an important role in determining restrictions that can be made on off-duty behavior of police officers.

Early Intervention Systems:
A Tool in Risk Management for the Police

In Chapter Five, early intervention systems (EISs) are described as the cornerstone of the new police accountability. EISs are databases that allow police supervisors to track and monitor the performance of police officers. These computerized systems can track a variety of outcome measures that directly impact accountability within police agencies including citizen complaints, use of force incidents, and involvement in litigation, to name a few.

EISs are a central tool used in risk management within police agencies as this system helps police administrators determine if changes need to be made to agency policies, practices, and training. Trend analysis using data over an extended period of time is needed in order to identify which policies and procedures should be altered to help reduce future exposure to risk. EIS databases are especially useful in this process as it allows for the analysis of multiple measures over an extended period of time. This aspect of EISs makes it the perfect tool for the risk management process—the risk management process is continuous and ongoing because risks can change over time and EISs collect the appropriate measures related to risk over an extended period of time.

The Prevalence of Risk
Management in American Policing

Over the past three decades, several professional groups and publications have identified the need for the use of risk management in police organizations. The Public Risk Management Association (PRIMA, a professional trade association of risk managers) published a police liability assessment guide that outlines activities that pose the greatest liability risks for police officers. PRIMA's liability guide identifies the use of firearms and other nonlethal weapons, police pursuits, defensive tactics, and hostage situations as police activities that pose a high level of risk. The PRIMA guide suggests that adequate training in high-risk incidents, along with the creation and enforcement of department policies that clearly define procedures in high-risk incidents, is critical in the control of police liability.[34]

The Commission on Accreditation for Law Enforcement Agencies (CALEA) suggests that risk management is one of the best ways that law enforcement agencies can protect themselves if ever faced with litigation. Specifically, CALEA contends that if agencies act in accordance with clearly written policies that meet accreditation standards and they have been assessed by CALEA representatives, they are taking the appropriate steps to protect themselves from litigation.[35] The CALEA website notes that there are financial incentives for agencies to adopt risk management as some insurance providers will offer discounted premiums, reimbursement for accreditation fees, and other "grants" as they believe that accredited agencies that use risk management cost them less money compared to nonaccredited agencies.

The CALEA website includes links to several articles providing information about the benefits of risk management. For example, an article published in 1999 by John Nielsen and Danny O'Malley describes how accreditation can save police agencies money. This article reports that accredited police agencies that are part of the Miami Valley Risk Management Association averaged losses of $314 per officer compared to $543 per officer for nonaccredited agencies.[36]

A 1998 study conducted by the Intergovernmental Risk Management Agency (IRMA) compared several measures of organizational loss of IRMA police departments that were both accredited and not accredited. This study examined data that included all liability claims and underwriting and loss control records from 1993 to 1997. Analysis of the data revealed that nonaccredited agencies had more claims (138) compared to accredited agencies (54), the number of claims per 100 officers was higher for nonaccredited agencies (10.28) compared to accredited agencies (8.61), and the severity of the payouts per 100 officers was greater for nonaccredited agencies ($97,771.21) compared to accredited agencies ($63,298.69).[37]

Another article on the CALEA website showcases two risk management studies that support accreditation.[38] First, a study by the Tennessee Municipal League (TML) in 2002 compared the loss experiences of accredited agencies with nonaccredited agencies that were part of the TML pool. Loss histories (July 1, 1994 – June 30, 2002) of five accredited agencies were compared to the loss histories of 23 nonaccredited agencies. Loss histories included information from workers' compensation, general police liability, police auto liability, and physical damage of police autos. Nonaccredited agencies had higher rates of loss in all four of the specified areas of organizational loss compared to the accredited agencies. The methodology of this study is weak as the groups being compared in the study were not closely matched. The second study, conducted by the Colorado Interlocal Risk Sharing Agency (CIRSA), compared the property/casualty and workers' compensation claims of 22 accredited and 22 nonaccredited agencies from 1999–2001. The results of this study found that accredited agencies had fewer property and casualty claims when compared to nonaccredited agencies. Specifically, accredited agencies had 8.3 percent fewer property/casualty claims and 7.5 percent fewer workers' compensation claims than nonaccredited agencies, and costs associated with property/casualty claims were 52.2 percent lower than nonaccredited agencies.[39] All of the studies featured on the CALEA website suggest that accredited agencies that utilize risk management tools are less likely to experience organizational loss, which in turn strengthens CALEA's assertion that risk management and accreditation can improve officer accountability and reduce exposure to liability.

Several publications geared toward police practitioners have featured articles on the importance of risk management in policing. In addition to highlighting the importance of using risk management, these publications suggest that risk management can potentially increase the level of professionalism and accountability in police agencies.[40] Many of these publications point out that only a few police agencies have risk management divisions, and that risk management programs can help police executives identify and manage the actions of problem officers.[41] The information provided in these articles is valuable; however, it is based solely on the experiences of risk managers and insurance professionals, not evidence-based research.

Research on Risk Management in Policing

Only within the last decade has any discussion of risk management been included in academic literature. In the book *Police Accountability: The Role of Citizen Oversight*, Samuel Walker reports that "one of the most notable failures of both police departments and other city officials has been their neglect of modern concepts of risk management and in particular their refusal to examine incidents that result in litigation and seek to correct the underlying problems."[42] He also describes the potential benefits that can result from using risk management, early warning systems, and citizen oversight as police accountability mechanisms.

Geoffrey Alpert and his colleagues devote an entire chapter to risk management and police liability in their book, *Police Pursuits: What We Know.*[43] In this chapter, risk management is discussed in the context of a "plan of action" to prevent costly payouts and injuries associated with vehicular police pursuits. The authors discuss how police agencies should take a proactive approach instead of a reactive approach to the implementation of risk management, specifically as it relates to vehicular pursuits.[44]

Policing and Misconduct, a book edited by Kimberly Michelle Lersch, includes an article by Samuel Walker that discusses the use of early intervention systems (EISs) as risk management within police agencies.[45]

The first empirical study on the use of risk management by American police agencies did not appear in print until 2004.[46] This study used interview and survey data from a national sample of law enforcement agencies, along with in-depth case studies of four police agencies that use risk management. In the first stage of this study, telephone interviews were conducted with local and county-level law enforcement agencies employing 200-plus sworn employees. The interviews were used to determine if and how police agencies use risk management. The interviews revealed that only 14 of the 354 (less than 4 percent) largest police agencies use risk management in the United States.[47]

In the second phase of this study, each of the 14 police agencies that reported that they use risk management were faxed a survey. Ten of the 14 agencies (71%) completed surveys (three agencies did not respond and one agency had only recently adopted risk management and felt that they were "too new" to provide information). The survey instrument collected a wide range of information about the use of risk management within these agencies. For example, most of the agencies reported that they adopted risk management out of necessity as they were experiencing an increase in lawsuits. Along with an increase in litigation, they reported that they needed risk managers to help them deal with changes in the legal and social environment in which police officers work, and to also deal with increased media scrutiny resulting from controversial incidents involving their agency. Most agencies adopted risk management in a reactive manner (as opposed to proactive).

The responsibilities of risk managers within their organizations consist of initiating reform of department policies, officer training, and the supervision of patrol officers. And finally, over half (60%) of the agencies reported that they believe that risk management has had an impact on liability management and accountability within their agencies; however, no agencies tracked the exact dollar amount of cost savings resulting from risk management efforts.

The final phase of this study included site visits to 4 of the 14 research sites for the purpose of in-depth case study analyses. The research sites include Charlotte, North Carolina; Los Angeles, California; Las Vegas, Nevada; and Portland, Oregon.[48] Each of the risk management programs were examined in great detail to see first-hand how risk management is incorporated into liability management within each agency. Details from the four case studies can be found in the book *Police Accountability, Risk Management, and Legal Advising.*[49]

Darrell Ross and Madhava Bodapati conducted a study that was published in 2006, which examined the risk exposure and law enforcement liability in the state of Michigan from 1985–1999.[50] This study used records that were collected and maintained by the Michigan Municipality Risk Management Authority (MMRMA), a group that provides insurance and risk management services to law enforcement agencies in the state of Michigan. The purpose of the study was to determine the common types of litigated cases brought against law enforcement agencies in Michigan and to also examine trends over time. Analysis of the data revealed that incidents involving automobiles without injuries was the most frequent type of claim, followed by use of excessive force, damage or destruction of property, vehicular pursuits without injuries, and false arrest/imprisonment.[51] The most costly type of claims involved wrongful death/fatalities followed by attempted suicide while in custody, medical care while in custody, suicide while in custody, and automobile accidents that involved injuries.[52] Overall, the study found that claims filed against Michigan police agencies along with costs associated with those claims are relatively low; annually, there was an average of 752 claims for 151 law enforcement agencies. The authors concluded that "risk management services and agency practices appear to be making a difference overall."[53] This study is important as it is the first published study to quantitatively assess the financial impact of risk management within police agencies.

Barriers to the Implementation of Risk Management

Although limited, there is evidence that risk management can have a financial impact when dealing with police liability. If there are benefits that result from using risk management, why isn't it more commonly used by American police agencies? Risk management professionals who have helped implement risk management programs in American police organizations identified what they believe are potential barriers to implementation. First, policing has traditionally been focused on crime fighting without any worry about financial costs.[54] With an increase in litigation involving police officers in recent years, more police executives are becoming as concerned with fiscal responsibilities as they are with their crime control efforts.[55] Police agencies need resources to be able to provide quality services to the public, which means that they need to utilize their resources in the most efficient way possible.

Another barrier is the cost associated with implementing risk management programs. Large cities are able to justify their need for hiring professional risk managers for reducing costs associated with police liability. Medium-sized and smaller cities have a harder time justifying the need for risk management as their exposure to liability may not be as great as police agencies serving communities with much larger populations.[56] Some less expensive alternatives to hiring full-time risk managers includes the expansion of the duties for individuals that work directly with police-related liability (such as city managers or city attorneys), employing only a few risk managers to service a large area or region that encompasses several small or medium cities with small populations or more rural areas, or an "as needed" risk management committee consisting of city attorneys, police department representatives, and insurance agents or risk assessors.[57]

Confusion about the best way to measure the impact of risk management within police organizations is another reason that so few police agencies use risk management. The monetary benefits of risk management are quantifiable in regard to impact; however, some would argue that it is impossible to measure the liability claims and lawsuits that have been prevented. The impact on police accountability and professionalism, along with an increase in the quality of police service provided to the community, are not easy to quantify.[58] Because resources are often limited in police organizations, it could be difficult to justify the need for an in-house risk manager if there are no outcome measures for the nonmonetary benefits.

Another barrier to the implementation of risk management within police agencies is the lack of research on the use of risk management by police agencies. As mentioned earlier, there have only been a few studies on the use of risk management by the police. There are several websites that provide information on risk management training for police agencies. For example, Lexipol provides various risk management resources for public safety agencies. This group helps police agencies alter and improve their department policy manuals.[59] The Spokane Police Department has worked with Lexipol to develop a policy manual that consists of law enforcement "best practices."[60] Several other police agencies in other states (including Iowa and Oregon) are also working with Lexipol to revamp their department policy manuals.[61] Legal & Liability Risk Management Institute (LLRMI) is another group of risk management professionals who provide consulting services to law enforcement agencies.[62] This group advertises that its goal is "to enhance professionalism and effectiveness while reducing liability risk through training, policy and procedure implementation, and legal support."[63] There are also training seminars offered by individual risk management experts that travel across the country training police personnel (such as G. Patrick Gallagher and Gordon Graham). The problem is that there has been very little evidence-based research on the use of risk management in police agencies.

Overcoming Barriers to Implementation: The Case of Risk Management in Medicine

The lack of published research on the use of risk management in police agencies is one of several barriers to its adoption. Police executives are left to wonder: Does risk management work? Is it an effective way to reduce liability and increase officer accountability in my agency? One way to answer these questions is to examine some of the published research on the use and impact of risk management in other high-risk/liability professions.

Risk management is a core component in the regulation of liability and accountability within medical facilities in the United States.[64] Doctors, nurses, and other medical care professionals are exposed to risk/liability every day when dealing with patients. In this profession, human error can result in minor and major medical complications, and in some cases, death. In November 1999, the Institute of Medicine (IOM) released the report *To Err Is Human: Building a Safer Health Care System*, which details how the health care system in the United States is not as safe as it could be or should be.[65] The report points out that "At least 44,000 people, and perhaps as many as 98,000 people, die in hospitals each year as a result of medical errors that could have been prevented."[66] It was also estimated that human errors cost between $17 billion and $29 billion per year in hospitals nationwide.[67]

The purpose of the IOM report was to bring awareness to the great human and monetary costs associated with errors made by medical professionals—specifically, the errors that are preventable. In an effort to help medical facilities make changes to reduce human error, the IOM report provided four recommendations: First, medical facilities have to "establish a national focus to create leadership, research, tools and protocols to enhance the knowledge base about safety." Second, facilities need to "identify and learn from errors by developing a nationwide public mandatory reporting system and by encouraging health care organizations and practitioners to develop and participate in voluntary reporting systems." Third, facilities need to focus on "raising performance standards and expectations for improvements in safety through the actions of oversight organizations, professional groups and group purchasers of health care." And finally, there needs to be an "implementation of safety systems in health care organizations to ensure safe practices at the delivery level."[68]

Since the publication of the 1999 IOM report, medical facilities across the country have adopted innovative and effective ways to reduce human error. An error reduction approach that has drawn a great deal of attention within the medical community in the United States and in several other countries is the use of "checklists."

Innovative Risk Management in Medicine: The "Checklist"

Dr. Peter Pronovost (critical care specialist at Johns Hopkins Hospital) experimented with the use of checklists to reduce infections in central-line catheters.[69] He created his checklist by writing down the steps it would take to avoid line infections (see Figure 7.2). He asked the nurses working in the

Intensive Care Unit (ICU) to monitor doctors as they put lines into patients for one month. The result of the nurses' observations was striking—doctors skipped at least one of the steps on Pronovost's checklist in more than one-third of the patients cared for during the previous month.[70] With permission from hospital administration, Dr. Pronovost instructed all nurses to stop doctors when they tried to skip any of the steps on the checklist. After one year of oversight by the nurses, Provonost found that the line infection rate dropped from 11 percent to zero. In an effort to confirm the findings from the previous year, Pronovost continued the oversight by the nurses for another 15 months. Once again there were very few line infections (two cases). Pronovost and his colleagues calculated that during the time that the checklist was being used in the ICU, 43 infections and eight deaths were prevented, and the hospital saved approximately $2 million.[71]

Figure 7.2   The Checklist

The following list is recommended to reduce the risk of infections:

Wash hands with soap or cleanser

Wear sterile clothing

Clean the patient's skin

Avoid veins in arms and legs (use veins in chest)

Check the line for infection every day and remove it as soon as it is no longer needed

---

Source: The Wall Street Journal, March 27, 2011. "The Secret to Fighting Infections: Dr. Peter Pronovost Says It Isn't That Hard. If Only Hospitals Would Do It," written by Laura Landro. Available at: http://online.wsj.com/article/SB1000142405274870436400457613196318589308 4.html.

In 2004, the effectiveness of Pronovost's checklist was examined even further when it was used in hospitals across the state of Michigan. The results of this study revealed that after 18 months, the checklist reduced the number of line catheter infections up to 66 percent. Further, it was estimated that the checklist saved more than 1,500 lives and $200 million over the course of the 18-month study.[72] The findings of this study were published in the prestigious *New England Journal of Medicine* in 2006.

After the findings of Pronovost's study were published in 2006, the adoption of checklists by medical facilities across the United States skyrocketed. Hospitals and clinics began to use checklists for a wide range of tasks in an effort to reduce human error. Research published in medical journals reveals that the checklists can be effective in oncology units[73] and surgical wards,[74] to name a few. The power of the checklist became even more evident when Health and Human Services Secretary Kathleen Sebelius urged hospitals across the United States to use checklists to reduce central-line infections in July 2009.[75]

Despite a plethora of empirical research confirming the utility of checklists, there are some roadblocks to the adoption of checklists. First, the culture within an organization needs to be open to the use of checklists. Dr. Pronovost faced resistance from doctors, nurses, and other medical professionals when the checklist was implemented in hospitals in Michigan. Specifically, the medical staff felt that they could do their job just as well without a checklist.[76] Some of the doctors felt insulted because they were being asked to do something so elementary.[77] If checklists are rejected by members of an organization it is unlikely that checklists will be used by them, and in the end, the checklists will not be effective. It is critical that administrators present the reasons why checklists are being adopted by the organization, the benefits that checklists can bring to the organization, and that adequate training will be available to everyone who will be asked to use checklists. Second, the use of checklists has to be integrated into daily operations so that it does not place a huge burden on members of an organization.[78] If checklists are short and easy to use, it is more likely that employees will use them as they are supposed to. And finally, extra time and resources are necessary when an organization adopts a checklist system. There are costs associated with the actual checklist (paper material or in some cases computerized checklists), and also with the collection, monitoring, analysis, and reporting of results from the use of checklists. Some organizations may not have the resources (or in some cases not want to use their resources) to adopt a checklist system.

Some people might be thinking to themselves, "A checklist . . . really?!" How can something as simple as a checklist have such a significant impact? In the case of the Pronovost checklist, it helped with memory recall for tasks that are considered mundane, and it spelled out the minimum steps that need to be taken to accomplish the task at hand while reducing liability and risk.[79] Even more important, it keeps everyone involved in the task accountable for their own actions. The reduction in errors and increase in accountability resulting from the use of checklists are precisely why this is an effective risk management technique.

Checklists and Policing: Could It Work?

Checklists have been used and have been found to be effective in several professions including banking,[80] child psychology,[81] real estate,[82] education,[83] and nutrition[84] to name a few. Could checklists be an effective risk management tool in police agencies attempting to manage liability and increase officer accountability?

Checklists could be an effective risk management tool for police agencies. In fact, there are some police agencies in the United States that already use checklists as part of officer training, investigations, and when dealing with incidents that often lead to litigation or some other negative outcome (such as citizen complaints). The Conroe Police Department in Texas uses checklists as part of their officer field training program.[85] The field training manual that is given to every officer who enters the field training program contains all of the training categories and training checklists that document the completion of all training tasks. The use of checklists in this department benefits the individual officers by requiring them to complete all aspects of training needed to be effective in this position. In addition, using checklists for training allows the police agency to be protected from litigation based on claims that they did not properly train their officers. The documentation of completed training is in line with the basic principles of risk management, as it results in a paper trail to prove that actions were taken (in this case training) by police agencies.

The Portland Police Bureau (PPB) uses checklists for a variety of police practices. First, the PPB uses a checklist when conducting investigations with police officers that use deadly force (see Figure 7.3).[86] The PPB also uses a checklist for in-custody deaths and serious use of force incidents. These checklists are modeled after those used by the Miami-Dade Police Department and the Los Angeles County Sheriff's Department.[87]

Figure 7.3 Officer-Involved Shooting Checklist*

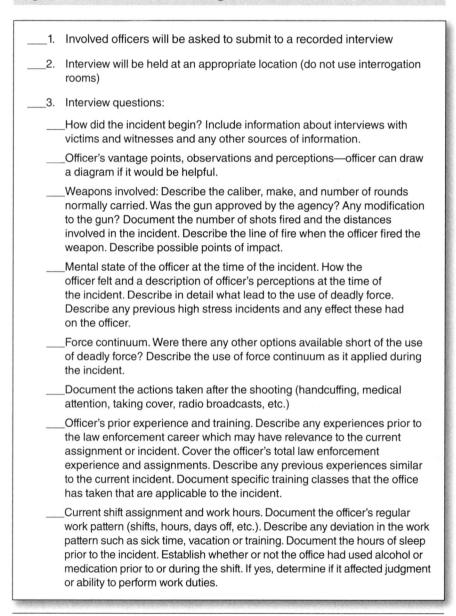

____1. Involved officers will be asked to submit to a recorded interview

____2. Interview will be held at an appropriate location (do not use interrogation rooms)

____3. Interview questions:

____How did the incident begin? Include information about interviews with victims and witnesses and any other sources of information.

____Officer's vantage points, observations and perceptions—officer can draw a diagram if it would be helpful.

____Weapons involved: Describe the caliber, make, and number of rounds normally carried. Was the gun approved by the agency? Any modification to the gun? Document the number of shots fired and the distances involved in the incident. Describe the line of fire when the officer fired the weapon. Describe possible points of impact.

____Mental state of the officer at the time of the incident. How the officer felt and a description of officer's perceptions at the time of the incident. Describe in detail what lead to the use of deadly force. Describe any previous high stress incidents and any effect these had on the officer.

____Force continuum. Were there any other options available short of the use of deadly force? Describe the use of force continuum as it applied during the incident.

____Document the actions taken after the shooting (handcuffing, medical attention, taking cover, radio broadcasts, etc.)

____Officer's prior experience and training. Describe any experiences prior to the law enforcement career which may have relevance to the current assignment or incident. Cover the officer's total law enforcement experience and assignments. Describe any previous experiences similar to the current incident. Document specific training classes that the office has taken that are applicable to the incident.

____Current shift assignment and work hours. Document the officer's regular work pattern (shifts, hours, days off, etc.). Describe any deviation in the work pattern such as sick time, vacation or training. Document the hours of sleep prior to the incident. Establish whether or not the office had used alcohol or medication prior to or during the shift. If yes, determine if it affected judgment or ability to perform work duties.

*This is a modified version of the checklist used by the Portland Police Bureau. The source from which this checklist was drawn can be found at http://www.parc.info/client_files/Portland/First%20Report/2%20-%20Appendix%201.pdf.

Checklists could be used by internal affairs divisions when they investigate citizen complaints filed against officers and when they investigate officers that are flagged by early intervention systems. Essentially, checklist systems could be used for police actions that are most likely to result in litigation, liability claims, and citizen complaints.

It is likely that there would be resistance to the adoption of checklists by patrol officers (for some of the same reasons that there was resistance by doctors presented with the Provonost checklist). In order to prevent some of the potential road blocks, police administrators would need to create a culture within their organizations that is open to the use of checklists and that sees the value of checklists. It is critical that police administrators present the reasons why checklists are being adopted by the organization, the benefits that checklists can bring to the organization, and that adequate training will be available to everyone who will be asked to use checklists. It is also imperative that checklists are easily integrated into daily operations so that it does not create an increased workload for patrol officers. If checklists are short and easy to use, it is more likely that patrol officers will use them. In addition, police administrators will need to find resources to adopt a checklist system.

There are costs associated with the actual checklist (whether it be paper checklists or computerized checklist programs that can be integrated into laptop computers already used in patrol cars). The collection, monitoring, analysis, and reporting of checklists used by patrol officers could become part of the responsibilities of internal affairs or public integrity bureaus within police organizations. It makes sense that this type of division or unit be responsible for watching the use of checklists as their role is one that already involves monitoring and tracking the behavior of patrol officers. Police executives could justify the costs associated with the adoption of checklists as it is likely that in the long run, checklist systems could save them money and more importantly, increase police accountability within their organizations.

Looking Ahead: The Future of Risk Management in Policing

Despite the increase in costs associated with police liability in the last four decades, very few police agencies use risk management and very little is known about risk management in policing in the United States. Other than the two studies conducted by Archbold, and Ross and Bodapadi, there have not been any in-depth studies of risk management and policing. Future research should include studies similar to the Ross and Bodapadi study in other police agencies across the United States to gauge the financial impact of risk management on police liability. The use of risk management by medium and small police agencies should also be examined in the future. It should not be assumed that medium and small police agencies do not have organizational loss related to liability incidents.

The use of early warning systems as a tool in risk management efforts should also be looked at more closely as there is a growing interest in the use of this particular oversight mechanism. The extent to which risk management enhances police professionalism and officer accountability should also be studied in the future. Research focused on the adoption and impact of checklists by police agencies will be critical in understanding if and how this particular risk management technique impacts liability and accountability in police agencies. In conclusion, there is still a lot to learn about the use and impact of risk management in American police agencies.

Notes

1 Peter Young, *The A, B, C's of Risk Management* (Washington, DC: International City/County Management Association, 1991).
2 Gerry Armitage and Helen Knapman, "Adverse Events in Drug Administration: A Literature Review," *Journal of Nursing Management* 11 (2003): 130–41. Dana Royce Baerger, "Risk Management With the Suicidal Patient: Lessons From Case Law," *Professional Psychology: Research and Practice* 32 (2001): 359–67. Thomas Baxter Jr., "Governing the Financial or Bank Holding Company: How Legal Infrastructure Can Facilitate Consolidated Risk Management," *Current Issues in Economics and Finance* 9 (2003): 1–8. James Harshfield, "Liability Issues of Using Volunteers in Public Schools," *NASSP Bulletin* 80 (1996): 61–6.
3 Steve Ashley and Rod Pearson (1993), *Fundamentals of Risk Management* (Liability Assessment & Awareness International, Inc). Available at http://www.laaw.com. See also Peter Young, *The A, B, C's of Risk Management* (Washington, DC: International City/County Management Association, 1991).
4 Peter Young, *Risk Management: A Comprehensive Approach* (Washington, DC: International City/County Management Association, 2000).
5 Ibid.

6   Robert Wennerholm, "Officer Survival Recommendations: New Civil Liability Concerns," in *Risk Management Today: A How-to Guide for Local Government*, eds. Natalie Wasserman and Dean Phelus (Washington, DC: Public Risk and Insurance Management Association and International City Management Association, 1985). See also G. Patrick Gallagher (1990), "The Six-Layered Liability Protection System for Police," *The Police Chief*, June, pp. 40–4.

7   Egon Bittner, *The Functions of the Police in Modern Society* (Washington, DC: National Institute of Mental Health, 1970).

8   Joyce Blalock, *Civil Liability of Law Enforcement Officers* (Springfield, IL: Charles C. Thomas Publisher, 1974). See also Rolando del Carmen, *Civil Liabilities in American Policing: A Text for Law Enforcement Personnel* (Englewood Cliffs, CA: Prentice-Hall, Inc., 1991). See also Charldean Newell, Janay Pollock, and Jerry Tweedy, "Financial Aspects of Police Liability," International City/County Management Association Baseline Report, International City/County Management Association, vol. 24 (1993), 1–8.

9   Steven Ashley and Rod Pearson, *Fundamentals of Risk Management*, Liability Assessment & Awareness International, Inc. (1993). Available at http://www.laaw.com.

10   Ibid.

11   Geoffrey Alpert and Lorie Fridell, *Police Vehicles and Firearms: Instruments of Deadly Force* (Prospect Heights, IL: Waveland Press, 1992). See also Concetta Culliver and Robert Sigler, "Police Use of Deadly Force in Tennessee Following *Tennessee v. Garner*," *Journal of Contemporary Criminal Justice* 11 (1995): 187–95. See also Antony Pate and Lorie Fridell, "Toward the Uniform Reporting of Police Use of Force: Results of a National Survey," *Criminal Justice Review* 20 (1995): 123–45. See also Jerry Sparger and David Giacopassi, "Memphis Revisited: A Reexamination of Police Shootings After the Garner Decision," *Justice Quarterly* 9 (1992): 211–25.

12   Dave Grossi, "Setting the Record Straight on Force Continuums," *The Police Marksman* (January/February 2006).

13   Thomas Petrowski, "Use of Force Policies and Training: A Reasoned Approach," *FBI Law Enforcement Bulletin* (October 2002): 25–32.

14   Richard Hough Sr. and Kimberly Tatum, "An Examination of Florida Policies on Force Continuums," *Policing: An International Journal of Police Strategies & Management* 35, no. 1 (2012): 39–54.

15   Steven Ashley and Rod Pearson, *Fundamentals of Risk Management* (Liability Assessment & Awareness International, Inc., 1993). Available at http://www.laaw.com.

16   Geoffrey Alpert, Dennis Kenney, Roger Dunham, and William Smith, *Police Pursuits: What We Know* (Washington, DC: Police Executive Research Forum, 2000), 154.

17 Geoffrey Alpert and Lorie Fridell, *Police Vehicles and Firearms: Instruments of Deadly Force* (Prospect Heights, IL: Waveland Press, 1992). See also Robert Crew, David Kessler Jr., and Lorie Fridell, "Changing Hot Pursuit Policy: An Empirical Assessment of the Impact on Pursuit Behavior," *Evaluation Review* 18 (1994): 678–88, and Robert Crew, Lorie Fridell, and Karen Pursell, "Probabilities and Odds in Hot Pursuits: A Benefit-Cost Analysis," *Journal of Criminal Justice* 23 (1995): 417–24.

18 American Civil Liberties Union of Southern California, *Analysis and Recommendations: Los Angeles Police Department K-9 Program* (Los Angeles, CA: Los Angeles California Police Commission, 1992).

19 Brian Reaves, *Local Police Departments (2007)* (Washington, DC: Bureau of Justice Statistics, 2011).

20 American Civil Liberties Union of Southern California (1992): 21.

21 Charlie Mesloh, "Barks or Bites? The Impact of Training on Police Canine Force Outcomes," *Police Practice and Research* 7, no. 4 (2006): 323–35.

22 Alec Campbell, Richard Berk, and James Fyfe, "Deployment of Violence: The Los Angeles Police Department's Use of Dogs," *Evaluation Review* 22 (1998): 535–61. See also Los Angeles County Sheriff's Department, *12th Semiannual Report* by Special Counsel Merrick J. Bobb and Staff (Los Angeles, 2000).

23 Edward Hickey and Peter Hoffman, "To Bite or Not to Bite: Canine Apprehensions in a Large, Suburban Police Department," *Journal of Criminal Justice* 31 (2003): 147–54.

24 Thomas Martinelli, "Minimizing Risk by Defining Off-Duty Police Misconduct," *Police Chief*, 74 (2007): 6.

25 Ibid.

26 Ibid.

27 See http://www.seattlepi.com/local/article/Bellevue-cops-profane-at-Seahawks-game-not-fired-4091126.php.

28 See http://www.nola.com/crime/index.ssf/2012/03/new_orleans_cop_suspended_inde.html.

29 Ibid.

30 See http://jobs.aol.com/articles/2012/08/09/police-officer-susan-graziosi-fired-for-facebook-criticism-sue/.

31 See http://www.sfltimes.com/index.php?option=com_content&task=view&id=9512&Itemid=199.

32 Ibid.

33 See http://www.nytimes.com/2011/04/07/us/07police.html?pagewanted=all&_r=0.

34 PRIMAFILE Online, "Police Liability Assessment Guide," PRIMAFILE Online, on file with author (2000).

35 See http://www.calea.org/content/risk-management-liability-insurance-and-calea-accreditation.

36 See http://www.calea.org/content/accreditation-saves-money.

37 See http://www.calea.org/content/intergovernmental-risk-management-agency-irma-report.

38 See http://www.calea.org/content/two-risk-management-studies-support-accreditation.

39 Ibid.

40 G. Patrick Gallagher, "Risk Management for Police Administrators," *The Police Chief* (June 1990): 18–29.

41 Hal Heazeltine, "Case Study: A Risk Audit of Law Enforcement," *Risk Management* 10 (1986): 60–3. See also Roberto Ceniceros, "Policing Their Own Risks: Formal Risk Management Growing in Law Enforcement," *Business Insurance* 32 (1998): 10–13. And also Joanne Wojcik, "Liability Lawsuits Rise Again for LAPD," *Business Insurance* 28 (1994): 20–2.

42 Samuel Walker, *Police Accountability: The Role of Citizen Oversight* (Belmont, CA: Wadsworth Publishing, 2001). See pages 100–1.

43 Geoffrey Alpert, Dennis Kenney, Roger Dunham, and William Smith, *Police Pursuits: What We Know* (Washington, DC: Police Executive Research Forum, 2000).

44 Ibid., 156.

45 Samuel Walker and Geoffrey Alpert, "Early Warning Systems as Risk Management for Police," in *Policing and Misconduct*, ed. Kim Michelle Lersch (Upper Saddle River, NJ: Prentice Hall, 2002), 219–30.

46 Carol A. Archbold, "Managing the Bottom Line: Risk Management in Policing," *Policing: An International Journal of Police Strategies & Management* 28, no. 1 (2005): 38–50. For the study in its entirety, see Carol A. Archbold, *Police Accountability, Risk Management, and Legal Advising* (New York: LFB Scholarly Publishing, 2004).

47 Ibid.

48 Carol A. Archbold, *Police Accountability, Risk Management, and Legal Advising* (New York: LFB Scholarly Publishing, 2004).

49 Ibid.

50 Darrell Ross and Madhava R. Bodapati, "A Risk Management Analysis of the Claims, Litigation, and Losses of Michigan Law Enforcement Agencies: 1985–1999," *Policing: An International Journal of Police Strategies & Management* 29, no. 1 (2006): 38–57.

51 Ibid., 46.

52 Ibid., 46.

53 Ibid., 53.

54 G. Patrick Gallagher, "Risk Management for Police Administrators," *The Police Chief,* (June 1990): 18–29.

55 Roberto Ceniceros, "Policing Their Own Risks: Formal Risk Management Growing in Law Enforcement," *Business Insurance* 32 (1998): 10–13.

56 Los Angeles County (2003), available at http://www.co.la.ca.us/bobb
.html.

57 L. O'Brien and Duane E. Wilcox, "Risk Management Organization and
Administration," in *Risk Management Today: A How-To Guide for Local
Government*, eds. Natalie Wasserman and Dean Phelus (Washington, DC:
Public Risk and Insurance Management Association and International
City Management Association, 1985).

58 Peter Young, *Risk Management: A Comprehensive Approach* (Washington,
DC: International City/County Management Association, 2000).

59 See http://www.lexipol.com/disciplines/enforcement-fq-1.html.

60 See http://www.spokanepolice.org/documents/Lexipol%20111711
.pdf.

61 See http://www.lincolncountysheriff.net/about/policy_manual.pdf,
http://www.tigard-or.gov/police/docs/policy_manual.pdf, and http://
www.desmoinesmail.com/webpdf/Police/RosieInvest/Policy_Manual_
RELEASE_20101216.pdf.

62 See http://www.llrmi.com/.

63 Ibid.

64 See http://www.healthcarefinancenews.com/news/hospitals-face-risk-
management-head.

65 See http://www.iom.edu/~/media/Files/Report%20Files/1999/To-Err-
is-Human/To%20Err%20is%20Human%201999%20%20report%20brief
.pdf.

66 Ibid.

67 Ibid.

68 Ibid., 3–4.

69 See http://www.newyorker.com/reporting/2007/12/10/071210fa_fact_
gawande.

70 Ibid.

71 Ibid.

72 Peter Pronovost, Dale Needham, Sean Berenholtz, David Sinopoli, Haitao
Chu, Sara Cosgrove, Bryan Sexton, et al., "An Intervention to Decrease
Catheter-Related Bloodstream Infections in the ICU," *New England Journal
of Medicine* 355, 26 (2006): 2725–32.

73 Sara Stubenrauch, Eva-Maria Schneid, Alexander Wünsch, Almut Helmes,
Hartmut Bertz, Kurt Fritzsche, Michael Wirsching, and Tanja Gölz,
"Development and Evaluation of a Checklist Assessing Communication
Skills of Oncologists: The COM-ON-Checklist," *Journal of Evaluation in
Clinical Practice* 45, 5 (2009): 274–78.

74 Gian Maria Cavallini, Luca Campi, Michele De Maria, and Matteo Forlini,
"Clinical Risk Management in Eye Outpatient Surgery: A New Surgical
Safety Checklist for Cataract Surgery and Intravitreal Anti-VEGF

Injection," *Graefe's Archive for Clinical and Experimental Ophthalmology* (November 2012): 1–6.

75 See http://www.ahrq.gov/legacy/news/press/pr2009/hhskeystonepr.htm.

76 See http://www.newyorker.com/reporting/2007/12/10/071210fa_fact_gawande.

77 Ibid.

78 Ibid.

79 Ibid.

80 Bruce Johnson, "Lender Liability Litigation Checklist: A Summary of Current Theories and Developments," *UMKC L. Rev.* 59 (1990): 205.

81 Matthew Speltz, Nancy Gonzales, Stephen Sulzbacher, and Linda Quan, "Assessment of Injury Risk in Young Children: A Preliminary Study of the Injury Behavior Checklist," *Journal of Pediatric Psychology* 15, no. 3 (1990): 373–83.

82 Charles Sink, "Negotiating Dispute Clauses That Affect Damage Recovery," *Constr. Law* 18 (1998): 22.

83 Carroll Thomason and Dusty Thrash. "Play It Safe: A Pre-Installation Checklist That Could Mean an Injury- and Liability-Free Playground," *Children and Families* 8, no. 1 (1999): 40–42.

84 Paul Branscum et al., "An Evaluation of the Validity and Reliability of a Food Behavior Checklist Modified for Children," *Journal of Nutrition Education and Behavior* 42, no. 5 (2010): 349–52.

85 See http://texasisdchiefs.com/images/ConroeISDPD-FTOManual.pdf.

86 See http://www.parc.info/client_files/Portland/First%20Report/2%20-%20Appendix%201.pdf.

87 Ibid.

EIGHT

The New Technology and Police Accountability

T he work of police officers occurs mostly in public places; however, direct and continuous supervision of police officers is quite limited. Police officers are also given a tremendous amount of discretion as they interact with the public. Limited supervision coupled with vast discretionary power may work for some police officers, but it can open the door for police misconduct with others. So how is it possible to increase the monitoring of police officers as they work the streets? The use of advanced technology is one answer to this question. In the past, advancements in technology were viewed primarily as a way to help the police do their job more efficiently and effectively. Today, advanced technology not only helps officers do their job better, but it also increases officer accountability.

Video Recording Devices Used by the Public

The use of video recording devices as an accountability tool began in 1991 when the videotaped beating of Rodney King by officers in the Los Angeles Police Department (LAPD) was placed in the hands of the media. The recorded beating brought concerns about police brutality to the forefront of public attention. It is also likely that the Rodney King incident would not be viewed as a significant event today if the incident had not been videotaped by a resident of the neighborhood. Back then it was difficult for citizens to make accusations of police abuse because there was no way to prove it unless there were witnesses present on scene. With the increase in public access to video recorders (by way of cell phones) it is no longer as difficult to prove allegations of police abuse as it was several decades ago.

Public access to video recording technology has increased as cell phones with video recording capabilities have become more affordable. In addition, the quality of video that is recorded by these devices has improved. These devices have also become more compact, which allows people to carry them almost anywhere. Today, many of the incidents of police misconduct that are presented by the media come from citizens who have recorded these incidents on their cell phones. In essence, the ease of access to this particular piece of technology has resulted in greater accountability of police officers.

The increase in video recordings of police activities has resulted in heated legal debates centering primarily on the invasion of privacy. Recent court case outcomes have helped determine whether or not it is legal for citizens to record the police in public places. For example, *Glik v. Cunniffe*, 655 F.3d 78 (1st Cir. 2011) determined that private citizens have the right to videotape public officials (including the police) when they are working in public spaces (see Figure 8.1).[1] This action does not invade privacy as the police are acting as government officials in locations that are considered open to the public.

Reporting Police Misconduct: Is There an App for That?

The American Civil Liberties Union (ACLU) of New Jersey has a free app available for smartphones that can help citizens record and store information from their interactions with the police—the app is called "Police Tape." This app allows smartphones to record both video and audio recordings of citizens' interactions with the police. A copy of the recording is saved to the citizen's phone and another copy is automatically uploaded and saved by the ACLU of New Jersey.[2]

Figure 8.1   Details of Glik v. Cunniffe, 2011

On October 1, 2007, Simon Glik was walking in the Boston Commons area when he witnessed three Boston police officers making an arrest. A bystander yelled at the police to stop hurting the man that they were attempting to arrest. Thinking that the police may be using excessive force, Glik pulled out his cell phone and began to record the incident. When the police officers realized that Glik was video recording the incident, they placed him under arrest for violating state wiretapping law, which forbids any secret audio recordings. Glik's criminal case was eventually dismissed. Glik filed a lawsuit against the city of Boston for infringing on his civil rights. On March 27, 2012, the city of Boston settled the lawsuit with Glik for $175,000.

Sources: Boston.com, Feb.1, 2010, and March 27, 2012.

Similarly, the New York Civil Liberties Union (NYCLU) now has a free app called "Stop and Frisk Watch," which allows citizens to monitor the activities of New York City police officers. Recent controversy surrounding the stop and frisk practices of NYPD police officers prompted the creation of this app. Recent statistics reveal that residents of New York City were stopped by the police 533,042 times in 2012. Most of these citizens (89%) were innocent, and a majority of the citizens stopped by the police were minority citizens (55% black and 32% Latino).[3] The app allows citizens to document any stop and frisk encounters they witness and also provide alerts when stop and frisks are in progress. According to the NYCLU website, the app has three primary functions:[4] First, the app allows citizens to record incidents by using a button on the smartphone's frame. When the video recording shuts off, the NYCLU sends a survey to the smartphone asking for a description of the recorded incident. Second, the app can send alerts to people who are near the area where a stop and frisk is taking place. By alerting citizens to these areas, it is more likely that someone will be able to record the interactions. This function of the app is useful to community groups who monitor the police in New York City. And finally, the app allows citizens to report any police interactions that they might witness even if they were not able to record the interaction.[5]

There are other apps that can record police and citizen interactions. "Open Watch.net" is a website that was launched in January 2011 that offers several smartphone apps designed to record citizen encounters with police officers in a discreet manner.[6] Any recordings captured by these apps can be uploaded to the Open Watch's database, which is available to the public. Rich Jones, founder of Open Watch, says that he has received thousands of uploads from app users since the app was made available to the public. Oddly enough, the Open Watch founder says that he receives requests from attorneys and police officers who want to use recordings in trials. Jones says that there are police officers who use his apps to record their interactions with citizens so that they can protect themselves if allegations of police misconduct are lodged against them.[7]

It is likely that smartphone apps of this nature will continue to grow in popularity as people continue to use their cell phones and smartphones in various facets of their lives. It is also likely that police officers will become more aware of the fact that they could be recorded at any time when they interact with the public. Hopefully this awareness will begin to transform the behavior of police officers in the future.

Video Recording Devices Used by the Police

The use of video cameras in patrol cars is becoming more common in police agencies across the United States. Recent statistics indicate that more than half (61%) of local police departments used video cameras in their patrol cars in 2007—this has increased since 2003, when 55 percent of local agencies used video cameras in squad cars.[8]

Video cameras in patrol cars can record interactions between the police and citizens. These recordings can be helpful to both police and citizens. For example, if a citizen alleges that an officer used offensive language or excessive force, video recorded evidence can provide both audio and visual recording of the incident to either support the claim or exonerate the officer in question. In many cases, if the video recorded evidence did not exist, citizens would have a hard time proving that they were victims of police abuse. Video recorders can also help police supervisors identify procedures used by patrol officers that may compromise officer safety.

Video recording devices have improved over time by becoming more compact in size, and also by producing higher-quality video recordings. Some innovative police agencies have figured out new ways to use video recording devices to help them with their work. Officers in Fort Smith, Arkansas; Cincinnati, Ohio; San Jose, California; and Aberdeen, South Dakota, are testing a new video camera device that attaches near officers' ears that allows them to record every encounter they have with citizens.[9] Some police agencies are using video recorders that can be attached to their uniform (near their badge).[10] And other agencies are using video recorders that are attached to glasses.[11] Vievu, the company that makes body cameras for police officers, reports that it has supplied body cameras to more than 3,000 police agencies across the United States.[12]

> Several citizens in San Jose, California, complained that the police disproportionately make Hispanic and African American citizens sit on the curb during routine encounters. As a result, the San Jose police auditor wants police officers to wear body cameras in an effort to document the ethnicity or race of every person they encounter. This data would reveal if police are using race-based procedures when interacting with the public.
>
> *Source:* MercuryNews.com, April 12, 2012.

The advantage of having officers wear video recorders instead of having them installed in patrol cars is that more activity can be captured as officers interact with the public. Some agencies also view body cameras as an important tool when they are called to crimes scenes. Body cameras allow the officers to record the conditions at the crime scene exactly how it looked when they arrived.[13] This type of recording could be useful in the courtroom when officers are accused of tampering with crime scene evidence or accused of using inappropriate techniques to collect evidence at crime scenes.

Police agencies that routinely have allegations of misconduct lodged against them might find the use of such technology helpful. This is the case with the Seattle Police Department. In 2011, the United States Department of Justice began an investigation of the Seattle Police Department after numerous allegations of race-based policing and use of excessive force.[14] Members of the Seattle City Council recently requested that the mayor include resources in the next budget to purchase body cameras for the Seattle Police Department.[15] The cameras being considered for the Seattle pilot project would not allow officers to turn cameras on or off whenever they want. Instead, the cameras would be recording every interaction that Seattle police officers have with citizens. The hope is that the body cameras will result in officers being on their best behavior at all times because they know that they are being recorded. In addition, by initiating such a program, the Seattle Police Department can begin to rebuild the fractured relationship with the community by demonstrating that they are committed to transparency and accountability.

Police unions have had mixed reactions to the use of body cameras by police officers. Some argue that the cameras might cause police officers to hesitate to use force in situations where use of force is justified and necessary.[16] Body cameras, then, could potentially compromise officer safety. Police union representatives also have concerns about officers invading the privacy of citizens, as officers are sometimes required to enter the homes of private citizens (e.g., for domestic violence calls). If officers are wearing body cameras that cannot be shut off before entering private homes, this might infringe upon the privacy of citizens as officers will no longer be recording in public space. In contrast, there are some police unions that view body cameras as a way of protecting officers from false allegations of misconduct.

The use of body cameras by police officers has to be negotiated by police executives and police unions. One particular issue that might disrupt negotiations between these two groups is deciding who will have access to the video recordings.[17] Police executives might want the video recordings made available to the public in order to show that they are committed to being transparent and accountable to their communities. In contrast, union representatives might want limitations placed on the people who have access to video recordings in an effort to protect their members. Police executives might also want to limit officers' access to recordings in situations where they have been accused of misconduct or have been involved in incidents where there are potential policy infractions. If officers have access to the recordings, they could fashion their explanations and reports around the events that are viewable on the recordings. To muddy the waters even further, there are some jurisdictions where such recordings could be categorized as public record, which means that anyone should be able to get access to the recordings generated by officer body cameras.[18]

There are other ways that police agencies are able to use video cameras to record incidents that are deemed high risk and that also often result in police-involved litigation. Some police agencies are beginning to outfit their stun guns with video recorders.[19] As stun guns have become more common in police agencies across the United States, the controversy and liability involving the use of stun guns has also increased.[20] Some police executives have acknowledged this increase in liability and outfitted their stun guns with video recording capabilities. The Taser company reported that they have attached video cameras to more than 55,000 Tasers used by police officers across the United States.[21]

Police body cameras sound like a good way to increase officer accountability—but how much do these cameras cost? The Greensboro (North Carolina) Police Department has adopted a video camera system that costs $1,100 per camera.[22] The San Jose (California) Police Department utilizes the high-definition Taser Axon cameras that cost $1,700 per camera and a monthly fee of $99 per camera to a third-party company that is tasked with managing all of the video footage generated by each of the cameras.[23] The cost associated with body camera systems might prevent some police agencies from adopting this technology. It could be argued, however, that in the long run the cameras could save police departments money that might otherwise be spent on payouts in lawsuits and liability claims. Further, the cost of cameras might be well worth the money if they help police departments restore or strengthen their relationship with the communities they protect and serve.

Police Use of Social Media to Inform the Public

Social media networks have revolutionized the way that information and news stories are transmitted from person to person across the United States and in other countries. A recent study found that 43 percent of online news sharing occurs through the use of social media networks.[24] This study also revealed that most (65%) stories shared on social media networks feature news stories that are ongoing. Another recent study by the Pew Research Center found that men and women are equally as likely to get their news from social networking sites (including Twitter and Facebook).[25] This study concluded that online sharing through social networks has contributed to a significant increase in news consumption in the United States.

It is clear that social networking sites have become (and will continue to be) an important source of information for the public. One group has begun to use social networking to transmit information about incidents of police misconduct to the general public. In 2012, The Cato Institute took over The National Police Misconduct Reporting Project (NPMRP).[26] The NPMRP analyzes national media reports every day for stories of police misconduct. The incidents of police misconduct are entered and stored in a database that is made accessible to the public. The NPMRP uses several social networking sites to transmit every reported incident of police misconduct by many national news sources to anyone that signs up for its news feed.

Based on statistics provided on its website, the NPMRP transmits thousands of incidents of police misconduct using social networking sites. For example, the 2010 NPMRP report notes that during 2010, 4,861 individual reports of police misconduct involving 6,613 sworn law enforcement officers and 6,826 victims were transmitted to anyone who is signed up to their newsfeed via a social networking site.[27] The transmissions provided by NPMRP include information about the number of estimated fatalities resulting from police misconduct, the types of misconduct officers are involved in, and finally, an estimated amount that is spent on misconduct-related civil judgments and settlements (not including settlements that are sealed by the court, court costs, or attorney fees).[28]

It is possible that the use of social media networks to transmit information about incidents of police misconduct can enhance police accountability by keeping the public informed about what is going on in their own communities and also across the country. There has been virtually no empirical research conducted on social media and police misconduct; thus, it is too early to determine if social media influences officer accountability.

Global Positioning System (GPS)

The GPS (global positioning system) is also becoming a popular tool in policing. This technology not only helps police officers conduct their work more efficiently, it can also serve as a police accountability tool. Police officers use GPS devices to track down vulnerable populations if they wander away from their guardian or home (including elderly persons with dementia or children with special needs) and also people who have been charged with crimes and are fleeing the area.[29] This technology can be used to track and monitor the movements of patrol cars and patrol officers. Some police agencies use GPS tracking technology to determine how they can reduce costs associated with labor hours and fuel consumption, and also police vehicle maintenance.[30] The ability to track patrol cars and police officers using GPS enhances officer safety (in case back-up is needed) and also enhances police accountability by monitoring the whereabouts of police officers.[31]

Internal affairs and professional standards divisions conduct internal investigations centered on police officer behaviors/actions. Some of these investigations reveal that police officers go home to sleep while they are on duty, they are in locations that are outside of their beat areas, they falsify information on reports regarding their whereabouts, and they also sometimes falsify their time sheets.[32] Some police agencies also use GPS to monitor the driving habits of police officers—specifically, to identify the officers who have a "lead foot" (speeding).[33]

Some police agencies have taken the use of GPS a step further and have installed GPS devices within the two-way radios that police officers wear as part of their standard uniform. By attaching the GPS devices to the officer instead of the patrol car, the location of the officer can be tracked if he or she gets out of their vehicle. This can serve as an officer safety mechanism when officers are required to get out of their cars and pursue suspects. In addition, GPS devices attached to officers can also provide critical information in cases where alleged misconduct has occurred.

In 2011, a police officer in Lowell, Massachusetts, was charged with having sex with prostitutes while he was on duty. During the overnight shift, the police officer approached prostitutes for sex, and would then drive to an isolated area (in either his patrol car or his personal vehicle) to engage in sexual acts.[34] If the police officer was wearing a two-way radio that had a GPS device in it, that could have helped the investigation by identifying his whereabouts on the days and times that the sexual acts were said to have occurred. In 2011, an on-duty Miami Beach police officer left his all-terrain vehicle (ATV) patrol unit to have drinks at a nearby bar. After having several drinks, the officer got back on his ATV patrol unit (with a female passenger) and severely injured several people who were enjoying the beach area located in his beat area.[35] These are only a few examples of how GPS could enhance officer accountability in police agencies across the country. As GPS devices become more affordable for police agencies to purchase, it is likely that this technology will become more commonly used by police agencies.

The Future of Technology and Police Accountability

In the future, if designed appropriately, technology could be used to not only help officers more efficiently and effectively do their work, it could also allow for review and oversight by people/groups both within police agencies (such as police executives and internal affairs) and outside of police agencies (police auditors, civilian review boards). Well-designed information technology systems could be created in a way where information is collected instantaneously, it cannot be tampered with by police officers, and it can be saved in comprehensive databases that can be accessed by people both within and outside of police agencies. Creating a culture of transparency will not only increase officer accountability, but it will also help maintain (or in some cases restore or increase) the legitimacy of the police in the eyes of the public.

Notes

1   See http://www.yaliberty.org/posts/glik-v-boston-court-affirms-right-to-record-police-actions-in-public.

2   See http://www.aclu-nj.org/yourrights/the-app-place/.

3   See http://www.nyclu.org/content/stop-and-frisk-data.

4   See http://www.nyclu.org/app.

5   Ibid.

6   See http://www.dmlp.org/blog/2012/citizen-counter-surveillance-police-theres-app.

7   Ibid.

8   Brian A. Reaves, *Local police departments, 2007* (Washington, DC: Bureau of Justice Statistics, December 2010).

9   See http://transcripts.cnn.com/TRANSCRIPTS/1004/24/sitroom.01.html.

10   See http://chicago.cbslocal.com/2012/02/29/police-use-of-body-cams-stun-gun-cameras-stirs-controversy/

11   See http://www.ksl.com/?nid=148&sid=22965087.

12   See http://www.vievu.com/.

13   See http://www.homelandsecuritynewswire.com/dr20121128-more-police-departments-make-officers-wear-headcams.

14   See http://www.justice.gov/crt/about/spl/seattlepd.php.

15   See http://www.npr.org/2011/11/07/142016109/smile-youre-on-cop-camera.

16   Ibid.

17   Ibid.

18   Ibid.

19   See http://chicago.cbslocal.com/2012/02/29/police-use-of-body-cams-stun-gun-cameras-stirs-controversy/.

20   See http://www.mcclatchydc.com/2012/05/04/147757/taser-cases-could-electrify-the.html#.UdwWN23YxZ8.

21   See http://www.nytimes.com/2012/02/21/technology/tasers-latest-police-weapon-the-tiny-camera-and-the-cloud.html?pagewanted=all&_r=0.

22   See http://wunc.org/post/greensboro-police-officers-smile-youre-candid-camera.

23   See http://www.sfgate.com/bayarea/article/Many-police-use-cameras-to-record-interactions-3180364.php.

24   See http://mashable.com/2010/10/07/cnn-news-study/.

25   See http://mashable.com/2010/09/13/news-internet-study/.

26   See http://www.policemisconduct.net/about/.

27   See http://www.policemisconduct.net/statistics/2010-annual-report/#_Summary.

28   Ibid.

29   See http://projectlifesaver.org/Lifesaver/resource-center/news-and-press-releases/.

30   See http://ravtrack.com/avl/tracking-police-vehicles-with-gps-10/.

31   See http://gcn.com/articles/2010/10/08/sl-baltimore-pd-gps.aspx.

32   See http://www.tracking-system.com/news/3-tracking-system-information/367-monitoring-police-with-gps-trackers.html.

33   See http://msbusiness.com/blog/2011/01/16/greenwood-putting-gps-in-police-cars/.

34   See http://www.lowellsun.com/todaysheadlines/ci_18344886.

35   See http://blogs.miaminewtimes.com/riptide/2013/01/miami_beach_police_union_reach.php.

NINE

Police Accountability and the Economy

I n April 2013, the Camden, New Jersey, police department began to go
out of business as a result of the city's economic decline, overly generous benefits for its unionized police officers, and finally, the economic recession. Gradually taking its place was the new Camden County Police Department. About 90 of its 118 officers were former Camden city officers. The city police department was already down to fewer than 200 officers, while the new county force was expected to grow to about 400.[1]

Camden was an extreme case, but it was not unusual as the economic recession that began in 2008 had a devastating impact on many American cities. The recession aggravated conditions that had been developing slowly for decades. Cities lost their population base and the need for large police forces along with their economic bases. Police union contracts, meanwhile, had gained a number of benefits and pension obligations that many people thought were unreasonable. A small but growing number of cities began filing for bankruptcy: Vallejo, California, in 2007 and Stockton, California, in 2012.

The recession affected every aspect of American society. As they face budget cutbacks, police chiefs almost always seek to maintain the basic services of patrol and respond to citizen expectations. In that context, accountability procedures are relatively hidden aspects of policing that are often the first things to be cut. As we discussed in Chapter Five, early intervention systems require considerable nonsworn personnel to enter data into the system. Late data, incorrect data, or no data renders an EIS useless.

In 2010, the Police Executive Research Forum (PERF) held a summit in Washington, D.C., for chiefs of police across the United States to discuss how the economic crisis impacts their organizations. Some chiefs reported that they are eliminating ranks to reduce costs—specifically, Garry McCarthy (Newark, New Jersey, police director) reported that his agency had to eliminate the position of captain.[2] Philadelphia Police Commissioner Charles Ramsey stated that he had to cancel the last two academy classes and has no plans to bring anyone into the academy in the next few years. Steve Conrad (chief of the Glendale, Arizona, Police Department) reported that his agency has had to let many of the civilian workers go because of financial issues, resulting in an increased workload for patrol officers. Ironically, many of the chiefs attending this summit reported that violent crime has been declining in recent years despite the cuts they have had to make with personnel and police services. There was a group consensus that the decline in violent crime might give the public the false impression that the police are able to do more with fewer resources.

Bernard Melekian, director of the Office of Community Oriented Policing Services (COPS), recently described how the economic downturn has required police agencies to reprioritize their delivery of service to the public.[3] He described the prioritization of services in the context of a multitiered hierarchical system. The first tier, emergency response services (911 emergency calls), will not change as a result of the economy because this type of service involves the immediate safety and well-being of citizens. Tier two consists of nonemergency services where officers respond to incidents that have already occurred in order to collect information to include in reports. And finally, tier three services include quality of life issues.[4] Despite public expectation that the police will continue to provide all three levels of service, the second- and third-tier services are most likely to be partially or completely cut as a result of limited financial and staffing resources.

So where does police accountability fit into this hierarchy of services? Is maintaining a high level of police accountability still a priority in police agencies that are dealing with shrinking budgets? To answer this question, it is important to first look at how the downturn in the economy has affected the delivery of police service in the United States.

Economic Conditions and Police Service

In 2010, the Police Executive Research Forum sent out a national survey to gauge how police agencies have adapted during a time of shrinking budgets. The survey revealed that over half (68%) of the agencies surveyed stated that they would reduce or discontinue training.[5] Over one-third (35%) of the police agencies reported that their ability to maintain contributions for police pensions is becoming difficult.[6] Nearly half (47%) of the police agencies surveyed reported that services provided to their communities have declined or will decline in the near future.

A 2011 COPS office report also identified several ways that police agencies have changed as a result of hard economic times in recent years. Staffing within police agencies has been affected by budget cuts in several ways.[7] Some agencies have laid off police officers because their budgets could no longer cover all of the officers' wages. In January 2012, the Miami-Dade Police Department in Florida laid off 118 police officers in order to balance their budget.[8] The Memphis (Tennessee) Police Department planned the possibility of laying off 200 sworn officers if their budget did not increase in coming years.[9] Other police agencies have turned to mandatory furloughs (temporary unpaid leave for employees) or hiring freezes to reduce labor costs.[10]

Services provided to the public have also been scaled back in many communities across the United States. Some police agencies will no longer respond to motor vehicle thefts/accidents, burglar alarms, minor property crimes, and other nonviolent crimes.[11] In some cases, citizens now have to go to the local police station and have less serious incidents handled there by nonsworn employees, or in some instances citizens are required to process minor incidents themselves instead of sworn police officers. A specific example of this includes police agencies that do not dispatch officers to noninjury traffic accidents and require citizens involved in accidents to file their own accident reports (either online or at the police station).[12]

The use of electronic information systems has been credited with helping police agencies save money at a time when resources are scarce. DigiTICKET is a program that helps police officers issue citations in a more efficient manner.[13] This system completely eliminates the old-fashioned pen-and-paper method of issuing citations. Officers simply scan drivers' licenses into the device and all pertinent information is instantly loaded into the handheld machine. Officers can quickly choose the type of violation using a stylus. The machine then prints out a ticket.[14] The eCitation system allows officers to generate and print digital citations faster than older systems. This electronic system is believed to reduce the citation writing process by several minutes. Some agencies have reported that the eCitation system allows officers to write more tickets, thus generating additional revenue.[15] This has allowed some agencies to reduce the number of police officers working the streets at the same time (which further saves the agency money). The swiftness of this process also reduces the amount of time that police officers have to stand near busy lanes of traffic; thus, this could result in fewer injuries to police officers. Some agencies that use this system have reported that it has saved them $70,000 in just one year's time.[16]

eCitation systems can be tailored to the individual needs of each police agency. For example, the Alvarado (Texas) Police Department wanted a system that could capture certain types of data, specifically, racial profiling metrics. The eCitation system can capture this type of data for later analysis.[17] The tracking of this type of data holds officers accountable if they are found to be stopping a significantly greater proportion of minority citizens compared to other officers working in the same beat area. As of June 2012, there are 11 states across the country that have adopted eCitation systems from Saltus Technologies.[18]

Another innovative way to deal with shrinking budgets is to cross-train all sworn personnel in police, fire, and emergency medical services. Sunnyvale, California, uses cross-training to reduce costs and eliminate the need for consolidation with other nearby cities.[19] The initial training costs are expensive, but there are long-term cost savings in all areas of public service as a result of cross-training.

In an effort to save money, some police agencies are cutting back on the number of patrol cars on the street at any given time. In order to reduce the number of cars but not reduce the number of police officers, some police agencies are moving away from one-officer patrol units to two-officer patrol units. By putting two police officers in one car, police agencies are able to use half the gas, which results in half of the cost for fuel.[20] It is significant that the economic crisis has caused some departments to reverse the long-term trend away from one-officer patrol cars and revert to an older approach. The Longwood (Florida) Police Department began using the two-officer per patrol car approach when their fuel costs reached $150,000 per year.[21] This approach also cuts down the wear and tear of patrol cars.

The Raleigh (North Carolina) Police Department has converted 20 of their patrol cars to run on propane.[22] This conversion was possible because they secured grant money. The department has saved $22,000 on gas expenses since the conversion took place in early 2012.[23] Many agencies have also purchased hybrid patrol cars as a cost-saving strategy. Some police agencies use hybrid vehicles for activities that do not require a high-powered engine such as traffic duty, investigative activities, and also routine patrol in areas where most of the roadways have low speed limits.[24] It has been reported that the switch to hybrid patrol cars has saved agencies up to $3,000 per month in fuel costs.[25] The method of patrol has also changed in some police agencies as a result of shrinking budgets. Foot patrol, bike patrol, and motorcycle patrol have all been used as more cost-effective ways to patrol the streets.[26]

Some police agencies are hiring more civilian (nonsworn) employees to complete tasks that are usually completed by sworn police officers.[27] Police management experts have recommended civilianization for decades, arguing that many tasks in a police department simply do not require a trained, sworn officer with arrest powers. Police unions, however, have long resisted civilianization in an effort to preserve jobs for their members. The economic recession, however, changes the dynamics, making civilianization a necessity and not an option.

Civilianization supplements sworn police forces or in some cases replaces sworn positions in an effort to reduce costs.[28] It has been estimated that nonsworn, civilian employees cost anywhere from one-third to one-half as much as sworn police officers.[29] Nonsworn employees can be hired to serve in roles such as communication and computer specialists, crime scene technicians, and to handle parking and traffic violations. The growth rate of nonsworn, civilian personnel in police agencies has more than doubled compared to that of sworn police personnel from 1992 to 2008.[30]

In an effort to continue police service at a level that is expected by citizens and to reduce costs, some police agencies choose to contract with private security companies.[31] In 2009, Oakland, California, was facing a budget shortfall of $80 million. Instead of hiring additional sworn police officers, which cost the city approximately $250,000 per officer annually (including benefits and salary), the city hired four security guards for $200,000 to supplement its police force.[32]

Private security companies are hired to help with video surveillance, traffic control, and computer and communication systems maintenance, to name a few.[33] For example, in Maine, a private security company has been hired to monitor weight limits of trucks crossing the Waldo-Hancock Bridge.[34] In St. Louis County, Missouri, private security companies provide a variety of services in place of sworn police including the maintenance of communication systems.[35] It is common for private security companies to monitor and maintain closed-circuit television systems (including the New York City Police Department)[36] to act as the eyes and ears for the police when they are not able to be present. The use of technology as a "force multiplier" is becoming more common as the cost to use such equipment is far less than paying several sworn police officers.[37]

In some jurisdictions, private security companies are used in place of municipal or county law enforcement agencies that employ sworn personnel. In 2011, Foley, Minnesota, hired a private security company to patrol the streets of the small town in place of a law enforcement agency with personnel.[38] Many cities across Minnesota have faced difficult economic times in recent years. The League of Minnesota Cities reported that 59 police departments have been dissolved or combined with other departments since 2000.[39]

The use of citizen volunteers is another approach that is used to save money and maintain levels of police service.[40] Volunteers working within police agencies have increased significantly from 2004 to 2010. The International Association of Chiefs of Police (IACP) estimates that American police agencies use approximately 245,000 citizen volunteers a year.[41] Some police agencies use citizen volunteers to aid in the process of conducting criminal history checks, enforcement of handicap parking regulations, fingerprinting, photography, and data entry.[42] The obvious benefit of using citizen volunteers is that there are no costs to police agencies.

Some police agencies have turned to consolidation as another way to save resources.[43] Consolidation can take several forms: two or more police agencies combining their resources; two or more police agencies merging to form a single agency; a number of police agencies within a region combining their resources to cover a large geographic area instead of individual jurisdictions; or contracting services from regional law enforcement agencies.[44] It is common for small, rural towns to contract with sheriffs' departments to provide police service instead of trying to fund a local police agency. The Los Angeles Sheriff's Department, for example, contracts with 40 cities in the county to provide the full array of police services. The cities range in size from 700 to 170,000 residents. The LASD is the largest contracting law enforcement agency in the country.[45]

Police Accountability and the Economy

An economic crisis has an enormous potential impact on police accountability. Police accountability programs cost money to implement and maintain. In a time of shrinking budgets, there are some people in local government that are more concerned about putting officers on the street to fight crime than in maintaining accountability-based programs. At a conference on the economic crisis, Philadelphia Police Commissioner Charles Ramsey pointed out that training is one of the first programs to be cut. Unlike patrol officers on the street, the training unit is hidden from public view and cutting it does not arouse public complaints. Nonetheless, Ramsey warned that cutting training programs costs a department in the years ahead when inadequately trained officers engage in misconduct that results in liability suits and loss of public confidence.[46]

> When I came into D.C. [Washington], there had been a lot of cutbacks in training, and a lot of bad things happened on the street—the things that resulted in officers getting sued or getting fired—a lot of that had to do with the fact that management had let them down and hadn't provided the training that they needed. I learned a lot of hard lessons from that, and I haven't forgotten it. In Philadelphia we've been cut a lot of places, but so far I've not cut training at all, and I have no plans to cut training.[47]

"Troubled" police departments that face federal "pattern or practice" suits face special costs resulting from their failure to develop and maintain standards of accountability over the years. Recently, the New Orleans Police Department agreed to sign on to what has been called one of the broadest Justice Department investigations ever conducted in the United States.[48] The bids from several companies competing to become the police monitor in New Orleans range from approximately $7 million to $12 million.[49] These multi-million-dollar bids have not been well received by some members of the New Orleans City Council. Council Member Cynthia Hedge-Morrell told local city leaders that the $7 million price tag to implement the mandated changes identified in the consent decree is a "ripoff."[50] The $7 million that Hedge-Morrell was referring to would be the first payment of what is expected to cost $55 million after the consent decree is fully implemented in the next five years.[51] This price tag could become larger if the NOPD does not comply or resists the mandated changes spelled out in the consent decree.

Police auditors/monitors are another accountability mechanism that comes with expenses. The police monitor (and staff) who were appointed by a federal judge to oversee reforms in the Oakland (California) Police Department have billed the city approximately $1.5 million since 2010.[52] This figure is much higher than expected because the Oakland Police Department has not fully complied with the stipulations in the original settlement agreement. In Detroit, the cost of monitoring the police is just over $1.1 million annually, and this department has made some progress since monitoring began a few years back.[53] The Los Angeles Police Department also faced high costs resulting from a consent decree as they paid $40 million over the course of several years.[54] It is important to note that despite the large amounts of money spent in each of these places, the police departments are better off today than they were before the consent decrees.

Early intervention systems (EISs) (discussed in Chapter Five) are expensive to create and maintain. There is a wide array of options for software systems including IA Trak, Blue Order, and IAPro, to name a few.[55] The amount of money spent on an EIS is contingent upon the level of customization that takes place to shape the EIS to the specific needs of a police agency. The more "bells and whistles" added into the EIS the higher the price tag for police executives. As discussed in both Chapters Five and Six, the Los Angeles Sheriff's Department encountered problems when it failed to enter data into its EIS, the Personnel Performance Index, in a timely fashion and when the use of force reports and citizen complaint data were not complete or accurate. These problems were largely due to a shortage of data entry personnel.[56]

The Pittsburgh Police Department had to build an EIS from the ground up in order to have a system that would allow them to fulfill the requirements of their consent decree. This required them to contract with a private software company. The creation of the EIS, along with working out some of the initial "bugs" in the software program, took quite a bit of time and resources. Specifically, the cost of the software development for the system was $500,000, along with $314,000 for computer hardware, $200,000 to a second software vendor, and another

$11,000 for miscellaneous computer services.[57] In the end, the total cost of the Pittsburgh Police Department's EIS was more than $1 million.

The processing of citizen complaints filed against the police is a costly activity. Each complaint consumes the time of an internal affairs investigator and the on-duty time of the officer or officers against whom the complaint is filed. The more serious the incident—several different allegations, more than one officer, multiple witnesses—the more expensive the investigation. In fact, it is possible to turn the economic issue on its head and argue that higher standards of accountability can be a cost-saving measure. Fewer citizen complaints and fewer internally generated complaints (see Chapter Four) means less time required for investigations. Higher accountability standards are also likely to reduce the number of civil suits against the department and the total costs of payouts. By the same token, as discussed above, cutting training programs as a short-term cost-cutting measure is likely to undermine accountability standards and raise long-term costs.

There is some empirical evidence that the use of mediation to resolve citizen complaints filed against the police can be a cost-saving strategy when compared to the traditional process of handling citizen complaints. The cost of processing citizen complaints filed against the police will vary among police agencies; however, there have been a few evaluations of EIS programs that have looked specifically at this cost.

In 2008, an evaluation report of the Pasadena Police–Community Mediation and Dialog Program (pilot program) identified the costs associated with the processing of citizen complaints using the traditional method where the internal affairs unit within a police agency handles the complaint, as well as the cost of using mediation to resolve citizen complaints against the police. Specifically, the report noted that "according to PPD's calculations, mediation cost approximately $144 per mediation case, including the cost of salary, benefits, and other miscellaneous expenses incurred during the average two-hour session. An internal affairs investigation of a case typically costs an average of $429 in salary, benefits, and other expenses incurred during an average investigation of 6 hours."[58] Based on these numbers, mediation appears to be the cheaper option; however, research has revealed that mediation is not used as much as it could be in many police agencies across the country.[59]

Some police agencies are beginning to outsource the tasks that internal affairs/professional standards units were usually responsible for in the past. Brian Howerton (chief of police in Schaumburg, Illinois) reported that his police agency has contracted out the Office of Professional Standards to a private company that is staffed by former Federal Bureau of Investigation agents.[60] Any formal investigations that would have been conducted within the Schaumburg Police Department are now forwarded on to the private company. Chief Howerton commented that he believes that the investigations are thorough and can truly be categorized as independent from the police agency because nonsworn people are conducting the investigations. The police union, however, is less enthusiastic about the department turning this responsibility over to civilians. This cost-savings approach may not be possible for larger police agencies that have a larger number of cases that need to be processed by an internal affairs or professional standards unit.

So what does all of this mean? It is clear that the lagging economy in the United States has altered the operation of police agencies, along with the services that they are able to offer the public. Police agencies will have to continue to adapt to an unpredictable economy in the future, as it has been predicted that they will continue to feel the effects of smaller budgets for several years to come.[61] How will police accountability be affected by the downturn in the economy? Will we see police agencies that currently have accountability mechanisms in place reduce the funding for those programs? Will police agencies with limited budgets abandon their plans for implementing accountability mechanisms? Only time will tell how the economy will impact police accountability in the United States. When local governments and police executives are making the tough decisions about how resources will be spent, it is important for them to remember that there is something far more important than the financial costs of running a professional police agency—maintaining (or in some cases re-building) a good relationship with the people they serve in their communities.

Notes

1 "New Camden, NJ Police Force Hits Streets," Officer.com, April 9, 2013.

2 Police Executive Research Forum, *Is the Economic Downturn Fundamentally Changing How We Police?* (Washington, DC: Police Executive Research Forum, 2010).

3 See http://www.cops.usdoj.gov/files/RIC/Publications/e101113406_Economic%20Impact.pdf.

4 Office of Community Oriented Policing Services, *Impact of the Economic Downturn on American Police Agencies* (Washington, DC: United States Department of Justice, Office of Community Oriented Policing Services, 2011).

5 Ibid.

6 Ibid.

7 Ibid.

8 See http://www.huffingtonpost.com/2012/01/15/miami-dade-police-lay-off_n_1207399.html.

9 See http://nashvillecitypaper.com/content/city-news/police-chief-laying-200-officers-would-be-devastating.

10 Office of Community Oriented Policing Services, 2011.

11 Ibid.

12 See http://www.nytimes.com/2012/11/04/us/after-deep-police-cuts-sacramento-sees-rise-in-crime.html?pagewanted=all&_r=0.

13 See http://www.saltustechnologies.com/alvarado-texas-police-deploy-digiticket-advanced-ecitation-system/.

14 See http://www.news9.com/story/10773646/e-tickets-could-save-police-officers-time-and-money.

15 See http://www.newson6.com/story/21656360/porter-police-department-goes-digital-with-new-ticket-system.

16 See http://www.newson6.com/Global/story.asp?S=13184963.

17 See http://www.saltustechnologies.com/alvarado-texas-police-deploy-digiticket-advanced-ecitation-system/.

18 Ibid.

19 See http://articles.latimes.com/2013/jan/01/local/la-me-sunnyvale-20130101.

20 See http://poststar.com/news/local/police-double-up-in-patrol-cars-to-conserve-fuel/article_73b770d4-7439-11e0-ae8b-001cc4c03286.html.

21 See http://www.wesh.com/news/central-florida/Longwood-police-making-changes-to-save-money/-/11788162/16286446/-/7ppoucz/-/index.html.

22 See http://triangle.news14.com/content/video_stories/644675/raleigh-police-unveil-new-hybrid-police-cars?ap=1&MP4.

23 Ibid.

24 See http://www.nj.com/news/index.ssf/2010/10/hybrid_vehicles_making_way_int.html.

25 See http://www.ksl.com/?nid=148&sid=19955111.

26 See http://forestlaketimes.com/2012/10/17/return-of-bike-patrol-deemed-a-success/. And also http://www.wilx.com/home/headlines/21823574.html?site=full.

27 Office of Community Oriented Policing Services, 2011.

28 Brian Forst, "The Privatization and Civilianization of Policing," in *Boundary Changes in Criminal Justice Organizations: Criminal Justice 2000, Vol. 2*, ed. Charles M. Friel (Washington, DC: National Institute of Justice, 2000), 19–79.

29 Forst, 2000.

30 Brian A. Reaves, *Census of State and Local Law Enforcement Agencies, 2008* (Washington, DC: Bureau of Justice Statistics, 2011).

31 Office of Community Oriented Policing Services, 2011.

32 See http://online.wsj.com/article/SB124027127337237011.html.

33 Forst, 2000, 23.

34 See http://archive.bangordailynews.com/2003/08/06/private-security-hired-to-enforce-bridge-limit/.

35 See http://www.stlouisco.com/LawandPublicSafety/PoliceDepartment/Services/OperationalSupportCAREandCommunications.

36 See http://www.nyclu.org/pdfs/surveillance_cams_report_121306.pdf.

37 Office of Community Oriented Policing Services, 2011.

38 See http://publicintelligence.net/minnesota-town-replaces-police-force-with-private-security/.

39 Ibid.

40 Ibid.

41 International Association of Chiefs of Police (IACP), *Policing in the 21st Century: Preliminary Survey Results* (Alexandria, Virginia: IACP, 2010).

42 See http://www.ci.fargo.nd.us/CityInfo/Departments/Police/Citizen Resources/CitizenVolunteerProgram/.

43 Office of Community Oriented Policing Services, 2011.

44 New Jersey State Association of Chiefs of Police, *Police Department Regionalization, Consolidation, Merger & Shared Services: Important Considerations for Policy Makers* (West Trenton, NJ: New Jersey State Association of Chiefs of Police, 2007).

45 "Municipal Police Services," at http://www.lasdhq.org.

46 Police Executive Research Forum, 2010.

47 Ibid., 18.

48 See http://www.nola.com/crime/index.ssf/2012/02/revamping_of_new_orleans_polic.html.

49 See http://thelensnola.org/2012/10/17/bids-for-police-monitor-posted/.

50 See http://thelensnola.org/2012/11/14/council-faults-consent-decree-budget/.

51 Ibid.

52 See http://www.ktvu.com/news/news/special-oakland-fed-cops/nHb95/.

53 See http://www.nola.com/crime/index.ssf/2012/02/revamping_of_new_orleans_polic.html.

54 See http://www.nola.com/crime/index.ssf/2011/10/consent_decree_leaves_los_ange.html.

55 Frank Hughes and Lisa B. Andre, "Problem Officer Variables and Early-Warning Systems," *The Police Chief*, 74, no. 10, October 2007.

56 Merrick Bobb, *16th Semiannual Report* (Los Angeles: Police Assessment Resource Center, 2003), 43–59.

57 Robert C. Davis, Christopher W. Ortiz, Nicole J. Henderson, Joel Miller, and Michelle K. Massie, *Turning Necessity Into Virtue: Pittsburgh's Experience with a Federal Consent Decree* (Vera Institute of Justice, September 2002).

58 Police Assessment Resource Center, *Evaluation of a Pilot Community Policing Program: The Pasadena Police-Community Mediation and Dialog Program*. COPS Evaluation Brief No. 2. Washington, DC: Office of Community Oriented Policing Services, U.S. Department of Justice, 2008. See page 14.

59 Samuel Walker and Carol Archbold, "Mediating Citizen Complaints Against the Police: An Exploratory Study," *Journal of Dispute Resolution* 231 (2000). See also Jon L. Proctor, Richard Rosenthal, and A. J. Clemmons, "Denver's Citizen/Police Complaint Mediation Program: A Comprehensive Evaluation" (2008).

60 Police Executive Research Forum, 2010.

61 Office of Community Oriented Policing Services, 2011.

PART IV

The Future of Police Accountability

TEN

The Future of
Police Accountability

A Quick Look Backwards

Much has changed with regard to police accountability in recent years. And when we look back a few decades, the changes can only be described as a revolution in thinking, and policies and practices designed to hold police officers accountable for their conduct. Forty years ago the policy that has become the standard model for police use of force policies had just appeared. The idea that traditional police officer responses to domestic violence incidents were problematic and should be governed by formal policies was just beginning to appear. Recognition that high-speed police vehicle pursuits were highly dangerous to citizens and officers was also something new. Today, policies on these aspects of police work are standard. In the early 1980s there were but a handful of citizen oversight agencies covering major city police departments. Thirty years ago the idea of early intervention systems had only just surfaced. It was unthinkable then that the Civil Rights Division of the U.S. Justice Department would sue some of the largest police departments in the country for violations of peoples' rights and reach settlements requiring sweeping accountability reforms. It has happened, however, and at a 2012 Police Executive Research Forum conference on federal pattern or practice litigation, chiefs or representatives from three major police departments that had been sued stated that they were better departments because of the experience. Two commented that it had substantially reduced lawsuits against their departments and the dollar costs associated with them. Another commented that the experience had increased the department's credibility with the public.[1]

Another important index of change is the terminology we use when discussing police accountability. The term "police accountability" is relatively new, particularly as it refers to a set of policies and procedures. The most important new term in policing is legitimacy, which is now recognized as arguably the most useful concept for understanding policing. The concept of legitimacy has supplanted "police-community relations" (PCR), which emerged in the 1960s because of the national racial crisis and the urban riots in particular. The idea of PCR and PCR programs were narrowly focused on police relations with the African American community. (It is fascinating to re-read the major documents of the 1960s and to discover that, with only rare exception, the Latino community virtually did not exist. Nor, for that matter, was there any concern about gender bias in policing.) Additionally, the areas of concern primarily involved a few key police activities: officer-involved shootings, use of excessive physical force, and discriminatory arrests.

Legitimacy, by contrast, shifts the focus in three ways. First, it is concerned about police relations with the entire community. Second, it recognizes that how people perceive the police as an institution is implicated in each and every form of police-citizen contact. Third, legitimacy recognizes that public attitudes about the police are a function of the process, of how they are treated, and not just the outcomes of encounters with officers. In the paradigmatic encounter, a citizen who is the subject of a traffic stop will be more likely to at least not think negatively about the police if the officer is polite, respectful, and responsive to the person's questions. Conversely, the person's attitude is very likely to be negatively affected if the officer is rude and disrespectful.[2]

Legitimacy has special relevance for police accountability because each and every policy and procedure discussed in this book is designed to reduce and hopefully eliminate officer actions that negatively affect perceptions of legitimacy and conversely replace them with actions likely to build legitimacy. Critical incident policies that reduce use of excessive force or rudeness are likely to enhance legitimacy. An early intervention system that corrects an officer's conduct at an early stage in his or her career is likely to reduce legitimacy-damaging incidents. An open and accessible citizen complaint procedure is likely to build confidence that concerns will be addressed quickly and effectively, and thereby build feelings of trust and legitimacy.

The State of Police Accountability Today

For the first edition of this book in 2005, the title was chosen to make the point that a "new world" of police accountability had emerged. The argument was that a package of interrelated accountability procedures had crystalized. The three core elements were state-of-the-art use of force policies, an early intervention system, and an open and accessible citizen complaint procedure. The Justice Department "pattern and practice" litigation played a major role in identifying and lending authority to that package.[3]

Today, nearly a decade later, the world of police accountability has moved far beyond that initial package of policies and procedures. As Chapter Three of this edition argues, formal written policies are needed to govern all critical incidents involving police authority when dealing with citizens. They also need to cover foot pursuits, response to people with mental health problems, and many others. The underlying principle of early intervention systems—the collection and analysis of systematic data on police performance for the purpose of proactively seeking to reduce unwanted incidents—has expanded to include broader pattern and trend analyses of police department conduct. Recognition that a department today must be data driven if it seeks to be fully accountable is far more widespread than it was a decade ago.

While there is much to celebrate in the developments in police accountability over the past decade, we should not lose perspective on the extent of that progress. One would be hard pressed to identify any one large police department that encompasses all the elements of the new accountability. Progress toward a comprehensive list of critical incidents covered by good policies is uneven at best. In fact, in the absence of a national survey that examines the content of such policies (and does not simply check a box to indicate that a department "has a policy" on a given subject), we don't really know where American policing stands in this regard. Nor do we know exactly how extensive early intervention systems are, especially if we probe deeper to determine exactly how they are used in different departments. The details of citizen complaint procedures, with respect to both internal affairs units and citizen complaint procedures, is another unexplored subject with regard to both formal procedures and day-to-day practices. In the absence of good, comprehensive data on these subjects, caution strongly suggests that we hold off before celebrating too loudly the state of police accountability today.

Perhaps the most worrisome problem today involves sustaining the accountability reforms that have been achieved. We discuss that issue at the end of this chapter.

Progress in Police Accountability: What Are "Best Practices"?

Throughout this book we have used the term "best practices" to characterize recommended policies, procedures, or practices. The term is widely used in policing today, and not just with regard to accountability reforms. But what, exactly, does it encompass? Does it refer to policies and procedures that have some official status? Is there a list of best practices somewhere? Should there be a list? And if so, who should prepare it? If there is no formal list, do best practices simply refer to the preferences of the person using it? This section discusses the term and what it does and does not mean.

Use of the term best practices is relatively recent in policing, and in certain respects it has emerged as part of the police accountability movement. Some points about the meaning of the term are very clear. There is no list of best practices in police accountability, official or unofficial. This contrasts with, for example, the CALEA accreditation standards for law enforcement, which is an official set of written standards adopted by a commission that broadly represents the law enforcement profession.[4]

The term best practices is also very different from Supreme Court decisions that, in the decentralized context of American law enforcement with about 18,000 law enforcement agencies, are the closest we have to national standards for the police. A Supreme Court decision does not represent a best practice, however; it represents a *required* practice as determined by the highest court in the land. Violation of a Supreme Court decision, moreover, has consequences, such as the overturning of a criminal conviction because of a Fourth Amendment violation. By contrast, there is little real penalty for a police department not being accredited by CALEA, apart from some measure of status. A police department will not lose federal or state funds as a consequence, for example. (Educational institutions, by contrast, suffer real and severe consequences, including loss of federal funding, for not being accredited.)

What then is this thing people keep referring to as "best practices"? As currently used, best practices in police accountability refers to ideas about policies, procedures, and customs that at least some experts in the field believe to be the best approach on a given issue. There is no list, and the ideas have no official status of any kind. Who are these experts, you might ask, and who appointed them? The plain truth is that they are people who have written and spoken on police practices, and on that basis are widely recognized as experts. But there is no list. There is no "academy" of experts, as there is in many fields of the sciences and the humanities, to which people are selected by the existing members. This is all very loose and informal, but as the discussion that follows argues, these are the virtues of the whole concept of best practices.

It is useful to contrast "best practices" with the related term "generally accepted police practices," which is used in civil litigation. Plaintiffs typically argue that a police department's use of force policy is not consistent with generally accepted police practices, while police departments argue the opposite. From the perspective of this book, however, it is likely that most "generally accepted police practices" can also be described as "unprofessional," "unwise," "harmful to community relations," "dangerous to citizens and officers," "illegal under state statute," or finally "unconstitutional." The very nature of the term "generally accepted practices" describes what is, without any normative framework. Historically, it is true that such practices as slavery and child labor were once generally accepted in the Western European/American world that shapes our culture and legal system. Generally accepted practices do not and never should determine what should be.

As it is generally used, the term "best practices" in policing does not necessarily mean "the best" but simply "better than" what currently exists (those "generally accepted practices"). A national survey, for example, might find that most police departments do not have a restrictive policy on foot pursuits as discussed in this book, or any policy for that matter. That would in fact be the "generally accepted practice." A restrictive policy is considered a best practice because it is better than what generally exists. It would be easy to cite many other examples.

The fact that "best practices" means "better than" highlights the related point that the specifics of particular police practices are constantly changing. It is fair to say that most police use of physical force policies today are different from the policies that existed several years ago. They are more detailed, more precise in their language, and cover more specific aspects of the use of force. Progress in policing is characterized by continual refinement. This point is illustrated by the Collaborative Reform Process report on Las Vegas, which found the department's deadly force policy to be very good but promptly went on to recommend a number of needed improvements.[5]

Constant change and refinement with respect to police accountability policies and procedures is not only the way it has been but is the way it should be. And it is also appropriate that there is neither an official list nor a formal list of "experts" whose word has some official status. The appropriate model is the classic theory of free speech and a marketplace of ideas. All of today's recognized best practices arose out of a free and unrestricted debate over police practices. As we pointed out in Chapter Three, there was a wide-ranging debate over the problem of officer-involved shootings in the decade leading up to the 1972 NYPD policy, which became the national model. And as Chapter Five explained, there was a long debate and some experimentation about "problem officers" that led to today's early intervention systems.

In the free market of ideas, no idea has any official status and no speaker has any claim to more authority than anyone else. Only the persuasiveness of the idea itself governs. And so the future of best practices in police accountability will be determined by the course of the already ongoing debate. Some new ideas will undoubtedly arise, and some existing best practices will be challenged and possibly even be dethroned.

The Challenge of Sustaining Accountability Reforms

The history of the American police is filled with examples of important reforms that achieved notice in their time but eventually faded away. This is a general problem that affects reforms in all aspects of policing, and it is a particularly important one with regard to accountability.

One of the most famous examples of reforms that disappeared is the anticorruption program instituted in the New York City Police

Department in the early 1970s by Police Commissioner Patrick V. Murphy. In the wake of the major corruption scandal that is popularly known by the name of one officer, Frank Serpico, Murphy created an elaborate program that decentralized anticorruption responsibility within the NYPD. Murphy soon left the department, however, and the anticorruption program withered away. A new corruption scandal erupted in the early 1990s, and the subsequent Mollen Commission investigation found few traces of meaningful anticorruption efforts.[6] Many other examples exist. For a brief period in the early 1970s, the concept of "team policing" swept through American policing. A half step in the direction of community policing, it sought to decentralize command and control within police departments in order to better address neighborhood problems and improve police-community relations. The concept was not fully thought out, however, and team policing programs were poorly planned and implemented. It vanished almost as quickly as it had appeared.[7] More recently, community policing and problem-oriented policing were embraced by departments across the country. One wonders, however, whether a rigorous national survey would find many programs still in existence in more than just name.[8]

To say that all police reforms have failed would be an overstatement. Most of the basic elements of the professional era of policing continue to endure: higher personnel standards, the rational allocation of police patrol through a workload formula, and the idea of policing as a profession. The control of police officer discretion through administrative rule-making is deeply entrenched in police organizations, at least with respect to certain police actions, and does not seem likely to wither away. These are enduring achievements, and we should not underestimate their continuing contributions.

The future of the more creative and demanding aspects of the new police accountability are cause for concern, however. Early intervention systems are an obvious example. They are extremely demanding in terms of resources and management attention. Once the EIS software is purchased and installed, the real challenge begins. Entering all the required performance data requires that many separate data systems (use of force reports, officer involvement in civil litigation, and so on) need to be complete and accurate and entered into the EIS in a timely fashion. The Los Angeles Sheriff's Department PPI, widely regarded as one of the best EISs, had serious problems with all of these issues.[9] Reviewing EIS data, identifying and selecting officers for intervention, and then delivering appropriate interventions are all extremely time-consuming tasks that call for making difficult judgments. The demands of day-to-day police operations, with the steady flow of crises, aggravated by periodic budget crises, make it difficult to maintain a focus on the goals of an EIS.

Internal review of critical incidents such as officer-involved shootings to identify needed changes in policies, training, or supervision also calls for a perspective and skills that are not a part of traditional police work. In Chapter Six we quoted a veteran officer who pointed out that it is difficult to ask hard questions and criticize current operations in ways that will embarrass colleagues. This is true in all organizations. Recommending changes in training and supervision, moreover, threatens the way members of the department do business. For all these reasons, meaningful internal review is a prime candidate for fading away.

The basic threat to the new accountability is the resistance to change that is inherent in all large organizations, including the police. As we have indicated at various points in this book, the new accountability seeks to change the way officers at all ranks work. Patrol officers are expected to de-escalate when faced with a disrespectful kid on the street; sergeants are expected to review officer conduct in a more critical way than they had before, and to engage officers about their conduct without being mere rule enforcers; an EIS expects sergeants to become data analysts and spend more time in front of a computer and less time on the street; and the EIS also asks higher-level commanders to become data analysts, to look for patterns and trends, and to think critically about existing policies and practices.

In a brief but highly illuminating essay, Wesley Skogan identifies the various reasons "Why Reforms Fail" in policing.[10] Most are directly relevant to the accountability policies and procedures discussed in this book. Two reasons are resistance from mid-level and top managers and from front-line supervisors. It should be clear that officers at these ranks play critical roles in most of the new accountability measures. If front-line supervisors do not fully enforce critical incident policies, the policies are undermined. An EIS depends entirely on proper actions by these officials. Skogan points out that rank-and-file officers can also undermine reforms because they are asked to change the way they do routine police work. Changing one officer is a challenge; changing the entire patrol force is an enormous one. In those departments with police unions, the power of the rank and file to resist change is even greater. Provisions of the collective bargaining agreement can be invoked to challenge disciplinary actions arising from new accountability measures. Skogan points out that police departments are faced with competing demands and expectations. Accountability measures, as we have argued, are often labor intensive, and police executives are tempted to cut them in the face of a budget crisis or public demands for putting more officers on the street. Finally, changes in leadership often undermine major reforms. The new police chief may simply be not as interested in new accountability measures. As in other organizations, moreover, a new chief often wants to put his or her stamp on the organization and pursue different priorities.

The threats to the new police accountability, in short, are many and powerful. How, then, to overcome them? Unfortunately, there has been little research on the dynamics of ensuring the continuity of reforms in policing. A study of institutionalizing reform on one large department, however, offers a promising model that can be applied to accountability reforms.[11]

Trend Ikerd studied the institutionalization of problem-oriented policing (POP) in the Charlotte-Mecklenburg (North Carolina) Police Department.[12] To develop a department-wide commitment to POP, a number of policies and practices were instituted. POP was incorporated into academy and inservice training programs, regular personnel evaluations, and promotional procedures. New recruits were required to develop a POP project as part of their field training experience. In a survey of officers, 87 percent of rank-and-file officers and 86 percent of captains reported that POP was part of their performance evaluations. Moreover, 85 percent of the captains reported that they had been rewarded for the POP efforts. Almost 90 percent of the captains indicated they discussed POP on a regular basis with other officers, indicating that POP had become a part of the culture of their work lives.

The training, personnel evaluation, and promotional changes effected by the Charlotte-Mecklenburg Police Department dramatizes what has not happened in virtually all major police reforms. We can begin with federal pattern or practice litigation because it involves accountability reforms. Consent decrees settling Justice Department investigations all required state-of-the-art use of force policies, an EIS, and changes to the citizen complaint process.[13] The consent decrees have typically been greeted with anger on the part of the officers in the departments affected (in some cases expressed openly, in others not so openly).[14] There is no evidence that any of the affected departments made efforts to explain the required reforms, including why they were necessary for constitutional policing, how they would work, and why the department would be a better organization in the long run as a result. A training/explanation process for all officers, moreover, would give officers the opportunity to ask questions and express their complaints. As we noted in Chapter One, the legitimacy literature holds that giving affected people a voice in a process helps to build a sense of legitimacy.[15] Nor is there any evidence that the Justice Department required or suggested that departments conduct an explanation/training session.

Even apart from consent decrees, reforms in policing have traditionally been implemented without providing officers with explanations and an opportunity to express their views. This is probably true of the implementation of most EISs. The PERF survey of police managers, for example, found that the most serious problems involved implementation and the lack of planning.[16] Critical incident policies are revised on a regular basis, and it is not clear that steps are taken to explain their rationale. Too often, policy revision is done in a crisis management atmosphere where the new policy is viewed as something the department had to do to avoid being sued (or sued again). With respect to community policing, apart from a few notable examples, there is no evidence that in departments that embraced it the concept was explained to all officers. The result was often misunderstanding and disdain for the program.

The Charlotte-Mecklenburg example provides a model for a program to ensure the continuity of police reforms. Specific accountability reforms, together with the broader concept of accountability, should be incorporated into inservice training for all officers. Specific programs— the EIS, a new policy on de-escalation, and pattern and trend analyses of officer-involved shootings—should be explained in detail, with officers having an opportunity to ask questions and voice their criticisms. In a broader sense, however, the training also needs to explain how these new programs are going to improve the quality of police services and make officers' work lives easier: fewer controversial use of force incidents, fewer citizen complaints and internal affairs investigations, meaningful discipline for those few officers that most other officers know to be unprofessional, and an improved public image and greater trust in the community.

Would such a program work? We don't know, mainly because it has never really been tried (and evaluated). Common sense, however, suggests that it makes sense and should be tried. This book has argued that much has been accomplished with respect to police accountability. Despite the flagrant abuses that make the national news, policing has come a long way since the troubled decade of the 1960s, and even since the mid-1980s. Most important, we not only have a coherent set of strategies, policies, and procedures designed to hold police officers to account for their conduct in dealing with citizens, but we understand how all of these elements fit together into a coherent package. It would be a terrible shame to let any of this progress slip away. Making accountability reforms endure must be a high-priority item on the policing agenda. And if the recent past is any indication, further progress toward fully accountable policing is within reach.

To sum up, there has been considerable progress in police accountability in recent years, but much remains to be done. Some departments have yet to fully embrace the strategies and tools of the new accountability. More seriously, they have not adopted the mindset of accountability, including the willingness to learn from and borrow what the better departments have done. Some other departments took important steps forward, only to slip back into the old ways. Learning how to sustain reforms, as we have argued, is a major challenge for the police profession. The most important indicator of recent progress is that we now have a clear set of strategies and tools likely to enhance accountability, reduce misconduct, and build legitimacy in the eyes of the community. As the lead author of this book put it at the 2012 PERF conference on pattern or practice litigation, "No police department should be in a position where it can be sued by the Justice Department, because the past cases make it clear what is expected of them to achieve professional, bias-free, and accountable policing."[17] We know what to do and how to do it. All that remains is the will and the administrative skills to do it.

Notes

1   Police Executive Research Forum, *Civil Rights Investigations of Local Police: Lessons Learned* (Washington, DC: Police Executive Research Forum, 2013), 34–5.

2   Lorraine Mazerolle, Sarah Bennett, Jacqueline Davis, Elise Sargeant, and Matthew Manning, "Legitimacy in Policing: A Systematic Review," *Campbell Systematic Reviews* 9 (no. 1, 2013).

3   Samuel Walker and Morgan Macdonald, "An Alternative Remedy for Police Misconduct: A Model State Pattern or Practice Statute," *George Mason Civil Rights Law Journal* 19 (Summer 2009): 479–552.

4 See http://www.calea.org.

5 James K. Stewart et al., *Collaborative Reform Process: A Review of Officer-Involved Shootings in the Las Vegas Metropolitan Police Department* (Washington, DC: Office of Community Oriented Policing Services, 2012). Available at http://www.cops.usdoj.gov/pdf/e10129513-Collaborative-Reform-Process_FINAL.pdf.

6 Commission to Investigate Allegations of Police Corruption and the Anti-Corruption Procedures of the Department [Mollen Commission], *Commission Report* (New York: City of New York, 1994).

7 Lawrence W. Sherman, Catherine Milton, and Thomas V. Kelly, *Team Policing: Seven Case Studies* (Washington, DC: The Police Foundation, 1973).

8 Michael S. Scott, *Problem-Oriented Policing: Reflections on the First 20 Years* (Washington, DC: Department of Justice, 2002).

9 Merrick J. Bobb, *16th Semiannual Report* (Los Angeles: Police Assessment Research Center, 2003).

10 Wesley G. Skogan, "Why Reforms Fail," *Policing and Society* 18 (March 2008): 23–34.

11 Samuel Walker, "Institutionalizing Police Accountability Reforms: The Problem of Making Police Reforms Endure," *Saint Louis University Public Law Review* 32 (no. 1, 2012): 57–93.

12 Trent Ikerd and Samuel Walker, *Making Police Reforms Endure: The Keys for Success* (Washington, DC: Department of Justice, 2010). The most serious attempt to institutionalize reforms in a police experiment is discussed in Robin S. Engel, Marie Skubak Tillyer and Nicholas Corsaro, "Reducing Gang Violence Using Focused Deterrence: Evaluating the Cincinnnati Initiative to Reduce Violence (CIRV)," *Justice Quarterly 30* (no 3, 2013): 403–439.

13 Walker, "Institutionalizing Police Accountability Reforms."

14 Robert C. Davis, Christopher W. Ortiz, Nicole J. Henderson, Joel Miller, and Michelle K. Massie, *Turning Necessity Into Virtue: Pittsburgh's Experience With a Federal Consent Decree* (New York: Vera Institute, 2002).

15 Mazerolle et al., *Legitimacy in Policing: A Systematic Review.*

16 Samuel Walker, *Early Intervention Systems for Law Enforcement Agencies: A Planning and Management Guide* (Washington, DC; Department of Justice, 2003).

17 Police Executive Research Forum, *Civil Rights Investigations of Local Police*, 9.

Index

About the Authors

Samuel Walker is Professor Emeritus of Criminal Justice at the University of Nebraska at Omaha. After retiring in 2005 he has continued his research, writing and consulting on police accountability, citizen oversight of the police, early intervention systems for police officers, and civil liberties.

Professor Walker is the author of 14 books, which have appeared in 33 different editions. His most recent book is *Presidents and Civil Liberties from Wilson to Obama* (2012). His other books include *The Police in America: An Introduction* (with Charles M. Katz) (8th ed., 2013), *Police Accountability: The Role of Citizen Oversight* (2001), *Taming the System: The Control of Discretion in Criminal Justice, 1950–1990* (1993), *Sense and Nonsense About Crime* (7th ed., 2011), *The Color of Justice: Race, Ethnicity, and Crime in America* (with C. Spohn & M. DeLone) (5th ed., 2012), and *In Defense of American Liberties: A History of the ACLU* (2nd ed., 2000). He is the author of *Early Intervention Systems for Law Enforcement Agencies: A Planning and Management Guide* (2003), published by the COPS Office of the U.S. Department of Justice.

Professor Walker has served as a consultant to the Civil Rights Division of the U.S. Department of Justice and to police departments, local governments, and community groups in more than 35 cities and counties across the country on different police issues.

Carol A. Archbold is an Associate Professor of Criminal Justice at North Dakota State University in Fargo, North Dakota. She earned her PhD from the University of Nebraska–Omaha in 2002. Dr. Archbold's research interests include women in policing, police accountability and liability, police handling of sexual assault cases, and police and race issues. She has published articles in such journals as *Police Quarterly*, *Policing: An International Journal of Police Strategies and Management*, *International Journal of Police*

Science and Management, Police Practice and Research: An International Journal, Journal of Criminal Justice, and the *Journal of Crime and Justice.* In 2004, Dr. Archbold published a book based on the first national study of the use of risk management in law enforcement in the United States, *Police Accountability, Risk Management and Legal Advising* (LFB Scholarly Publishing). This study was the focus of her dissertation. Along with Samuel Walker and Leigh Herbst (Culver), she was a contributing author for "Mediating Citizen Complaints Against Police Officers: A Guide for Police and Citizens," funded by the Office of Community Oriented Policing Services (United States Department of Justice, Washington, DC). In 2011, she was one of three authors of a reader, *Women and Policing in America: Classic and Contemporary Readings* (Aspen Publishing), with Dorothy Moses Schulz and Kimberly Hassell. Dr. Archbold authored "Policing: A Text/Reader" for SAGE Publications in 2012. She recently completed a study that examines how an increase in population from an oil boom impacts the police and crime in western North Dakota, and is currently working on a national study of police misconduct.

ⓈSAGE research**methods**

The essential online tool for researchers from the world's leading methods publisher

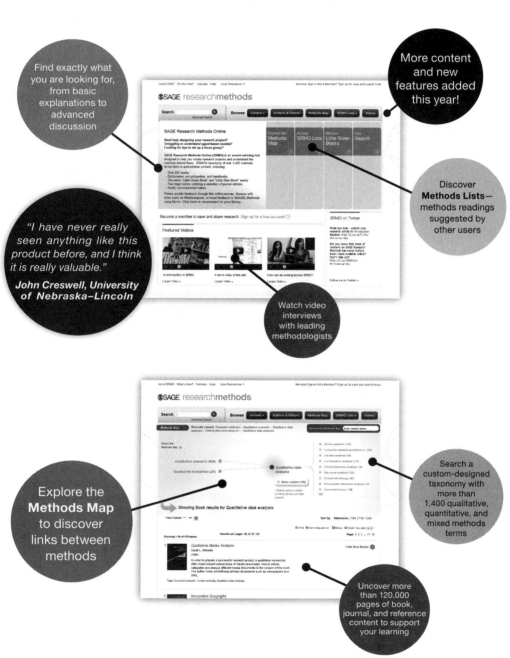

Find exactly what you are looking for, from basic explanations to advanced discussion

More content and new features added this year!

"I have never really seen anything like this product before, and I think it is really valuable."

John Creswell, University of Nebraska–Lincoln

Discover **Methods Lists**— methods readings suggested by other users

Watch video interviews with leading methodologists

Explore the **Methods Map** to discover links between methods

Search a custom-designed taxonomy with more than 1,400 qualitative, quantitative, and mixed methods terms

Uncover more than 120,000 pages of book, journal, and reference content to support your learning

Find out more at
www.sageresearchmethods.com